Decoding Platform Engineering Patterns

A Strategic Guide to Building, Scaling, and Succeeding with Platforms

Shweta Vohra

Forewords by Priyanka Sharma and Shalini Kapoor

Decoding Platform Engineering Patterns: A Strategic Guide to Building, Scaling, and Succeeding with Platforms

Shweta Vohra
Manchester, UK

ISBN-13 (pbk): 979-8-8688-2554-5   ISBN-13 (electronic): 979-8-8688-2555-2
https://doi.org/10.1007/979-8-8688-2555-2

Managing Director, Apress Media LLC: Welmoed Spahr
Acquisitions Editor: James Robinson-Prior
Editorial Assistant: Gryffin Winkler

Cover designed by eStudioCalamar

Distributed to the book trade worldwide by Springer Science+Business Media New York, 1 New York Plaza, New York, NY 10004. Phone 1-800-SPRINGER, fax (201) 348-4505, e-mail orders-ny@springer-sbm.com, or visit www.springeronline.com. Apress Media, LLC is a Delaware LLC and the sole member (owner) is Springer Science + Business Media Finance Inc (SSBM Finance Inc). SSBM Finance Inc is a **Delaware** corporation.

For information on translations, please e-mail booktranslations@springernature.com; for reprint, paperback, or audio rights, please e-mail bookpermissions@springernature.com.

Apress titles may be purchased in bulk for academic, corporate, or promotional use. eBook versions and licenses are also available for most titles. For more information, reference our Print and eBook Bulk Sales web page at http://www.apress.com/bulk-sales.

Any source code or other supplementary material referenced by the author in this book is available to readers on GitHub. For more detailed information, please visit https://www.apress.com/gp/services/source-code.

If disposing of this product, please recycle the paper.

*To Maa (**Sudesh**), and my silly Vohras – **Rajiv, Sanskriti, and Saisha**.
Thank you for the endless love, patience, motivation,
and blessings that made this book possible.
You are my courage on difficult days,
my laughter in long nights, and my reason to keep going.*

*And to my **Readers** – your trust, reflections,
conversations, and encouragement made the
first version of this book a success. This second, more
complete edition exists because you read, questioned,
shared, and believed. This book is as much yours as it is mine.*

Table of Contents

About the Author

 **Shweta Vohra** is a platform architect, author, and inventor with over two decades of experience designing and scaling digital platforms across industries and continents. Her work sits at the intersection of platform engineering, cloud-native systems, and AI-driven architectures, helping organizations build systems that are resilient, and built to evolve.

A practitioner at heart, Shweta brings grounded perspective on how platforms succeed in the real world, how teams operate, how systems grow, and how technical decisions shape business outcomes. She is a multiple patent holder, an international speaker, and a strong advocate for sustainable technology ecosystems and women in technology leadership.

She is also the author of *Dear Software & AI Architect*, a reflective guide on modern technical leadership in an AI-driven world.

Based in the UK, Shweta writes, speaks, and teaches globally on platform thinking, architecture, and the future of software-driven businesses.

LinkedIn: linkedin.com/in/shwetavohra

YouTube: youtube.com/@TheAIArchitectShweta

About the Technical Reviewer

Gineesh Madapparambath is an architect with over two decades of experience in IT service management and consultancy. He designs and implements end-to-end automation and containerization strategies for enterprises, specializing in Ansible Automation Platform, Kubernetes, OpenShift, and Terraform to streamline operations and modernize infrastructure. A published author of books on Ansible and Kubernetes, he is also an active community contributor and editor at techbeatly.com, regularly blogging and speaking on DevOps and open source. Throughout his career, he has held various roles, always focused on bridging the gap between technology and business outcomes.

Forewords

Priyanka Sharma

Shweta Vohra's book, *Decoding Platform Engineering Patterns*, arrives at a critical juncture in the evolution of technology platforms. The Cloud Native Computing Foundation (CNCF) has long recognized the transformative power of platforms and their role as cornerstones of cloud-native computing.

Our community's work to refine a maturity model in platform engineering is founded on the belief that platforms are essential to operational efficiency and scalability in the digital landscape.

Look across the industry, and you'll see high-profile platform successes in Silicon Valley startups and established corporations.

However, their lead seems difficult to follow: a surprisingly large number of platform projects fail to make it off the drawing board, and research suggests around 80%.

The biggest issue is that a single agreed definition of a technology platform needs to be defined clearly. Before the cloud, the phrase defined a set of on-prem, complex enterprise-class systems that provided a software infrastructure for developers, operations, and users.

The relational database was a prime example: it provided an essential set of valuable functions – storage and data processing, a development foundation for software engineers, and an API framework that third-party applications could plug into for additional functionality. One vendor controlled the code and the development roadmap.

The scale, complexity, and rate of change in the cloud have challenged both this definition of a platform and the practice of its development. A fresh understanding and approach are required.

The CNCF has stepped in to help. We define a platform as a collection of capabilities, documentation, and tools that support the development, deployment, operation, and management of products and services. It should let organizations deliver applications and services faster and more reliably. Three characteristics define the modern platform.

First, innovation comes not from one vendor but through community-driven open source, attracting those interested in making change, finding answers, and furthering innovation. Projects generate feedback and updates at a rapid pace. The stronger the output, the more participants will be attracted, meaning technologies will become robust and sustainable.

Next, the concept of experience is a priority. Competition is intense in digital services, and customers – developers, users, or those outside your organization – have heightened expectations. Yet the cloud is a complex environment of transactions, microservices, and scale. Building a customer-first platform means organizing the components to deliver a streamlined, cohesive, and integrated experience.

Finally, we must raise our game on design, build, and work to a new platform engineering standard. As systems, infrastructure, and services mature, those designing and building platforms can harvest best practices and develop resources such as templates, meaning the platform can be scaled, operated, and secured quickly and efficiently.

This is where Shweta aligns with the vision of CNCF. With *Decoding Platform Engineering Patterns*, Shweta distills years of experience into actionable insights. Her book is grounded in her extensive work with customers on digital transformation in various sectors. She offers unbiased advice and delivers a vendor-neutral perspective applicable across different technologies.

Her book is essential because it helps simplify the otherwise complex world of platforms – a goal that resonates with the CNCF.

As you embark on your platform journey, consider Shweta's valuable advice, patterns and case studies. These are not theoretical concepts but tested and proven practices. Whether wishing to innovate, optimize, or simply gain a deeper understanding of platform dynamics, *Decoding Platform Engineering Patterns* is an invaluable resource.

—Priyanka Sharma
Former Executive Director, CNCF

Shalini Kapoor

I have spent over 27 years at the forefront of technological innovation, with my journey deeply rooted in applying future technologies to create transformative solutions. Leading initiatives that harness emerging technologies such as AI and IoT to drive sustainable growth and deliver large-scale impact has been a central theme in my career. Whether it was creating the Watson Internet of Things and AI Lab in Bangalore or leading strategic engagements to develop groundbreaking projects, the essence of my work has always been about leveraging platforms to solve complex, population-scale problems.

As the first IBM Fellow in India, I had the privilege of mentoring and providing technical thought leadership within the industry during my tenure at IBM. It was a rewarding experience to guide talented professionals such as Shweta Vohra, and I am delighted to see her work come to fruition so successfully in this book.

As a fellow author, I understand the commitment and clarity of vision required to distill complex subjects into accessible, actionable insights. Having authored *AI for You: The New Game Changer*, I appreciate the depth of expertise and passion that has gone into creating this book. From one author to another, I see in this work a genuine desire to guide readers through the intricacies of technology-driven platforms, making it a valuable resource.

This book is not just another addition to the growing body of literature on technology platforms. It stands out by offering a comprehensive blueprint for success, drawn from real-world experiences and lessons learned. Whether you're a seasoned technology leader or new to the field, the insights within these pages are invaluable. Shweta has done an excellent job of cutting through the noise and providing clear, actionable guidance on how to effectively build, manage, and scale platforms.

I am confident that this book will become a go-to reference for technology leaders and innovators around the world. It is a powerful tool for anyone committed to harnessing the full potential of platforms to drive growth, innovation, and long-term success.

—Shalini Kapoor
Author, Former Chief Technologist at AWS, Former IBM Fellow

Introduction

Introduction: Why Platforms Fail and Why This Book Exists

"Everywhere there can be a platform; there will be a platform."

—MIT Initiative on the Digital Economy

This prediction has not just come true[1]; it has become the very fabric of our modern technological landscape. Today, almost every business either leverages technology platforms or has evolved into a platform company itself.

Technology platforms are the engines of innovation, crafted to enhance user experiences while propelling and maximizing business success. The leading tech giants such as Meta (Facebook, Instagram, WhatsApp), Apple, Microsoft, Google, Amazon, Netflix, and Tesla are prime examples of thriving digital ecosystems. They have reshaped industries and redefined consumer expectations across the world.

Yet despite their ubiquity, the concept of "platform" has become increasingly muddled. The term is now used so broadly that its true meaning often gets lost amid technological jargon and marketing hype. Studies show that despite the revolutionary impact of digital platforms, **over 80% of them fail**.[2]

Why Platforms Fail

Why do so many platforms fail despite all the intelligence, investment, and innovation behind them? The reasons are remarkably consistent:

- **Lack of platform thinking and product mindset**: Failing to recognize that platforms are a special form of software, designed to scale through ecosystems and continuous evolution rather than short-term project delivery.

---

[1] https://ide.mit.edu/insights/just-released-2018-platform-strategy-report/
[2] https://www.itm-conferences.org/articles/itmconf/abs/2023/01/itmconf_iess2023_05001/itmconf_iess2023_05001.html

- **Misaligned incentives and ownership**: Teams optimize for delivery, not sustained value.

- **Over-engineering and under-measuring**: Building complex systems without clear success metrics.

- **Neglecting the user experience**: Assuming developers or customers will simply adapt.

- **Scaling too early or too narrowly**: Expanding without foundational clarity or ecosystem maturity.

If these feel obvious, they are; they are drawn from years of real-world practice, and whether you recognise them yet or not, they will inevitably shape your outcomes.

This book stands out for its field-tested lessons, reflections from real failures, and its focus on bringing platform engineering, business, and technology together to help you build platforms that truly endure.

Why This Book Exists

Given this growing ambiguity around what platforms truly are, it is crucial to draw from lived experience to clarify their role and impact. My journey in the software and IT industry, spanning over two decades, has provided insights from serving more than fifty customers across telecom, banking, automotive, healthcare, travel, and government. Through these experiences, I have witnessed the evolution of platforms firsthand, seeing their rise, reinvention, and often failure due to not leveraging how humans build, adopt, and understand scale.

My involvement with technology platforms began unexpectedly in 2003–2004 while developing some of the earliest web hosting solutions. Coding in Perl and Python, integrating Linux platforms, and creating templated solutions laid the groundwork for my lifelong focus on technology platforms. Those early days were marked by challenges in infrastructure and the infancy of automated builds, but they also set the stage for modern digital experiences.

Over time, I transitioned to more complex projects, from developing features for automated driving tractors in Australia to designing enterprise integrations across automotive, defense, IoT, and healthcare ecosystems. In the past decade, I have witnessed the convergence of cloud infrastructure, AI/ML, and platform thinking, fundamentally transforming how we design, operate, and scale technology.

Today, AI is not just an enhancement; it is shaping the next generation of platforms: intelligent, adaptive, and self-optimizing. This book introduces frameworks and success patterns to help you build AI-ready platforms that are both future-proof and human-centered.

The patterns and insights I have gathered have become invaluable. This book is my attempt to decode the complexity of platform engineering, offering grounded, practical guidance for those who build and lead them.

What Makes This Book Different

This work blends the **architect's craft**, the **engineer's precision**, and the **strategist's clarity**, turning complexity into actionable design. It does not just tell you what platforms are; it shows you how to make them work sustainably – organizationally, technically, and economically.

By the end of this book, you will be able to:

- Develop a clear understanding of platforms, platform engineering, and key platform patterns to drive meaningful innovation in your area of work

- Understand **why platforms succeed or fail** and how to measure their impact

- Design and evolve **platform blueprints** aligned with your business model and technology stack

- Leverage **technology, AI, and automation** to scale intelligently and reduce operational drag

- Build **platforms as living systems**, continuously improving through feedback, governance, and product culture

Sam's Journey

To bring common experiences across industry to life, let's merge them into one persona:

Sam, a seasoned technology manager tasked with developing a digital banking platform.

This journey began with excitement and high hopes. But over four years, Sam encountered a series of challenges that tested his skills, leadership, and resolve.

- **Year 1: Skills and Workforce Development**

  Sam's first hurdle was equipping his team with new skills for a rapidly changing tech stack. Despite investing heavily in training, the learning curve and delivery pressures collided. What seemed like upskilling soon revealed layers of complexity – from mastering containerization and IaC tools to understanding CI/CD pipelines and cross-domain collaboration.

- **Year 2: Vendor and Support Management**

  External vendors became both enablers and blockers. Reliability issues caused delays until Sam learned to balance open source adoption with the right partnerships. In practice, this meant evaluating SLAs, version control risks, and integration dependencies, where every choice could either accelerate delivery or create long-term friction.

- **Year 3: Technology and Platform Integration**

  Integrating new features with legacy systems caused inefficiencies and downtime. Sam realized architecture is not just about technology; it is about rhythm, timing, and empathy for users. From infrastructure selection to observability and developer support to operations, each layer required deliberate design choices to ensure resilience, maintainability, and trust.

- **Year 4: Performance, Scalability, and Cost**

  As usage grew, performance issues surfaced. Sam needed scalable designs that did not break the budget or burn the team out. Scaling was not just about compute; it demanded optimization across caching, storage tiers, cost monitoring, and real-time analytics – every decision influencing user experience and business outcomes.

Meanwhile, three continuous threads ran through every stage:

- **Security, compliance, and risk management**: Vigilance became nonnegotiable. What looked straightforward on paper turned into a daily discipline of threat modeling, access audits, data encryption, and regulatory alignment.

- **User adoption and customer impact**: Trust and experience determined success more than code. Feedback loops, usability testing, and API consistency became as critical as system uptime.

- **Strategic and operational impact**: Alignment between leadership vision and platform reality became the defining challenge. Turning architectural intent into measurable outcomes required both governance clarity and cultural resilience.

Sam's story is not unique. It mirrors what thousands of teams go through every year across industries. The question is: *must every team learn it the hard way?*

This book aims to make the invisible visible: the patterns, pitfalls, and playbooks that define lasting platforms.

Who This Book Is For

This book is written for those who shape, build, and scale platforms in modern organizations.

- **Platform engineers, architects, and DevOps professionals** who want to move beyond infrastructure delivery and design platforms as evolving products that empower others to build faster and better.

- **IT leaders, decision-makers, and strategists** seeking a holistic approach to software delivery that goes beyond the limits of "you built it, you run it."

- **Technology executives – CTOs, VPs, and heads of engineering –** who ask why platform teams grow large yet struggle to deliver speed, value, or alignment.

- **Product and program leaders** who bridge business and engineering, ensuring platform investments translate into measurable outcomes.

- **Curious practitioners and innovators** exploring how platform engineering connects people, technology, and business to create ecosystems that scale sustainably.

Whether you are in a startup defining your first platform or in an enterprise evolving from infrastructure to platform thinking, this book will help you build with intent and lead with clarity. Like Sam, you may be building for internal developers or external customers; either way, it will serve as your companion and mirror, helping you design clarity into complexity and create platforms that endure.

How to Read This Book

This book is designed as a **strategic playbook**, which is a blend of theory, frameworks, and field-tested patterns. It starts by decoding foundational ideas and gradually advances toward practical design models, platform scaling strategies, and AI-ready architectures.

Each section of this book is intentionally designed to take you from **foundation to mastery**, creating a progression that mirrors how real platforms are understood, built, and evolved in the industry.

- **Section 1: Decoding the Platform DNA (Understand)**

  Builds the foundation. It clears the noise, differentiates products from platforms, and gives you the mental models to identify value, personas, patterns, and platform boundaries with confidence. This section answers the question: *What is a platform and why does it exist?*

- **Section 2: The Platform Patterns (Scale)**

  Moves you from definition to perception. You learn to identify platform types, archetypes, and ecosystem roles, along with the forces and maturity signals that shape them. This section trains your eyes to *see platforms in the wild* and understand why some thrive while others fail.

- **Section 3: The Platform Success Blueprint (Strategy)**

  This is the heart of the book. It introduces the Platform Success Blueprint, a universal framework to design clarity, purpose, value flow, architecture, governance, measurement, and scale. This section details out all elements of strategy required for platform success, including when a platform as a product really thrives. This section gives you a **repeatable playbook** for building platforms that endure.

- **Section 4: Building and Scaling the Platform (Build)**

  This section zooms in on the platform provider's world, who is primarily responsible for laying a strong platform foundation. It explains the engineering, architectural, operational, and ecosystem depth required to bring platforms to life. Providers carry the complexity that users never see. This section teaches you how to handle that complexity intentionally through design, technology strategy, development-to-operations flow, and platform engineering.

- **Section 5: Leaving a Legacy Through Platforms (Execute and Evolve)**

  Theory becomes practice. Through user journeys, provider journeys, and a detailed Apple case study, you see how principles turn into lived decisions. This section shows how real companies grow, stumble, recover, and mature into platforms that create cultural and economic impact.

- **Section 6: The Future of Platforms with AI (Transform)**

  Here, the journey widens into the next decade. AI-native platforms, agentic ecosystems, intelligent middleware, and adaptive architectures reshape what platforms can become. This section prepares you for the platforms of tomorrow and the leadership mindset required to build them responsibly.

Throughout the book, you will find ***visual frameworks, models, and checklists*** – from the Platform Success Blueprint to the Platform Maturity Model – designed to help you turn insights into action and create platforms that grow with purpose.

A Living Community

This book is not just a tool for learning but an entry point into a wider community of innovators and platform builders. You can connect, share experiences, and continue the dialogue by connecting with the author on LinkedIn.

Your reflections, stories, and questions will shape the next wave of learning for everyone involved.

Author's Note

Every concept and example in this book is drawn from real projects, field experience, and independent research. The ideas shared are entirely experiential. This book stands for originality, lived insight, vendor neutrality, and intellectual integrity.

Take your time with it. Annotate, argue, apply. This is your field guide to understanding and building platforms that endure.

Enjoy the read, and may every platform you touch become stronger because of it.

SECTION I

Decoding the Platform DNA (Understand)

Establishes clarity, urgency, and a shared vocabulary around what platforms and platform engineering truly are.

CHAPTER 1

The Platform Dilemma – Why Everyone Builds One and Few Succeed

"Technology platforms' public triumphs often mask private frustrations."

Platforms represent one of the most powerful fusions of technology and business. They reshape industries, redefine customer experiences, and drive growth at scale. Yet, their immense promise often conceals the very challenges that can derail them from within. As platforms expand, so do their complexities. Navigating this landscape requires both technical clarity and leadership composure.

Among entrepreneurs and investors, platform-based businesses have become the preferred model for scale. Studies show that more than half of recent unicorns operate as platforms – from ride sharing to digital marketplaces. But success is not guaranteed. Like traditional companies, platform businesses must outperform competitors, sustain financial discipline, and maintain regulatory credibility. The paradox is simple: *the more visible a platform's triumph, the less visible its internal tension.*

© Shweta Vohra 2026
S. Vohra, *Decoding Platform Engineering Patterns*, https://doi.org/10.1007/979-8-8688-2555-2_1

The Platform Dilemma Triangle

Every platform operates within a tension of three forces:

1. **Speed of change**: The drive for rapid innovation and developer velocity

2. **Integration depth**: The need to connect securely with existing systems, data, and controls

3. **Economic viability**: The financial and operational sustainability of the platform

You can optimize two, but rarely all three. Push for speed and deep integration, and your costs will rise. Focus on economics and speed, and integration quality will suffer. The art of platform engineering lies in knowing which corner to manage, when, and why.

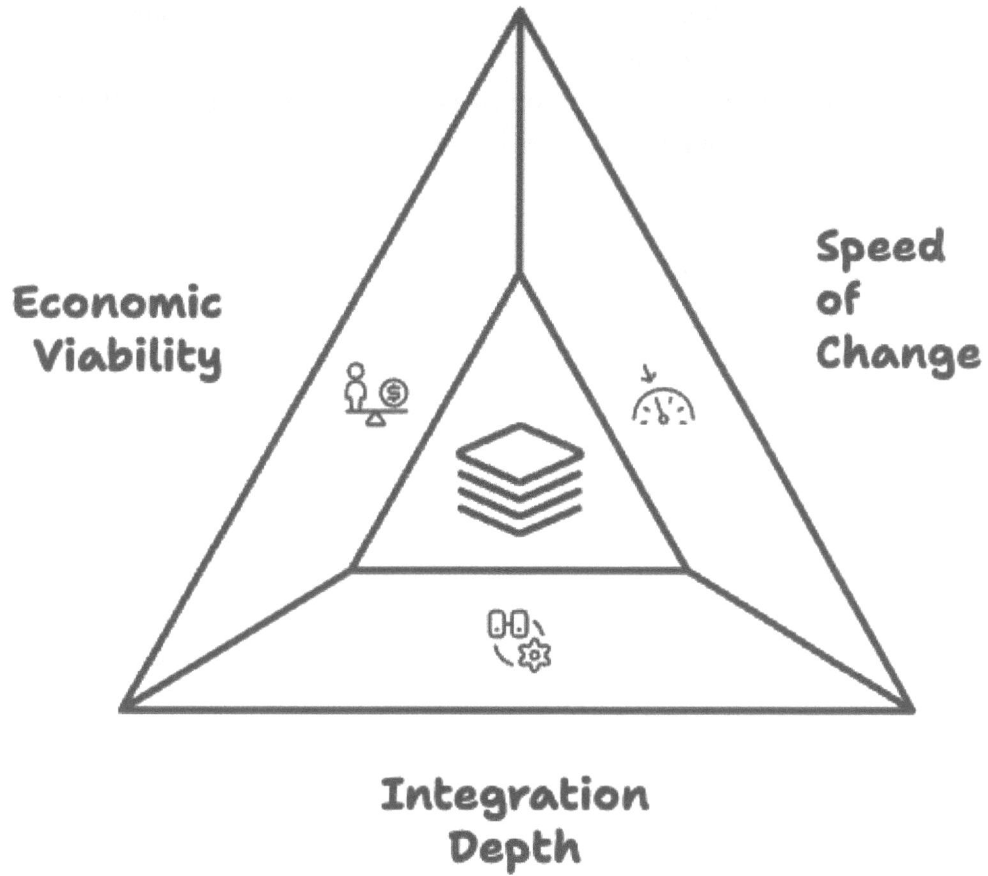

Figure 1-1. *Navigating the Platform Dilemma*

The dilemma: "You can build fast, deep, or cheap – but rarely all three. Choose consciously, not accidentally."

A Story from the Field

A few years ago, while leading a 20-member team for an automotive company, I faced this triangle firsthand. We set out to build a modern application platform – cloud-native, microservices-driven, and API-first. The excitement was contagious: *"Wow, all hail microservices!"*

For over two years, we built an MVP, integrating open source components, cloud services, and automation pipelines. Just as the finish line approached, a new technology emerged, promising faster results and lower costs. We faced a dilemma: continue with our hard-won foundation or pivot to something new.

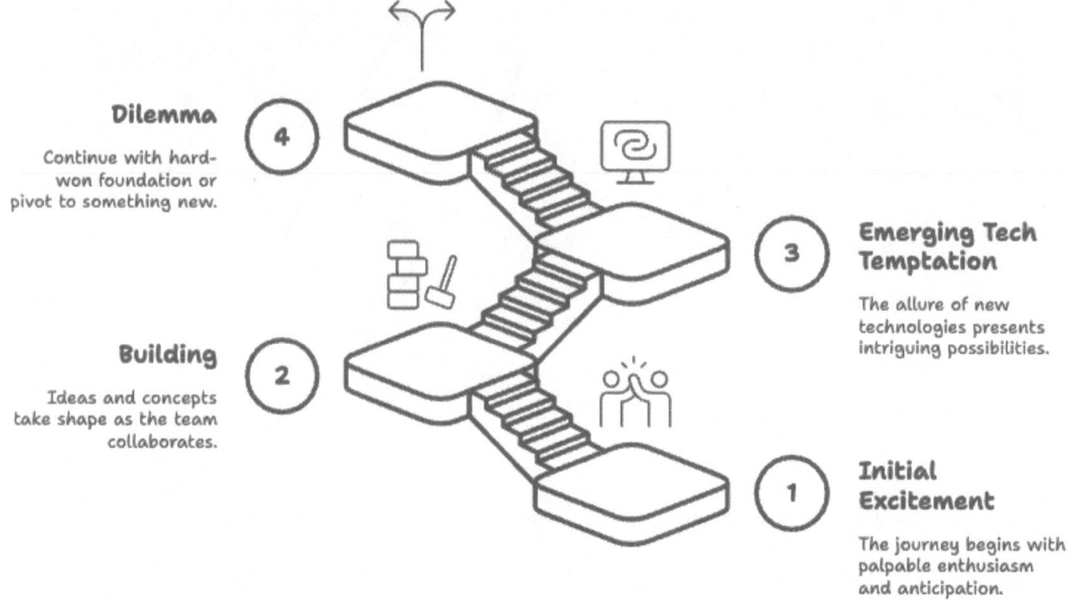

Figure 1-2. *Platform dilemmas with continuous emerging innovation*

The lesson was sharp that momentum without clarity becomes motion sickness. In platform work, innovation speed, integration depth, and cost discipline must stay in balance.

"A platform without strategy doesn't lose direction – it loses purpose, drifting from value to vanity."

Voices from the Field

Over the years, I've had countless conversations with people who live and breathe platforms, from CTOs to architects, engineers, and product managers. In this chapter, I'm bringing you four of those voices I've heard most often. Each one echoes a familiar pattern that repeats across industries and organizations, no matter how different their technology stacks or ambitions may seem.

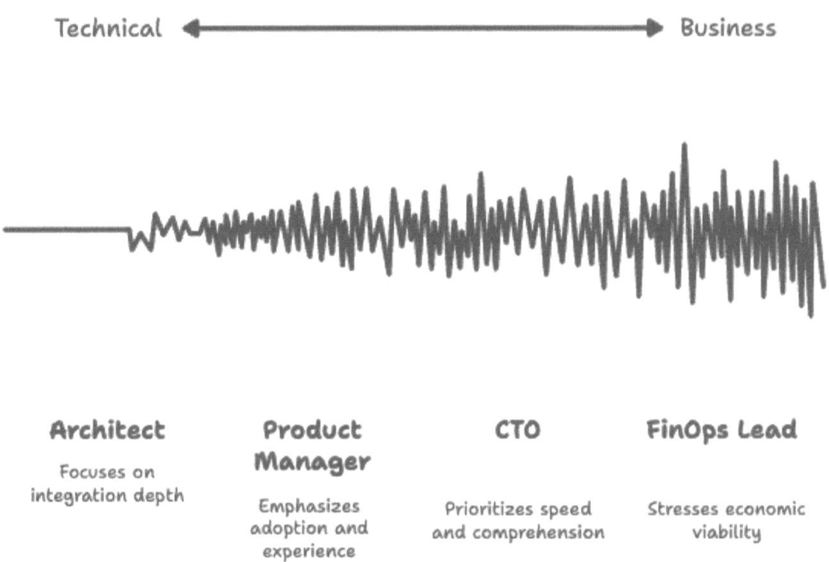

Figure 1-3. *Balancing technical depth with business value perspectives*

Voice 1 – CTO: Speed vs. Comprehension

"If we don't keep up, we fall behind."

For many CTOs, this isn't just a statement, but it's a daily dilemma. The relentless churn of tools, frameworks, and services creates a constant tension between keeping systems stable and pursuing innovation. Each new technology promises acceleration, yet every adoption cycle demands unlearning, retraining, and rebalancing operational reliability.

The real challenge is not choosing between innovation and stability but **synchronizing the two**. Serving what already exists while shaping what's next. Comprehension becomes the hidden bottleneck; when teams chase speed without shared understanding, decision-making slows, and cognitive debt accumulates faster than technical debt.

Technical reality: Establish clear service-level objectives (SLOs) and version lifecycle policies. Create *standard workflows* that protect stability without blocking progress. Encourage technical curiosity, but pair every innovation with a comprehension checkpoint – "Do we understand it deeply enough to operate it?"

Metrics:

- **Platform upgrade adoption rate:** Percentage of platform services running and adopted quarter on quarter.

- **Change comprehension index:** Ratio of successful rollouts to number of rollback incidents (indicating how well changes are understood before execution).

- **Innovation-to-stability ratio:** Number of new platform features shipped vs. critical incidents over a defined quarter – a balanced indicator of sustainable innovation.

Voice 2 – Architect: Integration Depth

"Hype or reality? How does it fit our data and integration model?"

Architects face the hardest balance of integrating the new with the old without breaking trust. Every new component, framework, or cloud service promises acceleration but quietly increases coupling and cognitive load. The real challenge isn't adoption; it's **integration depth**: ensuring that new layers speak the same language as existing systems, respect shared schemas, and maintain desirable observability boundaries.

Architectural coherence is not a constraint; it's the foundation of trust. When integrations are rushed or left implicit, platforms become brittle, data becomes unreliable, and incidents become harder to trace.

Technical reality: Treat integration as an architectural discipline, not a side effect of delivery. Design *contracts before code* – define APIs, data boundaries, and identity models upfront. Build shared observability and schema validation pipelines early. Align platform and application teams around integration reviews as part of the definition of done. Above all, measure *integration debt* just as you would technical debt because what's unclear today will cost exponentially more tomorrow.

Metrics:

- **Verified integration coverage:** Percentage of applications with signed-off API and data contracts

- **Trace completeness:** Ratio of services with full end-to-end observability or at least desirable observability across transactions

- **Identity consistency index:** Percentage of systems using standard identity and access patterns across environments

- **Integration rework rate:** Number of integration-related defects or rework cycles per release – a strong signal of underlying design misalignment

Voice 3 – FinOps Lead: Economic Viability

"Innovation scales fast, but so do costs. Maintaining healthy unit economics amidst constant variability is where discipline meets design."

Cost control is where idealism meets reality. Cloud platforms promise elasticity, but elasticity without accountability quickly turns into waste. Innovation adds value only when its cost curve stays predictable. The FinOps dilemma lies in balancing empowerment and governance – giving teams freedom to build while ensuring every build reflects economic awareness.

The complexity deepens when usage patterns fluctuate, services scale unevenly, or financial attribution blurs across shared resources. What seems efficient in isolation can collapse in aggregate if cost signals don't surface early enough.

Technical reality: Embed financial observability directly into the engineering workflow. Build cost visibility into CI/CD pipelines **and GitOps flows**, treating cost per deployment and cost drift as quality metrics. Use Git as the source of truth for infrastructure and policy changes, so cost guardrails are **versioned, auditable, and automatically enforced**. Introduce guardrails, not gates – policies that prevent runaway consumption without blocking delivery. Align finance, engineering, and product teams on shared dashboards that combine spend, utilization, and performance data. Make cost forecasts as iterative as your release cycles, evolving with every pull request and deployment.

Metrics:

- **Cost per successful deployment** (primary efficiency metric)

- **Infrastructure cost per customer transaction or API call** (unit economics)

- **Budget predictability ratio:** Forecasted vs. actual monthly spend

- **Idle resource ratio:** Percentage of unused or underutilized cloud resources beyond SLA thresholds

- **Automation efficiency index:** Percentage of workloads governed by automated cost policies or budgets

Voice 4 – Product Manager: Adoption and Experience

"Our platform is technically sound, yet adoption is hard to measure – or simply not there."

Even the most elegant platform fails if no one uses it. Adoption is the invisible success metric – it reveals whether the platform truly enables its users. Many teams mistake delivery for impact; they ship platforms that solve technical problems but ignore human friction. If developers or product teams avoid the "golden path," it's not rebellion – it's feedback.

True adoption isn't just about features; it's about *flow*. From command-line ergonomics to API consistency, from documentation clarity to onboarding speed, every friction point compounds into lost trust. The platform's experience layer determines whether it becomes a habit or a hurdle.

Technical reality: Treat developer experience as a product in itself. Define and iterate your "standard workflows" – the paved paths that make the right thing the easy thing. Instrument the platform to capture behavioral data such as onboarding time, success rates, and drop-offs. Pair analytics with direct feedback loops through user councils, surveys, and internal communities. Adoption doesn't improve with mandates; it improves with empathy and iteration.

Metrics:

- **Golden path adoption rate:** Percentage of teams consistently using standard workflows

- **Time to first successful deployment:** Measures onboarding efficiency

- **Developer satisfaction index:** Collected quarterly via surveys or feedback tools

- **Feature utilization rate:** Ratio of actively used platform capabilities to those deployed

- **Documentation completeness:** Percentage of modules or APIs with verified, up-to-date guides

Key Learnings and Opportunities

The following observations capture the recurring challenges and hidden opportunities revealed through decades of platform engagement. They serve both as lessons learned and as signals for change.

Misaligned expectations: A persistent issue with platform technologies is the gap between promises and delivery. Companies often expect seamless integration and instant transformation but end up battling complexity, integration delays, or unmet outcomes. The remedy lies in closing the gap with measurable outcomes – lead time, adoption rates, and service-level objectives (SLOs) that reflect real business value. *Lesson:* Clarity beats excitement. Define success in metrics, not marketing slides.

Misunderstood technologies: New technologies invite curiosity but often demand more readiness than assumed. Without understanding their limits, teams misapply them – leading to underutilized features, poor integrations, or productivity loss. Before full rollout, pilot a thin slice: validate contracts, observability, and rollback paths. *Lesson:* Curiosity needs discipline. Pilot to learn, not to impress.

Broken integrations: Seamless integration remains the most oversold promise in technology. Real-world platforms stumble here – APIs misalign, systems duplicate logic, and teams rely on manual fixes. Broken integration isn't a failure of code; it's a failure of shared understanding. Build contracts before code and automate schema validation. *Lesson:* Integration is not a feature; it's a relationship that must be designed and maintained.

Shallow products or promises: In the rush to adopt the latest trend, many organizations end up with half-mature solutions – technologies that look impressive but collapse under scale, regulation, or user friction. Running small, controlled experiments with clear exit criteria around cost, resilience, and usability protects both time and trust. *Lesson:* Resist the race to adopt; design the space to adapt.

Cultural overload: Sometimes the problem isn't the platform but the people building it in silos. Misaligned language between product, tech, and leadership turns shared goals into competing agendas. Establishing one platform vocabulary and rhythm of intent brings coherence to chaos.
Lesson: A common platform language builds more bridges than tools ever can.

In essence: The platform challenge is not just technical – it's cognitive, cultural, and operational. The variety and complexity of today's technologies can overwhelm even the most mature organizations. The real question isn't how fast you can keep up, but how clearly you can see what matters. The path forward lies in turning these learnings into disciplined platform practices. A theme that unfolds in the chapters ahead as we decode the evolution and innovation of modern platforms.

Five Early Signals Your Platform's in Trouble

1. Routine tasks require manual tickets; self-service usage falls below 70%.

2. When your so-called "standard workflow" takes more than three manual steps to ship, automation isn't working; it's waiting.

3. Version drift exceeds policy; upgrades become "projects."

4. Cost surprises during scale or new product launches.

5. Platform incidents without playbooks or clear ownership.

These are not symptoms of failure; they are early warnings. Platforms rarely collapse overnight; they erode slowly when ignored.

The Platform Readiness Pulse

Before we decode deeper platform patterns in the next chapters, take a quick self-assessment. Mark (✓) if you strongly follow the statement, and (X) if it is unclear, unknown, or weak in your context. Do this per platform if you operate more than one.

Strategy

Does the platform shorten time-to-market for your top products?

Is there a clear exit strategy from key vendors?

Are 3–5 success metrics agreed with business stakeholders?

Technology

Are identity, data contracts, and observability defined before new services ship?

What percentage of teams use the standard workflow with guardrails (often called a "golden path")?

Can you roll back any platform change within minutes?

Organization

Are product, platform, and security aligned on release cadence and SLOs?

Is documentation treated as a product with clear ownership?

Do developers have self-service environments and required access?

Finance and Compliance

Do you track cost per deploy and cost per customer transaction?

Are compliance checks automated in the delivery pipeline?

Can you forecast platform costs for twice the load without firefighting?

Now Act on It

- If you have not completed the checklist, pause and prefer doing it now in the flow.

- Count your total ticks (✓) out of 12.

- Circle two areas with the most X and define one improvement you will start this month.

- Pick one metric to track for each and schedule a 30-day check-in after finishing this book.

Platform Pulse Interpretation

- **>10 – Strong platform strategy and alignment:** Your teams show clarity, integration maturity, and operational discipline. Next focus: scale automation and refine developer experience.

- **6–9 – Moderate maturity with uneven depth:** Strategy and intent are visible, but deep technical integration and financial consistency may be suffering. Strengthen cross-functional alignment and cost transparency.

- **Below 6 – Weak platform foundation:** Likely fragmented strategy, unclear ownership, or low automation maturity. Go back to the drawing board, revisit your core vision, rebuild alignment, and set the right anchors before scaling further. We will explore how to do this in Section 2.

The Platform Dilemma Triangle: balancing speed, integration depth, and economic viability. It shapes every meaningful decision in platform engineering. Understanding which corner you are optimizing for, and why, is the first step toward sustainable success.

Use the *Platform Readiness Pulse* as your early diagnostic. It reveals where your platform truly stands today, not just in maturity but in clarity of intent and operational strength. Identify the top two levers you can improve immediately, whether that's integration depth, cost visibility, or alignment across teams.

Before moving ahead, define your compass. Establish three measurable platform success indicators you will track each month, such as time to deploy, self-service adoption rate, and cost per environment, and review them regularly with your product or business counterpart. These signals will guide your platform journey far more reliably than hype or assumptions.

Platforms are intricate systems, ecosystems of technology, people, and economics. Complexity can stall progress, but clarity, alignment, and discipline turn it into momentum.

Key Takeaways

- Platforms drive innovation and growth but demand disciplined management for lasting success.

- Evaluate technologies beyond their promises and ensure they align with your strategic and operational needs.

- Use data, not optimism, to measure platform success through adoption, reliability, and economic outcomes.

- Establish clarity between product, engineering, and leadership to prevent cultural overload and wasted effort.

- Treat this chapter as your foundation check before diving into the deeper design and innovation patterns that follow.

As you turn the page, imagine tracing the timeline of how we arrived here and how early digital systems evolved into platforms, how innovation cycles reshaped what we call a platform, and why understanding that history is essential to designing the next generation of platform success. Let's dive in.

CHAPTER 2

The Innovation Unfolded – How Platforms Changed Everything

"When you truly understand the problem, the platform innovation becomes a matter of time."

Every generation of technology promises progress, but each leaves behind unfinished transitions. What we now call *the platform dilemma* is, in truth, the story of evolution itself – every breakthrough creates both opportunity and complexity.

We're witnessing an unprecedented surge in platforms and in the confusion that accompanies them. So, you might think, what's the big deal? Digital transformation isn't new. It's been unfolding for decades, from mainframes to mobile, from hardware to cloud. What makes *platforms* distinct today is their scale, speed, and stakes.

Platforms don't just automate but orchestrate. They don't just connect but compound.

Yet, beneath their public triumphs lie private frustrations – rising costs, skill shortages, integration breakdowns, and shifting business models. To understand why, we must trace where these pressures began and how they shaped the modern platform economy.

The Four Forces of Platform Acceleration

Four key forces have driven the last three decades of platform growth. Each has accelerated innovation but also multiplied complexity. Together, they form the foundation and friction of every modern platform story.

© Shweta Vohra 2026

S. Vohra, *Decoding Platform Engineering Patterns*, https://doi.org/10.1007/979-8-8688-2555-2_2

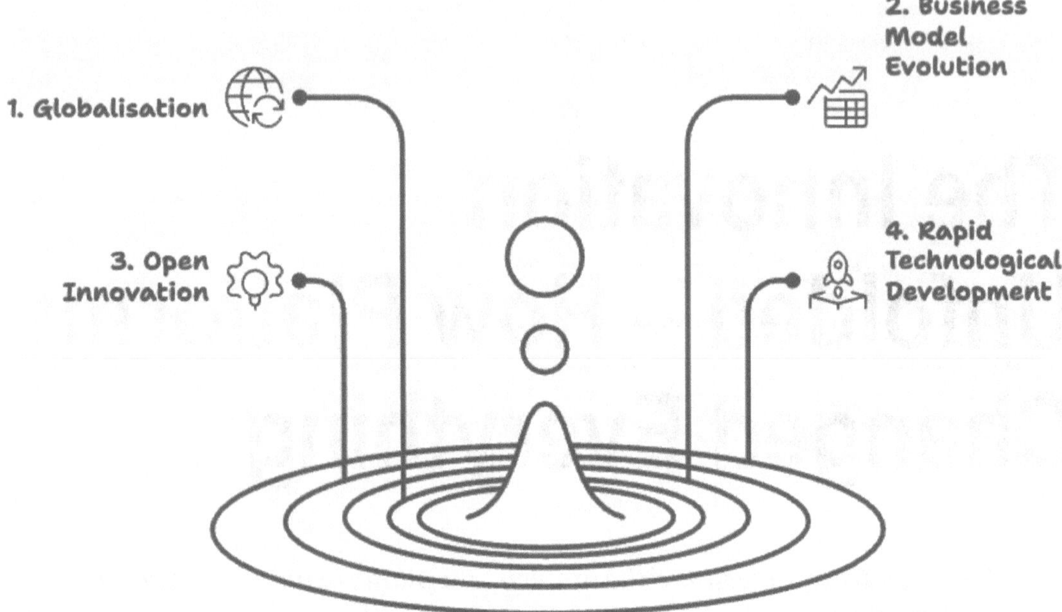

Figure 2-1. *Forces Driving Platform Evolution*

Each of these forces locks into the other like puzzle pieces – remove one, and the platform's balance falters.

1. **Globalization – Expanding Reach, Multiplying Complexity**

   The internet dismantled geographical barriers, allowing businesses to innovate and operate globally. Platforms now serve diverse markets, languages, and regulations – scaling opportunity while amplifying risk.

   Globalization reshaped technology through improved network infrastructure, high-speed connectivity, and decentralized collaboration. Yet, as reach expanded, regulation became regional. Data residency laws, privacy mandates, and geopolitical fragmentation now influence even the smallest design decisions. Globalization enabled innovation everywhere but also increased the need for regulation as systems evolved from centralization to decentralization.

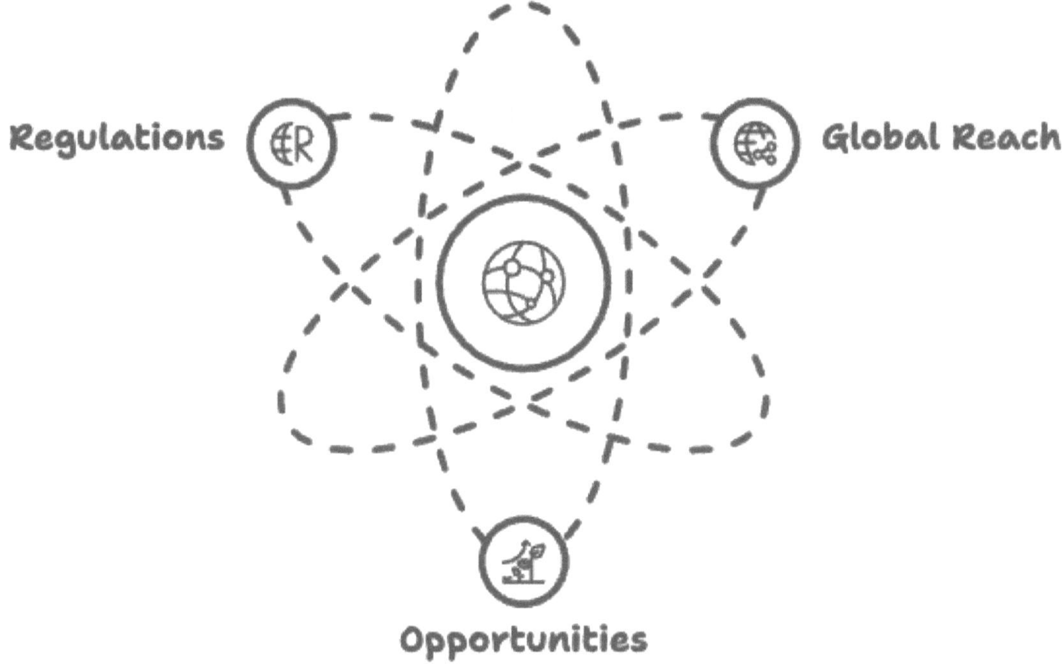

Figure 2-2. *Global reach multiplied opportunities and regulations*

2. **Business Model Explosion – The Redefinition of Value**

The rise of digital platforms has created new economic blueprints. We've moved beyond traditional **B2B** and **B2C** into hybrid and participatory models that reshape who creates, who consumes, and who profits.

Figure 2-3. *Business Model Explosion*

- **C2C (Consumer-to-Consumer):** Airbnb, eBay, Uber – direct exchanges between individuals.

- **C2M (Consumer-to-Manufacturer):** Alibaba, Nike By You – users influencing production.

- **D2D (Developer-to-Developer):** GitHub, Stack Overflow – ecosystems built on shared code.

- **H2H (Human-to-Human):** LinkedIn, Facebook – connections as currency.

- **M2M (Machine-to-Machine):** IoT and AI automation creating self-operating networks.

- **A2A (Agent-to-Agent):** Intelligent agents collaborating autonomously, exchanging data, negotiating tasks, and optimizing outcomes without human intervention.

These models blurred the boundaries between producer and participant. Every interaction now generates data, and every dataset becomes a business advantage. The result: a network economy that thrives on integration.

3. **Open Innovation – The Power and Paradox of Openness**

Open innovation, powered by open source ecosystems, has accelerated progress across the entire technology spectrum. Communities collaborate to build shared frameworks at a pace no single enterprise can match.

But openness brings trade-offs. Integrating a diversity of tools, licenses, and governance models adds operational complexity and accountability risks.

From Linux Foundation to CNCF's 180+ projects, open innovation has become both an engine and a maze. Every contribution expands capability – and every dependency multiplies fragility.

Open innovation democratized power – but also decentralized control.

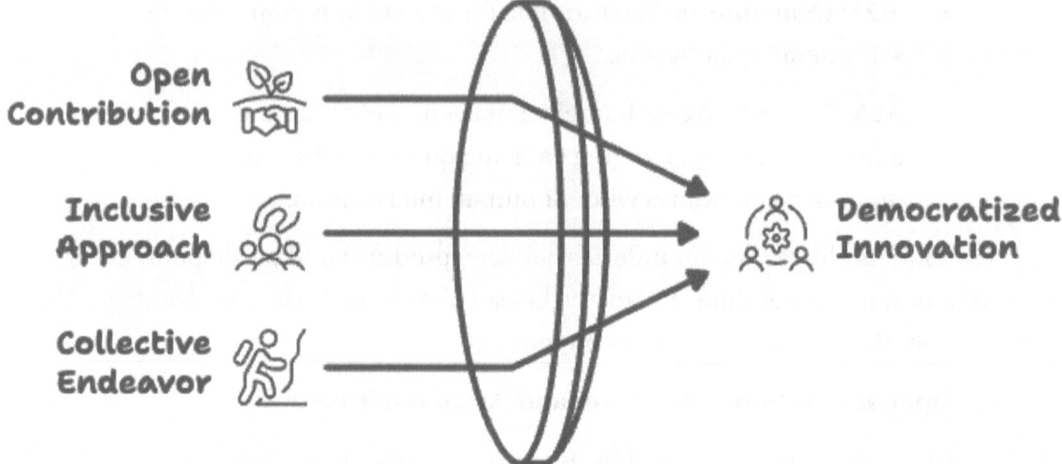

Figure 2-4. *Open contribution democratised innovation, but decentralised control*

4. **Rapid Technological Development – The Compression of Time**

Technology cycles no longer run in decades; they unfold in quarters. From cloud computing to AI, the pace of progress forces businesses to adapt faster than they can restructure.

Each innovation abstracts another layer of complexity. First, we abstracted **hardware**, then **software**, and now **decision-making itself** through automation and AI. The higher we abstract, the faster we move – but the less we fully understand.

a) **Evolution of Programming Language**

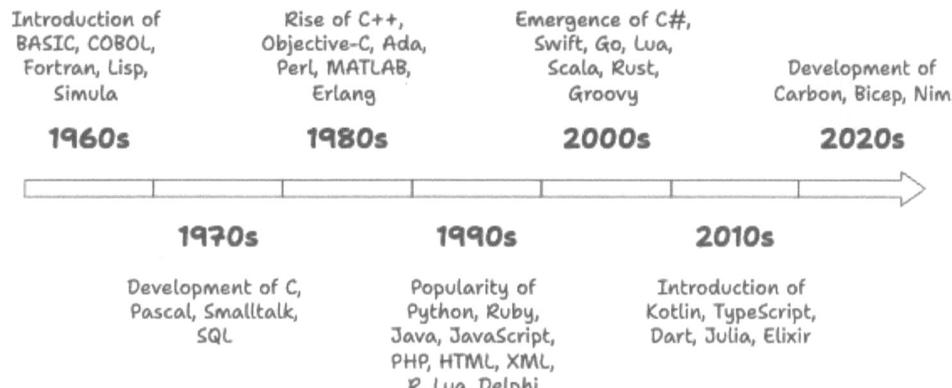

Figure 2-5. *Evolution of Programming Languages and Paradigms*

Every leap simplified expressions but demanded new skills, new tools, and new mental models.

b) **Database Technology Evolution**

Databases became the heart of platforms, shifting from relational to distributed, from consistent to adaptive.

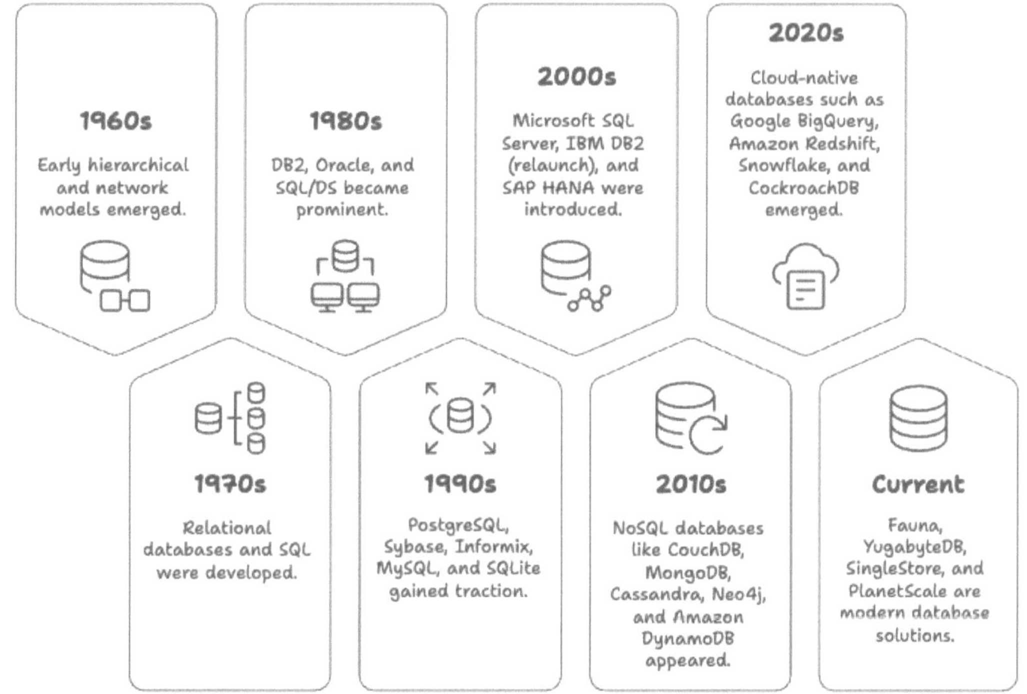

Figure 2-6. *Database Evolution Over Decades*

c) **Virtualization to Containerization Path**

What began as resource optimization became orchestration and then the art of control through abstraction.

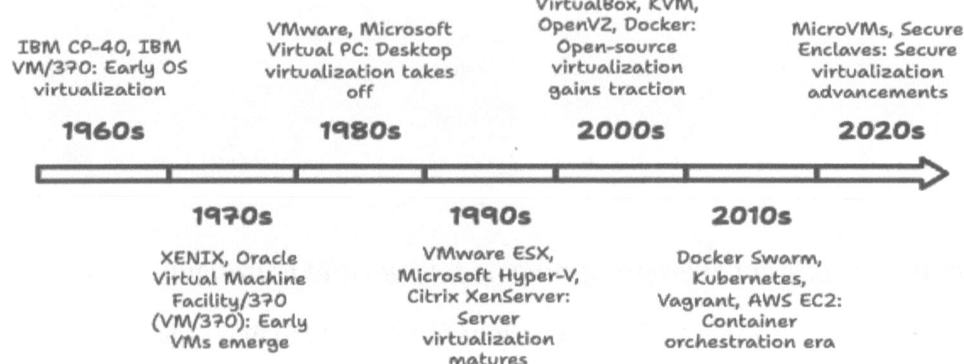

Figure 2-7. *Evolution of Virtualization Technologies*

Decades of Innovation – Patterns Beneath the Progress (1960–2020s)

Platforms didn't appear overnight. Their story spans six decades of ambition, iteration, and correction. Each decade solved one bottleneck and introduced another. Let's look at that closely and bring out your own observations as you read this data.

The 1960s – Foundations and Friction

Centralized computing enabled progress but came with high cost and low reach. Skill shortages and system rigidity limited access.

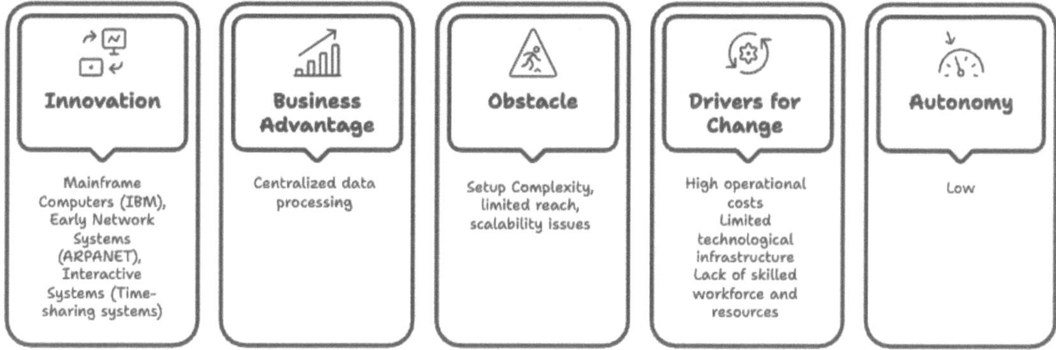

Figure 2-8. *Decades of Platform Innovation - 1960s*

The 1970s – Standardization and Entry

Personal computers and early operating systems like UNIX introduced accessibility but also complexity and regulatory hurdles.

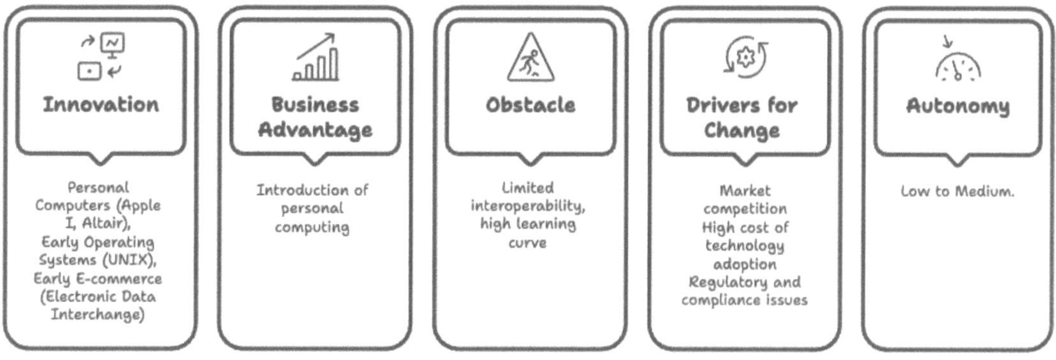

Figure 2-9. *Decades of Platform Innovation - 1970s*

The 1980s – Democratization and Security

PCs and LANs decentralized computing, but security and planning weaknesses emerged.

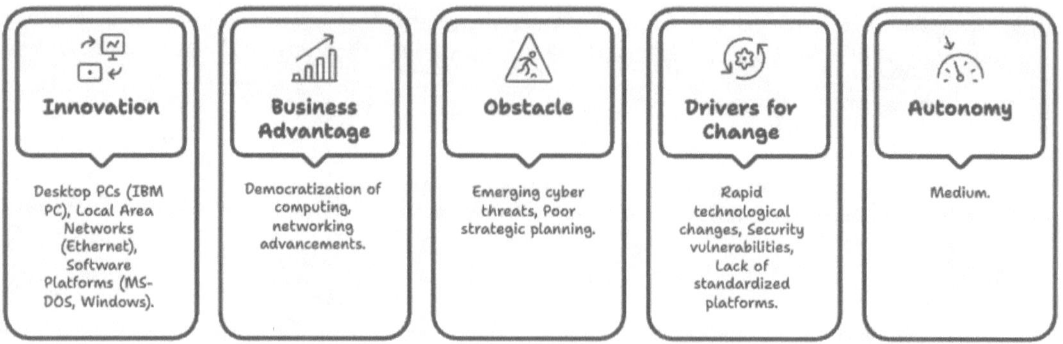

Figure 2-10. *Decades of Platform Innovation - 1980s*

The 1990s – Connectivity and Collapse

The web brought connection at scale, but the dot-com bubble revealed how speculation outpaced comprehension.

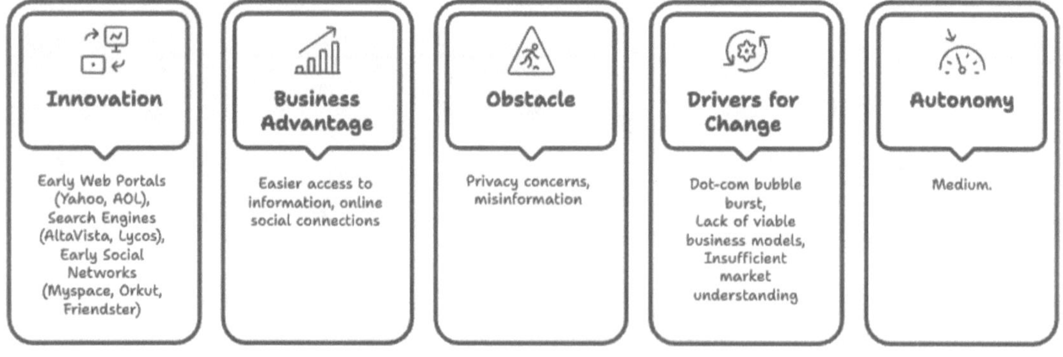

Figure 2-11. *Decades of Platform Innovation - 1990s*

The 2000s – Platforms as Economies

Social, e-commerce, and media platforms turned user participation into currency. Overinvestment, privacy breaches, and lack of discipline followed.

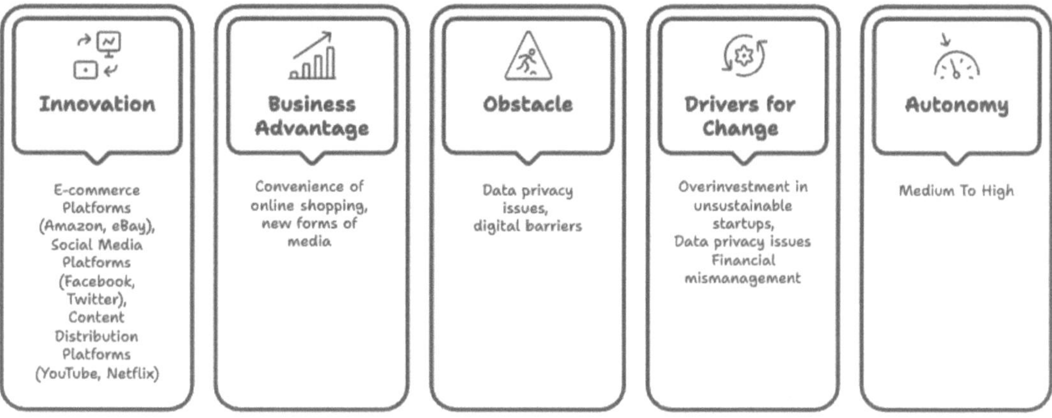

Figure 2-12. *Decades of Platform Innovation - 2000s*

The 2010s – Mobile Explosion and Experience Economy

App ecosystems, the gig economy, and crowdfunding empowered individuals but widened regulation gaps and worker instability.

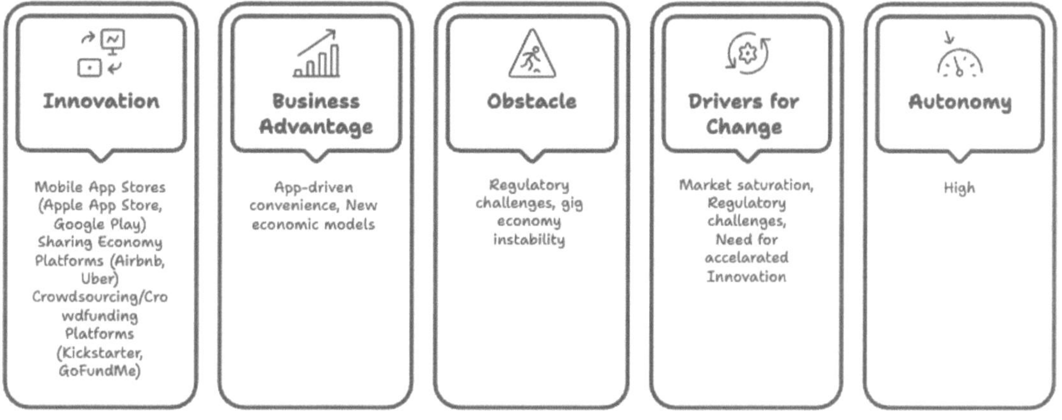

Figure 2-13. *Decades of Platform Innovation - 2010s*

The 2020s – Autonomy and AI

AI, blockchain, and decentralization brought adaptive intelligence – and fresh anxiety over privacy, security, and control.

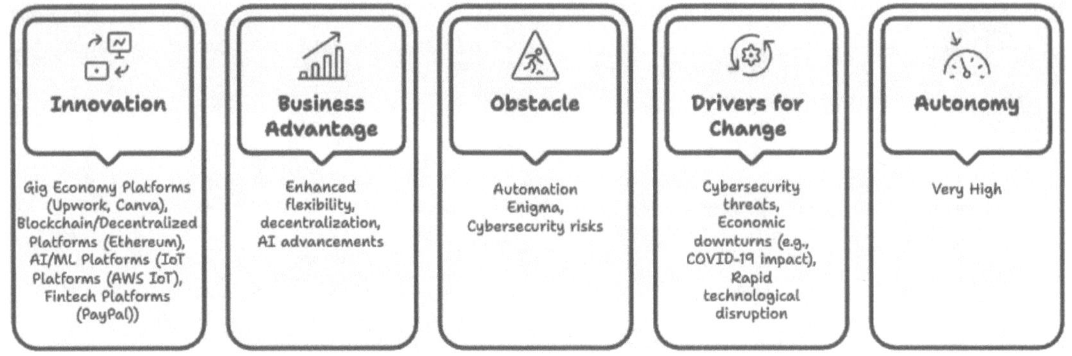

Figure 2-14. Decades of Platform Innovation - 2020s

"Each decade promised clarity and delivered new complexity."

Compounding Realities of Platform Innovation

If you look closely across these visuals, you'll see that the story of technology is not one of replacement but of compounding realities. Every decade adds a layer of progress, but none resets the system.

Security, skills, integration, and economic discipline have always existed. What's changed is their magnitude and interdependence.

Decade	Innovation Pulse	Persistent Challenge	Amplified by
1960s–70s	Centralized computing, early networks	High cost, low skill, limited reach	Globalization, early standardization
1980s	Desktop and network expansion	Cybersecurity gaps, poor planning	Software dependency
1990s	Internet revolution	Market speculation, data privacy	Early digital openness
2000s	E-commerce, social media	Overinvestment, misuse of data	Open innovation, mass participation
2010s	Mobile-first, gig economy	Regulatory gaps, skill instability	Social media scale, easy learning
2020s	AI, decentralization	Cyber threats, skill obsolescence	Instant learning, global dependence

Each era introduced solutions that eased previous pain points but spawned new interdependencies. What began as **technical debt** has now become **ecosystem debt** – a system-level imbalance that spans teams, tools, and time zones.

The **four forces** amplified exponentially:

- **Globalization** turned physical reach into digital omnipresence.

- **Business models** multiplied into crowd-led ecosystems.

- **Open innovation** grew from collaboration to hyper-dependence.

- **Rapid development** compressed years of maturity into months of churn.

As learning became accessible to everyone, mastery became scarce. We now live in an era of *velocity without synthesis* and *innovation without integration*.

Platform Revolution: Insights from Decades of Innovation

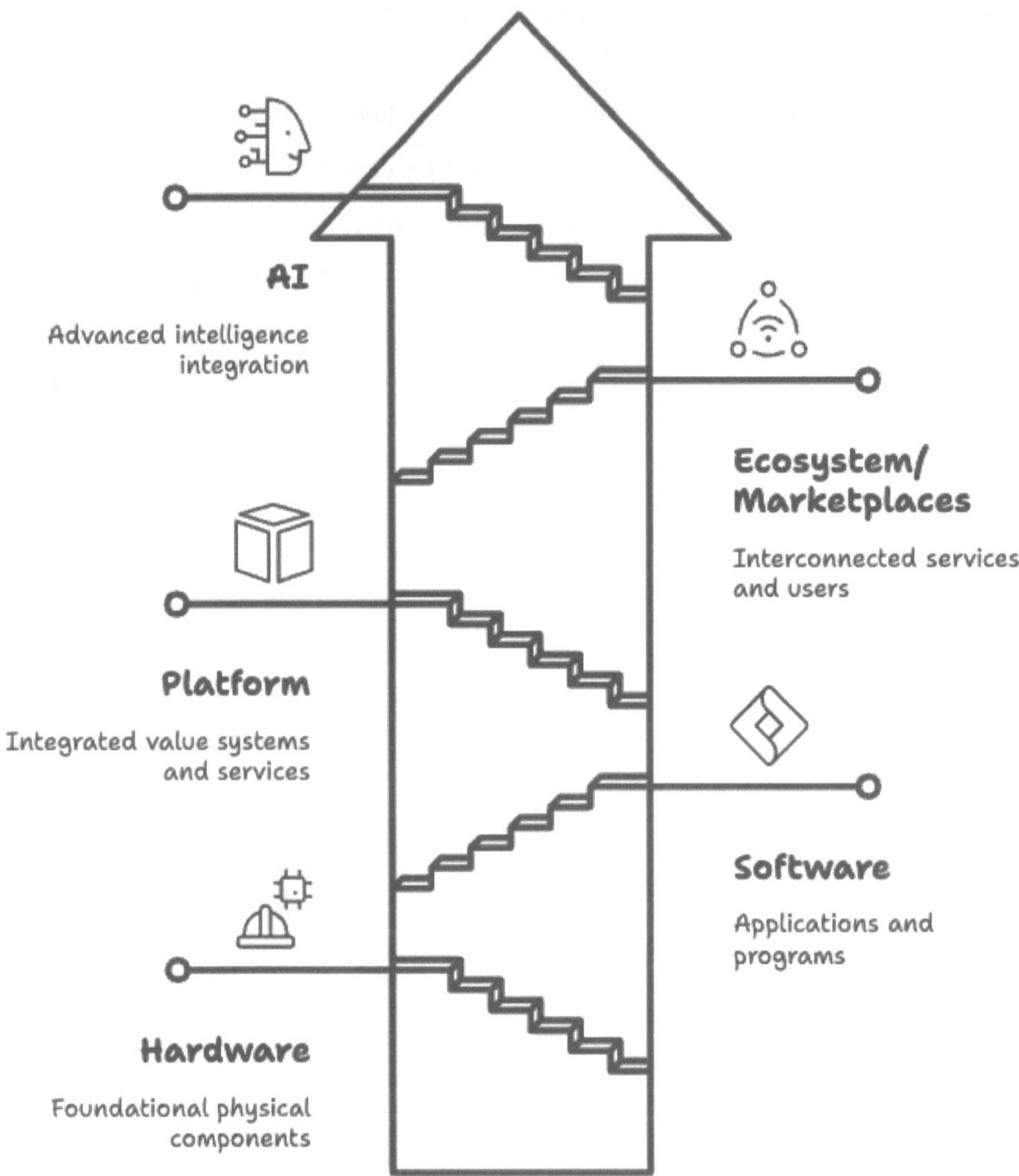

Figure 2-15. *Platform Maturity and Progression Ladder*

1. **Shift from Hardware to AI Platforms**

   Each era built on the last. Hardware gave capability, software gave usability, and AI gives adaptability.

2. **Centralization to Decentralization**

   What began in mainframes now thrives in distributed clouds. Resilience improved, but complexity multiplied.

3. **Autonomy and Oversight**

   Systems self-heal and autoscale, yet they require human ethics and governance more than ever.

4. **Security as a Recurring Constant**

   Every leap forward has carried new vulnerabilities. Today's scale simply amplifies them.

5. **Economics and Technology Intertwined**

   Every innovation cycle follows an economic curve of excitement, adoption, correction, and maturity.

6. **Infrastructure Sets the Ceiling for Innovation**

   Tools evolve, but infrastructure maturity still dictates how far platforms can scale.

7. **Clarity as the New Advantage**

   In an era where everything connects, the ability to design with awareness, not speed, defines resilience.

8. **Integration as the New Competitive Edge**

   As technology compresses time, the ability to integrate becomes the true differentiator.

We've inherited extraordinary tools and extraordinary expectations. Each era promised simplicity and delivered more layers of complexity. Yet, the patterns are visible now: platforms evolve, collide, and reform, each cycle leaving behind wisdom and warning.

If you've read this far, pause and reflect: Which decade or era mirrors your organization's platform journey today? What lessons from its evolution resonate with you and could shape your next leap forward? Use the reflection box below to capture the insights that stand out before moving ahead.

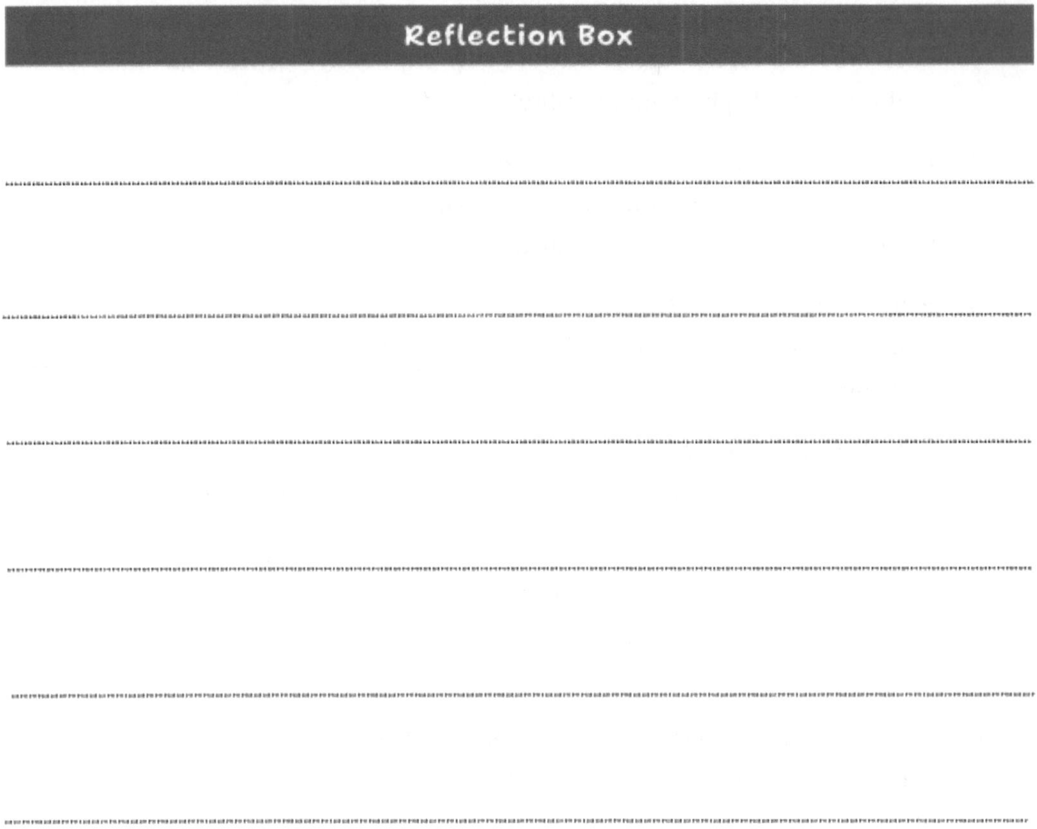

Reflection Box

Figure 2-16. *Reflection Box*

Now that we've unfolded how platforms came to be, the next step is to define what a *true platform* really is – and how to tell whether yours deserves to be called one.

Key Takeaways

- The evolution of platforms reflects a compound story, not a linear one where progress is built on persistent challenges.

- Four forces: Globalization, business models, open innovation, and rapid tech development accelerated innovation but deepened interdependence.

- Each decade amplified existing problems around security, skills, cost discipline, and integration.

- Open access to knowledge increased speed but reduced synthesis, creating the modern dilemma of innovation fatigue.

- The new advantage lies in clarity, connectedness, and comprehension – designing for understanding, not just for scale.

CHAPTER 3

Shattering Platform Myths – What a Platform Isn't (and What It Must Be)

"A real platform earns its name through action, not just a title."

Platform engineering is everywhere right now. Walk into any organization today, and you'll hear teams using the word *platform* for almost everything – from CI/CD pipelines and portals to cloud dashboards and data lakes. Somewhere along the way, the word lost precision. But important question to ask ourselves is are we all really talking about same thing.

In the previous chapters, we explored the vast opportunities platforms create and the immense innovation space they unlock. These platforms are not just shaping industries; they are redefining how businesses think, operate, and scale. Yet, as their popularity grows, so does the confusion. While platforms are inherently composable by design, not every composition qualifies as a platform. Simply connecting tools, APIs, or workflows doesn't automatically make it one. A platform is more than the sum of its components – it's a system of enablement that balances technology, people, and purpose.

Before we dive deeper into defining what a *true* platform is and how to leverage it effectively, we must first clear the noise. Misconceptions around platforms often distort strategy, leading teams to chase the wrong goals or reinvent what already exists. These myths blur the line between frameworks, products, and platforms, creating more friction than clarity.

© Shweta Vohra 2026
S. Vohra, *Decoding Platform Engineering Patterns*, https://doi.org/10.1007/979-8-8688-2555-2_3

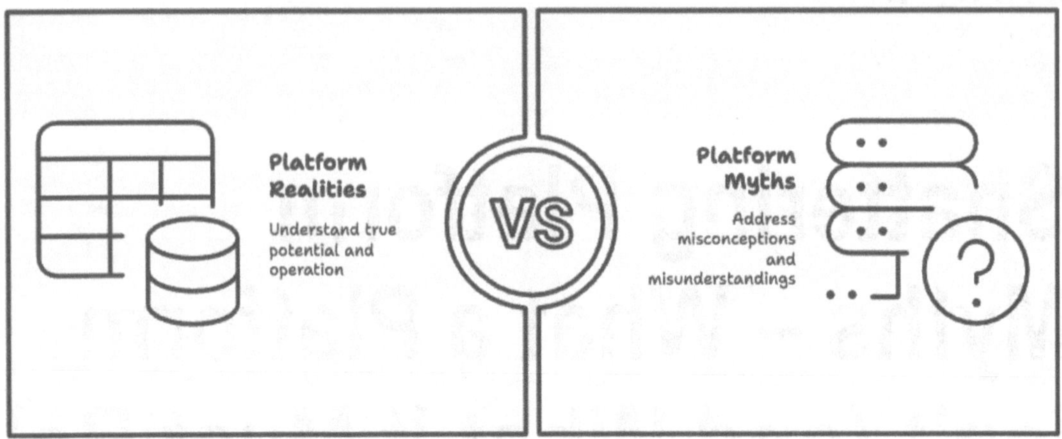

Figure 3-1. *Platform vs. Myths - Everything is not a Platform*

In this chapter, we'll address a simple but foundational question: **What is *not* a platform?** Through practical examples and real-world distinctions, we'll dismantle these myths to set a clear foundation for everything that follows.

Let's begin by separating fact from fiction. There are a handful of myths ahead; feel free to jump to the ones that spark your curiosity or address your biggest platform questions.

Platform vs. Myths – Let's Begin

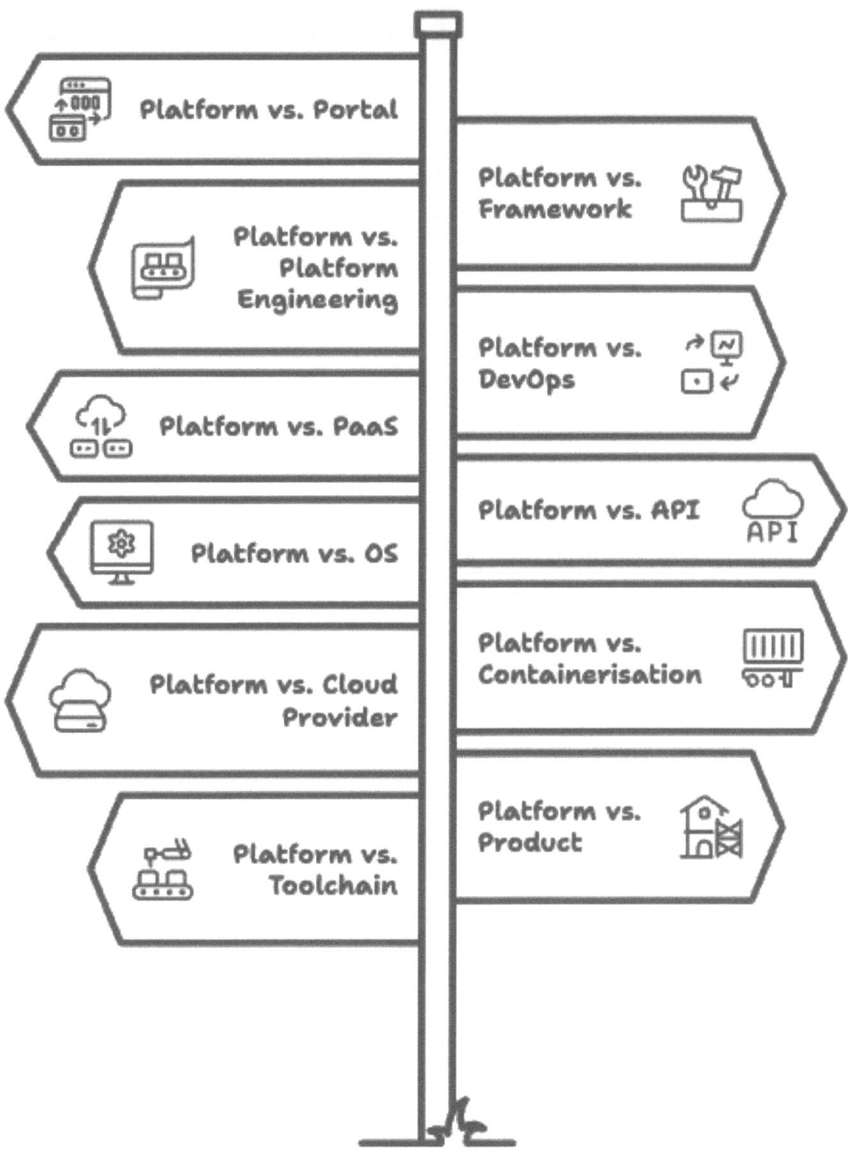

Figure 3-2. *Common Platform Myths*

Myth 1: Platform vs. Portal

Misconception: Platforms and portals are interchangeable.

Reality: A portal is an *access point*; a platform is an *ecosystem*. While they may appear similar, their purposes are entirely different. A portal focuses on aggregation and presentation – helping users access content, tools, or applications within a defined environment. A platform, on the other hand, provides the underlying foundation, structure, and orchestration layer that enables development, scalability, and continuous delivery.

Acceptance: Platforms may include portals as part of their service offering, but their scope extends far beyond the user interface – into enablement, lifecycle management, and the infrastructure that sustains innovation.

Example: Udemy serves as a great illustration. Its website acts as a portal where learners access courses, videos, and resources. Yet, beneath that portal lies a robust platform that empowers instructors to create, manage, and deliver content; process global payments; and support analytics and scalability. The platform is what sustains Udemy's entire learning ecosystem – not just what users see on screen.

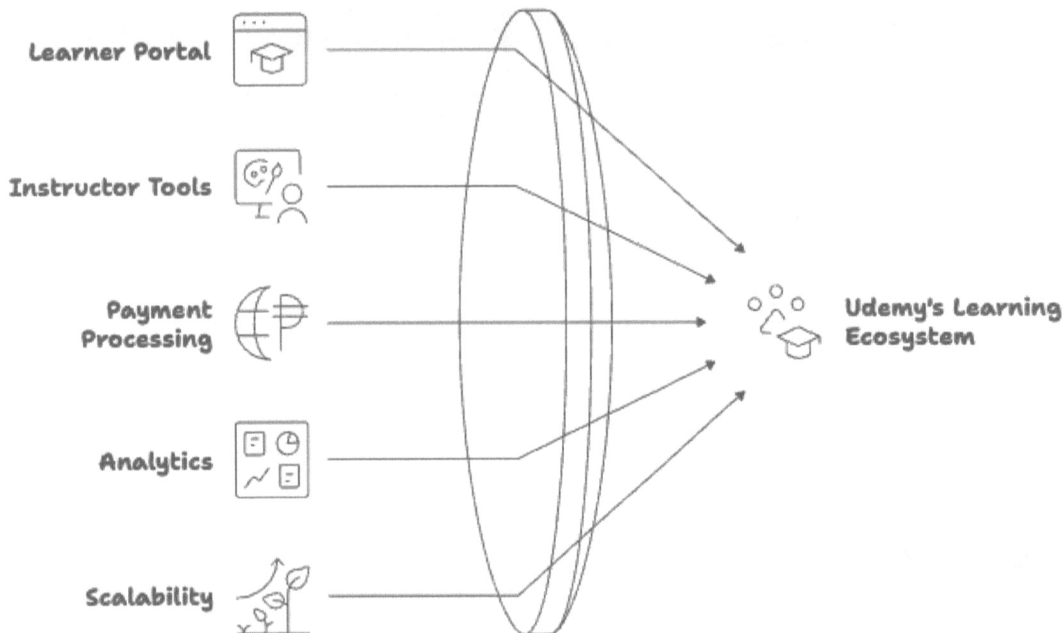

Figure 3-3. The Pillars of Udemy's Success

Myth 2: Platform vs. Framework

Misconception: A framework and a platform are the same thing.

Reality: A framework provides guidance; a platform provides governance and execution. A framework offers reusable patterns, libraries, and templates for developers to follow, while a platform operationalizes these frameworks to deliver scalability, observability, and consistency across teams and base for use cases built on top of that.

Acceptance: Frameworks define patterns; platforms make them practical by embedding governance, automation, and lifecycle management.

Example: The **AWS (Amazon Web Services) Well-Architected Framework** guides architects on secure and resilient design, but the **Turbonomic Platform** goes further by automating resource management in real time. Similarly, the **NIST (National Institute of Standards and Technology) Cybersecurity Framework (CSF)** defines risk management standards, while platforms like **Palo Alto Networks Cortex XSOAR** or **IBM Security QRadar SOAR** operationalize them through automation and integration.

Myth 3: Platform vs. Platform Engineering

Misconception: Platform engineering is everything about platforms - and this is the biggest one in industry.

Reality: Platform engineering is a discipline within the broader platform journey. Its set of engineering practices that focus on tooling, automation, developer experience. etc. But platform success extends far beyond engineering – it includes platform thinking, persona experience, business alignment, governance, security, and long-term sustainability.

Think of it like baking a cake. Platform engineering is the process of mixing ingredients, perfecting the oven temperature, and decorating with precision. The platform itself is the cake – the final entity in its own right that must taste good, look inviting, and serve a purpose. You can perfect the baking process and still end up with a cake that no one wants. The platform, like the cake, succeeds only when the whole experience works, not just the process behind it.

Acceptance: Platform engineering accelerates maturity, but it is not the definition of the platform or a replacement.

Example: A platform engineer builds reusable CI/CD pipelines or developer self-service systems – essential ingredients and techniques. The platform as a whole, however, includes governance, measurement, security, ecosystem value, and strategic enablement across the organization.

Myth 4: Platform vs. DevOps

Misconception: DevOps and platform engineering are the same.

Reality: **DevOps** is a cultural and organizational practice that bridges development and operations for faster delivery. **Platform engineering** implements that culture at scale – creating the shared systems, interfaces, and automation needed to sustain DevOps practices long-term.

Acceptance: DevOps reduces delivery friction; platform engineering sustains delivery ecosystems by embedding reliability, observability, and developer productivity.

Example: DevOps focuses on deploying features faster; platform engineering ensures that every team can do so securely, consistently, and independently without reinventing the pipeline each time.

Myth 5: Platform vs. PaaS (Platform as a Service)

Misconception: All platforms are PaaS.

Reality: PaaS is one valid form of platform delivery – offering managed runtime environments where developers can build and deploy applications without worrying about infrastructure. As seen in the previous chapter, various **business and technology models** can also operate as platforms, each enabling value creation in distinct ways.

Acceptance: PaaS provides environment abstraction; a complete platform provides **end-to-end enablement** – from identity and governance to developer experience and measurement.

Example: AWS Elastic Beanstalk is a PaaS, while an internal developer platform (not portal) built on AWS with capabilities, security policies, golden paths, and observability pipelines represents a true enterprise-grade platform.

Myth 6: Platform vs. API (Application Programming Interface)

Misconception: Platforms are just APIs.

Reality: APIs connect; platforms compose. An **API (Application Programming Interface)** defines how software components communicate, but a platform weave APIs together into a cohesive ecosystem that drives outcomes. APIs are the arteries, not the heart.

Acceptance: A strong platform treats APIs as enablers of self-service and interoperability, not as the product itself.

Example: Stripe[1] provides programmable payments with built-in analytics, fraud protection, and compliant workflows, operating as a full financial platform rather than just an API. It exposes powerful APIs, but its platform offers analytics, fraud detection, payment workflows, and developer experience – forming an ecosystem, not just a code interface.

Myth 7: Platform vs. Operating System (OS)

Misconception: A platform is just another operating system.

Reality: In fact, it's often the other way around. An **Operating System (OS)** manages hardware and provides services to applications – and is itself one of the most elegant examples of a platform. It enables economies of scale, allowing virtualization, containerization, and distributed computing to thrive across diverse hardware environments.

---

[1] https://stripe.com/gb.

A modern technology platform, however, operates at a higher abstraction layer. It manages business logic, integrations, developer workflows, and scaling processes across distributed systems – extending the principles of the OS from machines to organizations.

Acceptance: While an OS powers machines, a platform empowers people and processes, turning compute into capability and a plethora of possibilities.

Example: **Linux** is an operating system; **Kubernetes-based developer platforms** build on this foundation, orchestrating workloads, enforcing access controls, and managing lifecycle automation at enterprise scale.

Myth 8: Platform vs. Containerization

Misconception: Docker or Kubernetes *is* the platform.

Reality: Containerization is a **technology concept** – an ingredient, not the dish. It enables portability and isolation, but platforms build on it to add identity, security, cost tracking, and lifecycle automation.

Acceptance: A platform uses containerization to deploy and scale efficiently, but it also wraps it with governance, observability, and automation guardrails.

Example: Kubernetes orchestrates containers, but an enterprise platform adds provisioning workflows, policy enforcement, and developer self-service built atop Kubernetes.

Myth 9: Platform vs. Cloud Provider

Misconception: "We use AWS or Azure, so we already have a platform."

Reality: Cloud providers offer **building blocks**, not finished platforms. AWS, Azure, and GCP (Google Cloud Platform) provide infrastructure and managed services, but true platforms shape these components into opinionated, integrated systems aligned to organizational needs.

Acceptance: The cloud is the canvas; your platform is the artwork that brings it to life.

Example: AWS provides EC2 and Lambda; a platform architect defines golden paths, monitoring, access, and automation policies that turn these into scalable systems of enablement.

Myth 10: Platform vs. Product

Misconception: Every product is a platform.

Reality: A product *delivers* value; a platform *enables* others to create value. Platforms foster ecosystems where products and services can thrive and evolve.

Acceptance: A platform is a multiplier – it amplifies the reach, scalability, and interoperability of products and services. While a platform can be delivered as a product, this works best in organizations that already have a mature product culture. If that foundation doesn't exist, it's wiser to build it first and then layer platform thinking on top. Trying to enforce both at the same time usually leads to stagnation, and nothing truly moves forward.

Example: Spotify's consumer app is a product; its capabilities and developer API ecosystem that enables third-party integrations is the platform.

Myth 11: Platform vs. Toolchain

Misconception: A connected DevOps toolchain equals a platform.

Reality: Toolchains streamline workflows; platforms unify them with shared standards, governance, and self-service capabilities. If your developers still need to coordinate manually between tools, you have a toolchain – not a platform.

Acceptance: Integration without intention is just noise. A true platform brings coherence, shared purpose, and measurable flow across teams.

Example: Tools like Jenkins, GitHub Actions, Terraform, Kubernetes, and Backstage each automate parts of the delivery chain – but an internal platform weaves them together through access control, observability, and cost awareness. It transforms disconnected tools into a unified user or developer experience where teams can truly thrive and evolve.

Other Popular Misconceptions

Even after addressing the major myths, a few persistent misconceptions continue to shape how teams think about platforms. These are often subtler, born from overenthusiasm, vendor marketing, or incomplete understanding, yet they influence how organizations design, fund, and measure platform success. Let's set the record straight.

Platform must always expose a UI (User Interface): Not necessarily. Some of the most powerful platforms, such as operating systems or Terraform Cloud, are *API-first* and operate entirely behind the scenes. These backend systems deliver immense value without necessarily showing a graphical interface, enabling automation, scalability, and service integration across ecosystems.

Platform as a one-time setup: Platforms are *living systems* that evolve continuously. They require constant iteration, observability, and user feedback loops to stay relevant. A stagnant platform quickly turns into a silo, losing the very agility it was built to create.

Platform is only for large companies: Platforms are not exclusive to tech giants. Many small and mid-sized firms run *micro-platforms* from internal systems designed for developer enablement or service reuse. We are going to explore many platform examples in this book of all sizes and scales.

Platform eliminates complexity: Platforms don't erase complexity; they *manage* it and sometimes extend it due to scale and network effects it brings. By abstracting repetitive layers, they allow teams to focus on higher-value activities, but complexity merely shifts, not disappears.

Add Your Reflection

Breaking these myths lays the groundwork of true understanding for yourself and your organization. Many misconceptions come from overuse or misplaced confidence in tools that only appear to be platforms. Before moving ahead, take a moment to reflect: in your organization

- Which tools or systems are being called "platforms"?

- Are they truly enabling others, or just connecting what already exists?

Jot them down, and in the next chapter, we'll begin building the real foundations of platform understanding and test these against the Platform Success Blueprint.

Key Takeaways

- Not everything connected qualifies as a platform; only systems that enable and scale value creation do.

- A platform is more than tooling; it's the fusion of strategy, structure, and service design.

- Myths often emerge from marketing hype or oversimplified analogies; clarity begins with context and intent.

- Evaluate every system through one lens: **Does it enable others to create value autonomously and sustainably?**

- With these myths cleared, you're ready to explore what truly defines a technology platform – its anatomy, principles, patterns, and success measures.

CHAPTER 4

Defining the Platform – Clarity Before Capability

"Every successful platform begins not with technology, but with understanding the problem it exists to solve."

After clearing the fog of myths, it's time to ground ourselves. What truly makes a technology platform?

The word "platform" is used everywhere in modern technology, yet its meaning shifts depending on who you ask. Does this mean anything can be called a platform? That's the distinction we want to explore in this chapter.

Here, we'll simplify the definition, establish a shared vocabulary, and connect conceptual clarity with real-world examples. The goal is simple yet vital: by the end of this chapter, you should never again fall for vague marketing claims that label any software or service as a platform. You'll know precisely what qualifies and what doesn't.

If you haven't read the earlier chapters, I recommend revisiting them first. They provide the grounding needed to make this one come alive. Those chapters helped separate platforms from tools, frameworks, and other common confusions. This one builds on that clarity to define what a technology platform truly is and why precise definitions matter when turning ideas into scalable realities.

Having a shared understanding isn't just an academic exercise. It shapes how organizations design systems, allocate investments, and sustain innovation. Societies evolve when their innovations rest on strong foundations, not on vague metaphors. The same principle applies to platforms – clarity of definition leads to clarity of design.

© Shweta Vohra 2026

S. Vohra, *Decoding Platform Engineering Patterns*, https://doi.org/10.1007/979-8-8688-2555-2_4

What Makes a True Technology Platform

Let's begin with the simplest way to understand what a technology platform really is. Think of it from a user's perspective first:

> *"If it elevates you with stability and clear integration, it's a platform; otherwise, it's just a fancy or unfinished technology."*

A short sentence, yet it captures decades of evolution we explored in Chapter 2. Clear definitions give teams and leaders a shared mental model, a common language to design, scale, and govern technology effectively. When that clarity is missing, strategies drift, investments scatter, and platforms turn into costly, disconnected silos.

That's exactly what happened to **Sam**, whom we met in the Introduction chapter. His team built platforms based on technical feasibility first and thought about scale, integration, and ecosystem much later. Years of effort produced working systems, but not a true platform because the foundation began with tools rather than a shared understanding of the platform and the problem space.

Sam's challenge reflects a broader truth: clarity precedes capability. Experimentation is essential, but once you've learned, pause to define the platform's purpose. When teams gain clarity on the problem the platform solves, capability and success naturally follow.

Defining a Platform and Its Characteristics

A technology platform is a comprehensive system that provides complete functionality, whether serving a single or multiple business purposes. It becomes a true platform when it is stable across its lifecycle and integrates its users' needs.

Consider these five defining characteristics:

> **Self-sufficient:** Operates independently without constant intervention or manual dependencies, whether for one function or many.

> **Adaptable:** Designed to adjust to changing needs and scale to meet new demands.

> **Repeatable:** Executes consistent processes and functions across different contexts.

Integratable: Connects seamlessly with external systems, offering clear integration points and mechanisms that create minimal friction for its intended users.

Ecosystem-enabling: Fosters growth and collaboration by creating opportunities for others to build, innovate, and connect, turning integration into genuine co-creation.

Together, these five attributes form the **Platform V-ARISE Model**, a quick way to test the maturity and intent of any platform.

V-ARISE stands for **A**daptable, **R**epeatable, **I**ntegratable, **S**elf-sufficient, **and E**cosystem-enabling.

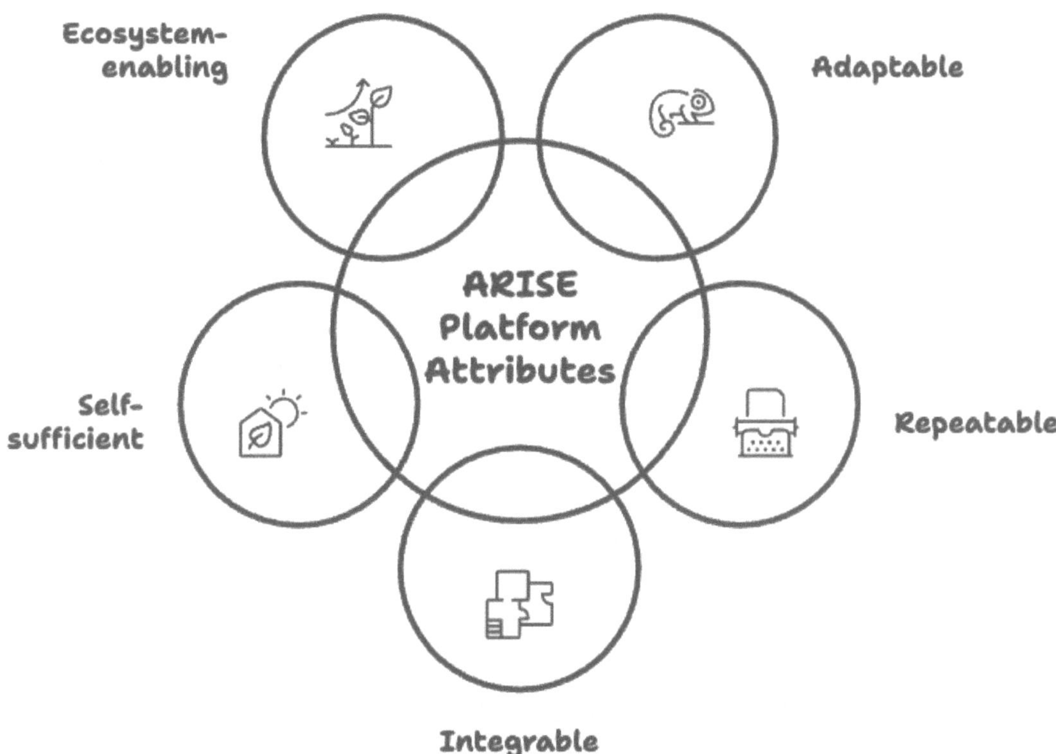

Figure 4-1. *V-ARISE Platform Attributes for Collective Value Creation*

Every platform, no matter how advanced, should demonstrate these traits at varying degrees of maturity. If its purpose is to serve as a true platform, these foundations must be present from conception.

Ask yourself: Does this Platform ARISE? If it fails in even one of these areas, it might be a useful product or connected toolset, or an unfinished piece of technology; but it isn't yet built to become a platform.

Platforms don't just serve; they amplify. They enable ecosystems to thrive by making participation easier, integration smoother, and innovation faster. The more a platform embodies the V-ARISE traits, the more value it creates – not just for its creators, but for everyone connected to it.

Example Case: Netflix and the V-ARISE Attributes

Let's bring this to life with a familiar example: Netflix.

Netflix perfectly illustrates the V-ARISE model in action.

Adaptable: Continuously adjusts recommendations and streaming quality based on user behavior, bandwidth, and device performance.

Repeatable: Delivers a consistent experience across geographies, networks, and devices, reflecting true platform maturity.

Integratable: Connects effortlessly with smart TVs, voice assistants, and partner systems such as Alexa or Chromecast.

Self-sufficient: Excels at one thing – video streaming. It manages global distribution, caching, and scaling without visible downtime.

Ecosystem-enabling: Nurtures a growing network of creators, partners, and device manufacturers who expand its reach and innovation boundaries.

You can now start to see how the Platform V-ARISE Model comes alive in practice. Let this framework settle in. Test it against your own context and observe how it shapes your view of platform maturity.

Throughout this book, we'll explore real-world examples and case studies – from complex business ecosystems to foundational technology models such as internal developer platforms – all connecting back to the V-ARISE.

The simplicity of this definition is intentional. Many digital transformation efforts fail because organizations overcomplicate what platforms are meant to achieve. Strong platforms are not built by stacking tools or chasing trends but by designing with clarity, intent, and platform thinking from the start.

Platform Engineering

Platform engineering is a disciplined and measurable approach to developing, operating, and evolving platforms that exhibit V-ARISE characteristics. It applies engineering principles to build reliable, efficient, and scalable ecosystems. It spans the entire lifecycle, from solving a core business need to shaping experience, and enabling continuous evolution and maintenance.

Platform success extends beyond engineering. It requires platform thinking, strong persona experience, business alignment, governance, security, and long-term sustainability.

To simplify this, think of it like baking a cake. Platform engineering is the process: selecting the right ingredients, controlling the temperature, and executing with precision. The platform itself is the cake, or even the entire cake-making system, a complete entity that must serve a purpose, deliver value, and be desirable to its users.

You can perfect the process and still create something no one wants. A platform, like a cake, succeeds only when the entire experience works, not just the system behind it. The chapters ahead will bring this to life with examples and patterns you can apply in practice.

Platform Thinking and Key Terminologies

Behind every successful platform lies a way of thinking – **platform thinking**. How do we define that thinking?

Besides, the V-ARISE model is now in your hand. It's important to understand platforms are not just about building software; it's about designing **enablement**. Platform thinking shifts the focus from delivering features to creating systems that allow others to deliver faster, safer, and smarter. It's about anticipating reuse, encouraging participation, and building capabilities that multiply value over time.

If V-ARISE defines how platforms behave, platform thinking defines how people build and scale them. Let's see a few more common and useful terms to complete the foundational definition of platforms.

Platformization

Platformization is the process of extending this mindset across products, teams, and business domains. It reflects the understanding that a platform isn't a one-time construct – it's a way of operating.

When organizations embrace platform thinking, teams stop repeatedly solving the same problems. Instead, they enable shared solutions that accelerate everyone's work.

> **Platforms are no longer just technology stacks; they are operating models for innovation.**

Platform Economy

The **platform economy** represents the larger landscape where platforms mediate value – connecting producers and consumers, data and insights, services and ecosystems.

From global marketplaces like **Amazon** and **Apple's App Store** to enterprise backbones like **Salesforce** or **Azure**, platforms now power a substantial portion of global GDP.

They reshape supply chains, redefine customer experiences, and create entirely new industries based on connection rather than ownership.

Even within enterprises, platform economics apply internally. The more teams adopt and integrate with shared internal platforms, the more valuable those platforms become – mirroring the same network effects that drive public platform success.

Network Effects

Network effects occur when the value of a system increases as more participants use it. This is the engine behind every thriving platform.

Direct network effects: Each new participant directly adds value for existing users. For example, the more professionals who join **LinkedIn**, the richer the network becomes for everyone.

Indirect network effects: Growth on one side attracts complementary growth on the other. For instance, as more gamers use **PlayStation**, more developers create games for it – amplifying value for both groups.

Even internal developer platforms mirror these same effects. The more teams use shared pipelines, APIs, or observability standards, the more efficient and valuable the organization becomes.

In essence, platform thinking transforms isolated tools into thriving ecosystems, where every new user, service, or idea strengthens the whole.

Platform Prism and Key Roles

A platform is like a **prism** – a single structure that refracts different experiences depending on where you stand.

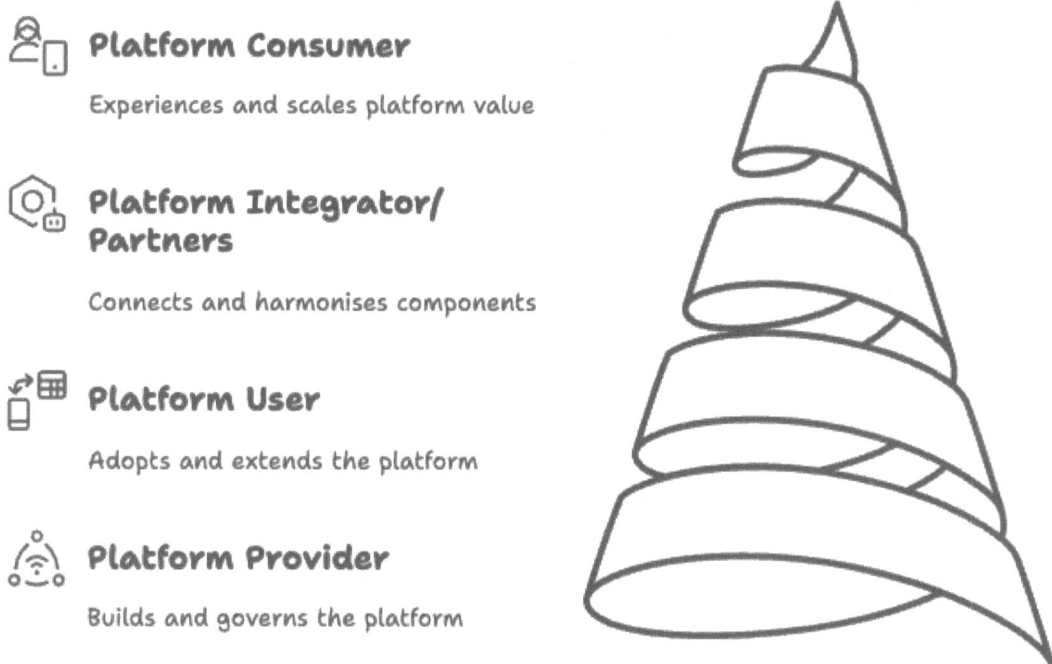

Figure 4-2. Platform Prism & Dynamics

- To a **consumer**, it feels like a seamless product or a service or a app, such as ordering on Amazon or streaming on Netflix.

- To a **platform user**, it is an environment they populate, configure, or extend – a seller listing a product or a developer publishing an app.

- To a **provider**, it is the architecture, governance, and enablement system that keeps everything running. It works best when nurtured as a product, evolving continuously and staying aligned across the value chain.

- And to an **integrator**, it is the connective tissue that makes different systems and data sources work together behind the scenes.

Each side sees a different color of the same prism, yet the value emerges only when these perspectives align.

Understanding this refracted view of roles is key to appreciating how platforms truly operate as shared systems of value creation, exchange, and feedback.

Platform providers: The creators and maintainers of the platform. They design, develop, and evolve core capabilities while ensuring security, adaptability, and business alignment.

Platform users: The builders on top, such as product teams, developers, or partners, who use the platform's services to deliver value.

Platform consumers: The end beneficiaries, the customers who experience value through apps, services, or products.

Platform integrators/partners: The connectors, those who sometimes bridge systems, data, and workflows to enable composability and reduce friction.

At its core, platform success depends on continuous value exchange: providers create capability, users drive adoption, integrators ensure cohesion, and consumers generate scale. Together, they form the **Platform Prism**, where every perspective amplifies the other to create a unified ecosystem of innovation.

More Real-World Examples

Let's bring the prism to life with two familiar examples.

Amazon

Amazon operates as a global e-commerce ecosystem that embodies every side of the platform prism. For consumers, it simplifies discovery and purchasing; for users such as sellers and partners, it offers a ready-made marketplace; for integrators, it seamlessly connects fulfillment, analytics, and payment systems behind the scenes; and as a provider, it designs and maintains the architecture, logistics, and governance that keep everything stable and scalable. Its true strength lies in its ability to scale through stability, adaptability, and repeatability – the essence of the V-ARISE model in action.

Platform provider: Amazon itself

Platform users: Sellers and business partners

Platform integrators: Service providers connecting inventory, analytics, and fulfillment

Platform consumers: Shoppers like you and me

LinkedIn

LinkedIn connects opportunity and talent, demonstrating how design, trust, and feedback sustain a thriving two-sided ecosystem. For consumers, it enables visibility, networking, and learning; for users such as recruiters and advertisers, it offers reach and insight; and as a provider, it continuously refines its recommendation systems to balance growth with trust.

Platform provider: LinkedIn Corporation **Platform users:** Companies, recruiters, and advertisers **Platform integrators:** Third-party tools and APIs extending LinkedIn's ecosystem **Platform consumers:** Professionals using the platform for networking, learning, or hiring

Both Amazon and LinkedIn demonstrate what makes a true platform: they evolve continuously, integrate seamlessly, and sustain value across multiple roles.

In Summary

This chapter transforms the abstract idea of a platform into something clear, testable, and actionable. A platform is not a collection of tools but a foundation that turns repeatable capability into scalable value. By understanding the roles of providers, users, consumers, and integrators, you now have the vocabulary to analyze any platform and assess its maturity and balance. While the real world may feature additional platform-centric entities, ***this book focuses on these four roles – especially the responsibilities, success factors, and pitfalls of providers, users, and consumers.***

With these foundations in place, we're ready to move from understanding to application. The next section introduces the **Platform Success Blueprint**, a universal structure that helps every reader – whether provider, user, or strategist – to build and scale platforms with clarity and intent. It's time to connect the dots between patterns, principles, and performance.

Key Takeaways

- A true platform is not just connected technology but an enabler of repeatable, scalable value creation.

- Simplicity drives clarity. The more your platform embodies the V-ARISE traits – adaptable, repeatable, integratable, self-sufficient, and ecosystem-enabling – the stronger and more resilient it becomes.

- The platform ecosystem revolves around providers, users, integrators, and consumers. Understanding these roles is key to designing sustainable, value-driven systems.

- Ecosystem integration and network effects amplify both external and internal platforms. The more adoption, the greater the collective value.

- With shared definitions and a common vocabulary in place, you are now ready to explore the patterns, principles, and measures that define successful platform engineering.

SECTION II

The Platform Patterns (Scale)

Explores foundational platform patterns, perspectives, and early scaling lenses.

CHAPTER 5

Understanding Platform Patterns, Perspectives, and Effects

"The moment you stop calling everything a platform, you start understanding what a real one truly is."

We have reached a point where we can separate what is truly a platform from what only wears the label. This chapter takes that clarity one step further. You will explore the most common platform patterns, how they differ in nature and design, and the effects they create. The goal is not memorization. It is pattern recognition in the wild: looking at products, systems, and organizations and knowing what you are seeing, for whom it works, and why it scales.

A thoughtful architect or product leader looks at any digital ecosystem and asks a simple question: What kind of platform is this, and from whose perspective? That is the thread we will pull through the chapter as we study how platforms are built, how they are experienced, and how they sustain themselves responsibly.

Seeing Through the Platform Prism

Earlier, we introduced the Platform Prism as a way to understand that the same platform can look entirely different to different people.

A **consumer** experiences need fulfillment. Open an app like Uber, and you feel convenience – a car arrives when you need it.

A **user** contributes value. A driver expects fair routing, transparent earnings, and timely payouts.

S. Vohra, *Decoding Platform Engineering Patterns*, https://doi.org/10.1007/979-8-8688-2555-2_5

A **provider** steers the business engine. They are the creators of the provider and their role is to blend business, logistics, data, and experience.

An **integrator or partner** extends capabilities through payments, mapping, identity, or logistics.

In this book, we will keep returning to the first three roles – consumers, users, and providers – because they form the heartbeat of every platform. Hold on to these perspectives as you move through the chapters; they will help you see patterns and decisions more clearly.

These perspectives coexist and rely on one another. A platform weakens when one dominates for too long. Many companies fall into this trap and continue optimizing only for consumers or chasing short-term monetization while neglecting developers, partners, or the internal teams that keep the ecosystem alive.

Platform Perspectives and Responsibilities

Each perspective carries responsibilities.

Consumers determine relevance through repeated choice.

Users sustain energy through participation and contribution.

Providers are custodians of strategy, quality, and scale. Keeping things glued as platform.

Integrators and partners keep the platform connected to the wider world.

Balanced attention across these roles creates durable platforms. Neglect creates cracks that show up first in experience, then in trust, and eventually in scalability.

Various Popular Platform Patterns

Figure 5-1. *Popular terminologies used around platforms*

Not all platforms are built the same. Some are born for public interaction. Others exist solely inside a company. Some thrive on external contributions. Others depend on internal discipline. Positioning your platform correctly starts with recognizing these distinctions.

Pure-Play Platforms

These are born digital and designed for interaction and exchange from day one. Instagram and YouTube are a few good and clear examples. People create and consume visual content. The platform curates, recommends, and monetizes. The network becomes valuable as those layers amplify one another.

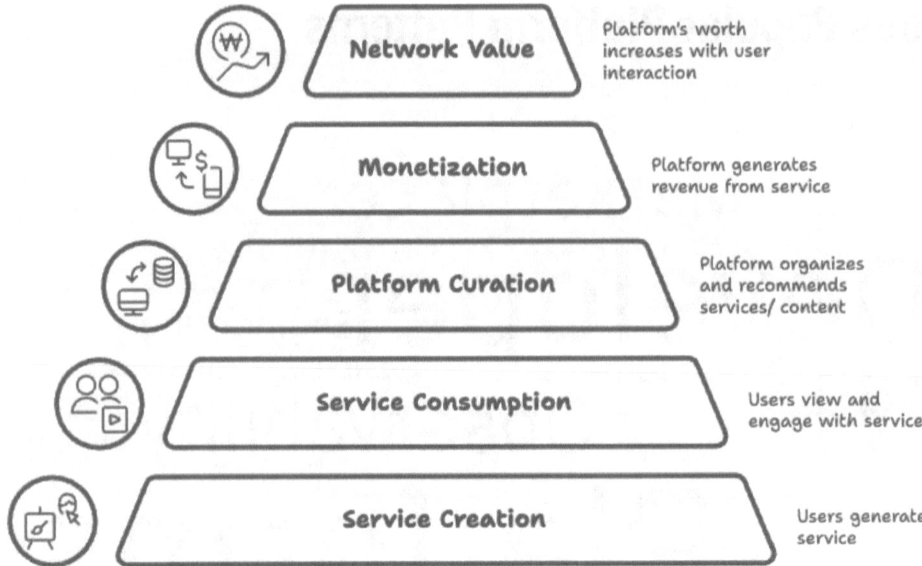

Figure 5-2. *Pure-Play Platform Dynamics*

Internal and External Platforms

External platforms face the market and power end-user experiences such as ride sharing, learning, payments, or retail. Internal platforms are built for teams inside an organization. They standardize how software is built, tested, deployed, observed, and secured.

Internal platforms are not new. For decades, engineering teams have maintained automated testing systems, developer toolchains, and workflow engines. What is new is the discipline and shared language around them. External platforms create reach. Internal platforms create readiness. Sustainable growth needs both.

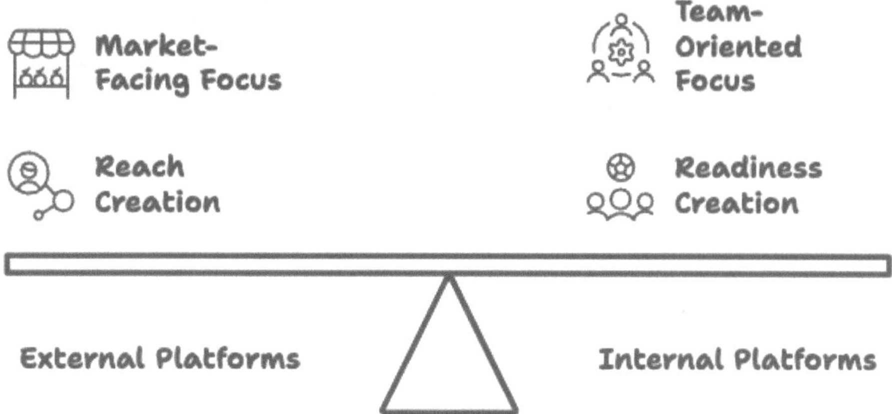

Figure 5-3. *Balancing External and Internal Platforms*

Enablement Platforms

External enablement platforms expose core capabilities to outside developers and partners. **Stripe** enables payments. **Slack** enables communication. **Snowflake** enables data sharing. These platforms multiply value by allowing others to build confidently on strong, well-designed primitives.

Internal enablement platforms function in a similar way but within the organization. They help teams deploy software, automate testing, manage observability, and integrate security without reinventing the basics. The guiding principle is simple: enable others to create value faster and more reliably.

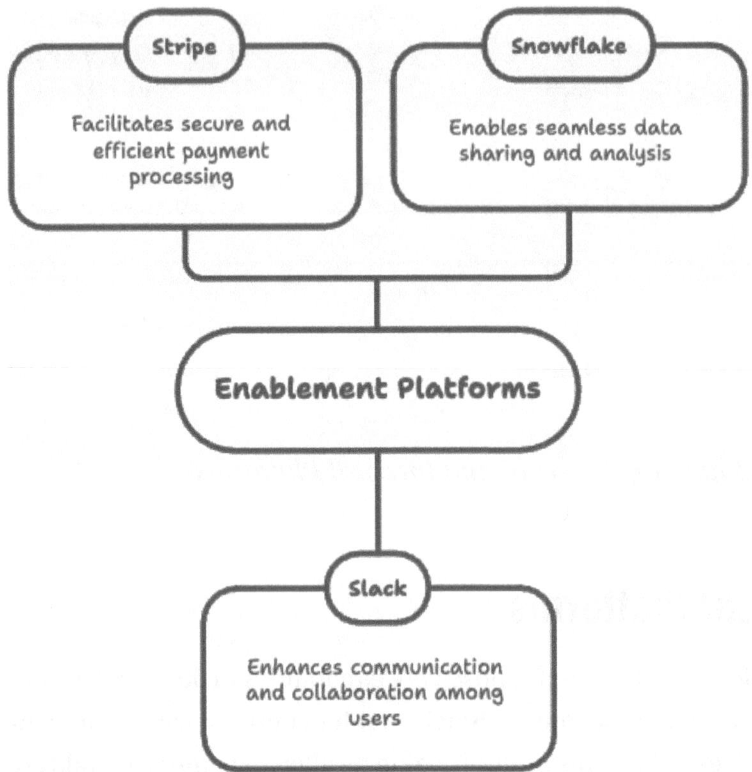

Figure 5-4. *The Pattern of Enablement Platforms*

Not everything in this space should automatically be called a platform, but understanding enablement in this sense helps you see where true platform characteristics begin. And when in doubt, your first tool for evaluating it remains the **V-ARISE model**, which helps you assess whether what you are looking at truly qualifies as a platform.

Platform of Platforms

No meaningful platform operates alone anymore. Amazon's retail ecosystem sits on top of its own cloud foundation. Uber depends on mapping, payments, messaging, and telco rails. YouTube thrives because devices, networks, and clouds form an invisible backbone. Android and iOS are platforms of platforms, supporting countless applications and services built by others. Once you see these interdependencies, you stop thinking in layers and start thinking in living ecosystems that consume and enable each other.

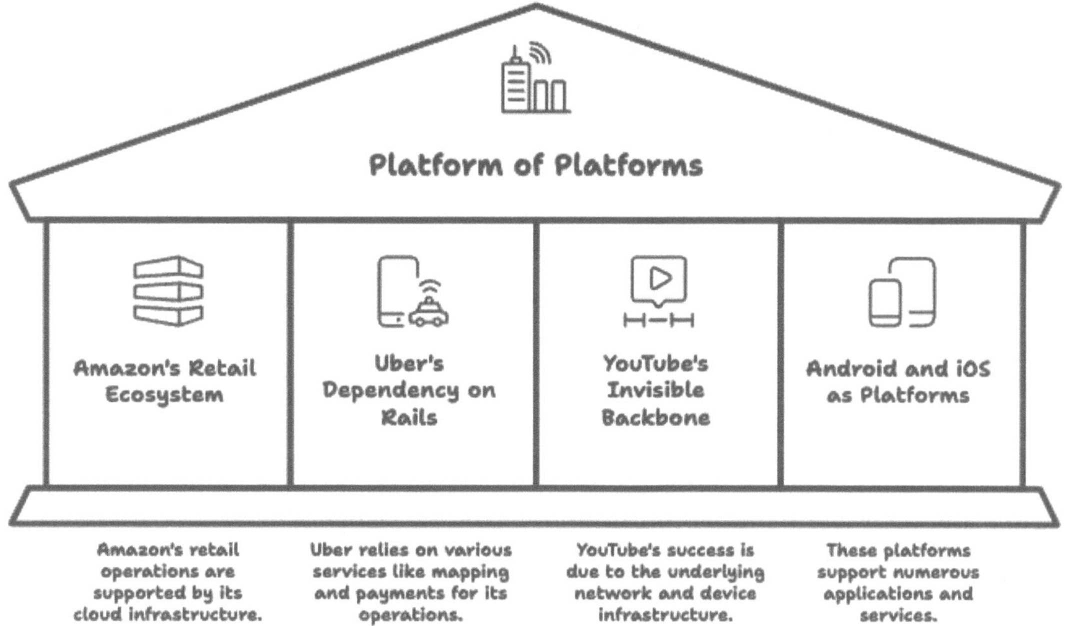

Figure 5-5. *Platform of Platforms*

Foundational and Business Platforms

At the base of many ecosystems sit foundational platforms. Cloud providers such as AWS, Azure, and Google Cloud deliver compute, storage, data, and AI capabilities as services. These are heavy lifters that power almost everything else.

Above them sit business platforms that people interact with directly: streaming, e-commerce, fintech, travel, learning, and more. Between the two live hybrid layers, such as data platforms, learning platforms, and analytics systems, that translate technical capability into business outcomes. The guiding principle remains constant. A real platform enables others to create, contribute, and grow.

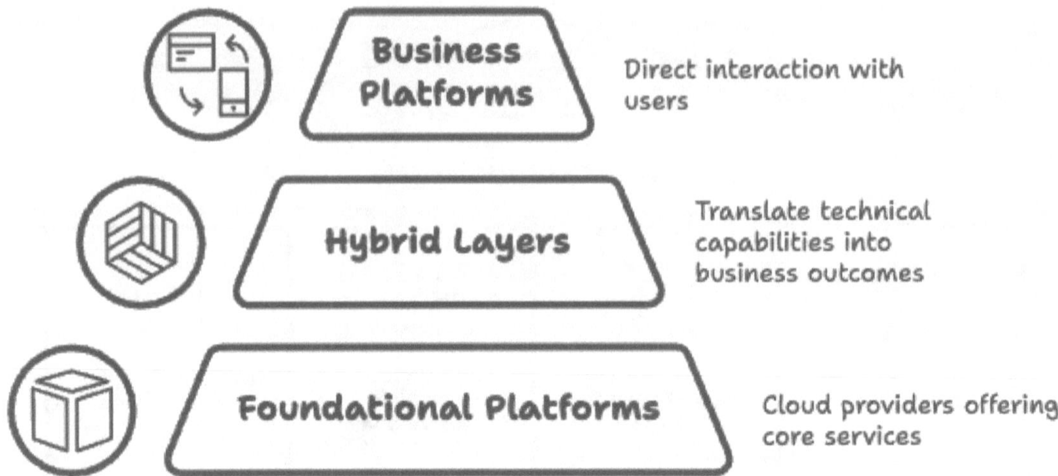

Figure 5-6. *Ecosystem and Foundational Platform Dependency*

Platform Effects

Different patterns create different effects.

Pinterest and Canva serve similar audiences but with distinct value loops. Pinterest is for inspiration and discovery. The more content people pin, the richer the discovery graph. Canva is for creation and sharing. The more people design and collaborate, the more templates improve, and the more teams adopt it. Both generate network effects, but they compound value in different ways. Knowing which effect you are designing for shapes your incentives, content policies, and product loops.

Cloud ecosystems offer another useful contrast. AWS Marketplace aggregates and distributes solutions from third parties, creating an exchange effect. Individual services such as S3 or Lambda enable and execute, creating a utility effect. One thrives on aggregation. The other thrives on enablement. Mixing them without design intent leads to overreach or confusion.

Transition Paths: From Service to Platform

Most companies do not become platforms on day one. They begin as products or services and evolve when they realize others could build on top of what they have created.

Salesforce started as a CRM product. With Force.com[1], it invited others to extend its core, transforming a product into an ecosystem.

Amazon built its internal infrastructure to power retail operations, but when it opened that same capability to the world, it became AWS – one of the largest and most transformative cloud platforms in history.

Shopify began as an e-commerce product helping merchants build online stores; over time, it opened an app marketplace so partners and developers could extend and enrich its offerings.

Each of these transitions required more than technology. They demanded governance, documentation, and collaboration.

"The platform mindset is not about serving customers, but about enabling others to serve customers through you."

The lesson is simple. Platforms are born from repeated success and deliberate openness. You do not necessarily jump to being a platform. You grow into one by helping others grow through you.

And if you want to tread this path with structure and foresight, the next sections of this book will take you there. The Platform Success Blueprint brings together all the essential elements needed to build, sustain, and scale platforms with intention, not accident.

By now, you should see platforms with greater clarity – what they are, how they differ, and why their patterns matter. From pure-play social platforms like Instagram to layered ecosystems such as iOS, AWS, or Shopify, each follows its own rhythm. Some begin as products, others as services, but the ones that endure become foundations for others to create value.

Every successful platform shares a simple truth: it started by solving a problem and ended by enabling others to solve their own.

---

[1] https://www.salesforce.com/news/stories/the-history-of-salesforce/

Up next, we move to the three essential pillars that shape every platform's journey – scale, metrics, and security. These forces appear in every platform's lifecycle, no matter when or how it begins.

Key Takeaways

- A platform always looks different through the Platform Prism. Design with all four lenses in mind – consumers, users, providers, and partners – because a platform weakens when any one of them is ignored.

- Identify your platform pattern early. Whether it is pure-play, enablement, internal, external, or a platform of platforms, each demands a distinct approach to design, governance, and evolution.

- Remember that platforms often grow out of products or services. Openness, documentation, and strong governance are the bridges that turn a successful capability into a thriving ecosystem.

CHAPTER 6

The Three Pillars of Platform Strength – Scale, Security, and Metrics

"Every platform's strength is not defined by how fast it grows, but by how gracefully it sustains that growth."

Building a platform that lasts requires more than good technology or market timing. It requires strength. The kind that comes from balance, discipline, and long-term design. Across every industry, from cloud ecosystems to consumer applications, three pillars determine whether a platform stands tall or collapses under its own ambition: scale, security, and measurement or feedback loops.

Before we go deeper, you may wonder why only these three have been placed upfront. Why not experience, development practices, or architecture choices. The question is valid. Those aspects are essential too, but their presence and importance differ depending on the platform pattern you are working with. Internal platforms, external platforms, business platforms, pure-play platforms, and foundational platforms each emphasize those dimensions differently. However, the three pillars you will explore in this chapter appear everywhere without exception. Pick any platform of your choice, in any industry, of any size, and you will find scale, security, and measurement shaping it at every stage. These are the universals, the structural forces that every platform must master.

S. Vohra, *Decoding Platform Engineering Patterns*, https://doi.org/10.1007/979-8-8688-2555-2_6

These three are not isolated functions. I want to address these essential factors of every platform, regardless of its type or pattern, right from the start. Together, they form a cycle of resilience. Scaling tests the platform's foundation. Security tests its integrity. Measurement tests its self-awareness and ability to learn from the market. When these three evolve in harmony, platforms thrive. When one falls behind, the entire system weakens.

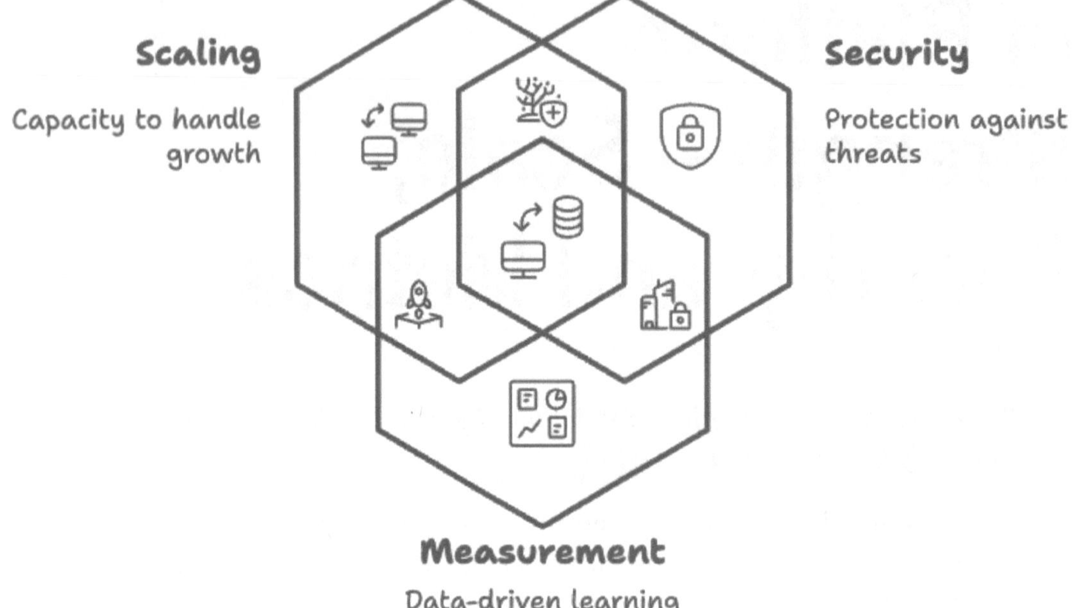

Figure 6-1. *The Synergy of Platform Resilience*

This chapter explores these three essentials: how to design for scale, secure platforms in a world of growing complexity, and measure what truly matters. Let us begin with understanding scale.

Designing for Platform Scale

Scaling a platform is one of the hardest challenges in technology and business. It is not about turning on more servers or enabling autoscaling; it is about scaling the people, teams, and governance that hold the ecosystem together. This can remind you of Sam's multiyear journey we discussed in Introduction of this book, and more important is the reason he went through that churn without knowing he needed these aspects from the beginning.

True platform scale happens in three interconnected dimensions.

The first is business and market scale.

This involves growing your user base responsibly, expanding into new markets, and managing the diversity that comes with scale. Netflix, for example, scaled its global footprint not by simply adding servers but by investing in localization, content partnerships, and region-specific pricing strategies. Airbnb did something similar, adapting policies, support systems, and user verification models to fit cultural and legal norms in each geography. Platform scaling is as much about cultural adaptation as it is about technical capacity. We will be diving deep into this pillar in Section 3.

The second is internal readiness and technology scale.

Inside the organization, systems and teams must evolve to handle higher velocity and growing complexity. Internal developer platforms play a central role here. They allow teams to build, test, and deploy software consistently across different business units, reducing friction and uncertainty. When Spotify scaled its engineering organization, it relied on internal platforms and portals orchestrated through Backstage, a well-known open source project. This helped teams coordinate services, manage dependencies, and gain shared visibility. That is how platforms stay stable even as their footprint expands. We will dive much deeper into this in Section 4, but the point is clear. A team's readiness for scale and continuous nurturing determines whether the business can grow smoothly across markets, rollouts, and all platform personas.

The third is governance and global scale.

The third dimension is governance and global scale. As platforms expand across borders, they encounter new challenges around regulation, latency, availability, and cultural expectations.

A fintech platform entering Europe must navigate General Data Protection Regulation (GDPR), localized consent flows, and region-specific data storage. A logistics platform expanding across Asia must handle infrastructure diversity and localization needs. Amazon Web Services built regional data centers not only to reduce latency but also to meet data residency laws and earn customer trust in each geography. Scaling globally therefore requires thoughtful governance, redundancy, regional autonomy, and cultural sensitivity. While this cannot always be preplanned, strong awareness and continued adherence to this aspect help avoid big mistakes.

Scaling, therefore, is less about technology and more about foresight. It is about knowing what kind of growth your foundation can sustain and what kind might quietly weaken it. From the next section onward, we will begin weaving these lessons into a practical framework for platform strategy and solutioning. Many businesses start with bold plans and early wins but overlook the foundations that make scale possible. By the time they realize the gaps, it is often too late or too costly to fix. This is not something you patch after success; it is something you build into the system from the beginning. That is why we are addressing scale here before we step into Section 3, where the Platform Success Blueprint brings these essentials together.

Securing Platforms – Regulation, Trust, and Compliance

No platform discussion is complete without addressing security and compliance. In today's interconnected world, even the smallest breach can leave lasting damage. Three pillars define a secure and trusted platform: trust, regulations, and compliance.

As AI becomes more deeply integrated into platforms, a fourth dimension – explainability, auditability – will soon take center stage. We will explore that in detail in Section 6 of this book.

Trust begins with intent. Every short-term gain achieved by compromising user trust becomes a long-term liability. The most successful platforms have learned that trust is non-negotiable, and once lost, it rarely returns. Trust is built through integrity, transparency, and consistent protection of user data.

A good example is **Apple's stance on privacy**. The company's design philosophy prioritizes data protection by default. Features like on-device processing for Face ID and local photo analysis demonstrate that privacy can coexist with innovation. This trust has become a differentiator for Apple's ecosystem, especially as users become more aware of how their data is collected and shared.

Regulations form the second essential. Every region enforces its own frameworks to safeguard users and promote responsible innovation. The General Data Protection Regulation (GDPR) in Europe grants individuals control over their personal data. The Payment Card Industry Data Security Standard (PCI-DSS) governs global payment safety. In healthcare, the Health Insurance Portability and Accountability Act (HIPAA) ensures patient privacy while enabling digital transformation.

Even if your platform does not directly operate in these domains, you may need to integrate with systems that do, thereby making regulatory literacy essential. For instance, **Stripe** – a financial infrastructure and payment processing company that provides a suite of online tools for businesses to accept payments, manage their finances, and accelerate growth. Invested heavily in meeting local financial and privacy laws across multiple jurisdictions before scaling globally. That foresight built trust with banks, regulators, and customers, enabling its rapid and safe expansion.

Compliance is where risk meets complexity. As studied by MIT Sloan Management Review[1] Mature platforms classify their markets along these two dimensions to guide their growth strategy. A platform like LinkedIn operates in a low-risk, low-complexity space, managing largely self-disclosed professional data. In contrast, PayPal operates in a high-risk, high-complexity environment, navigating multiple financial regulations simultaneously.

Regulatory preparedness is not about ticking boxes. It is about designing systems that adapt as laws evolve. The ability to reconfigure data storage, update consent mechanisms, and modify audit trails defines a platform's maturity. Microsoft Azure continuously updates its compliance frameworks to align with evolving privacy laws, allowing customers to stay compliant without reengineering their systems.

A word of caution: Many organizations delegate security to a single "security team" – often isolated from design and development. Unfortunately, that approach rarely works, leading to friction. Security cannot be an afterthought; it must be **baked into architecture and everyday decision-making**. When every engineer and architect shares responsibility for security, it stops being a barrier and becomes a foundation for trust.

---

[1] `https://learning.oreilly.com/library/view/platform-scaling-fast/53863MIT62303/`

When security becomes shared, it turns from a defensive layer into an enabler of credibility. That is the true hallmark of a platform built to last.

(More on secure architecture and design integration will follow in Section 4.)

Measuring What Matters – Platform Metrics and Impact

Measurement gives meaning to ambition and informs every feedback loop a platform depends on. But measuring a platform is very different from measuring a product.

A product can be judged with simple indicators such as usage or revenue. A platform, however, lives inside an ecosystem of technology, people, contributors, partners, and business loops. Measuring one layer gives an incomplete picture. A healthy platform demonstrates balance across all layers of its ecosystem, from infrastructure reliability to experience quality, from internal readiness to long-term value creation.

Amazon's growth captures this principle well. The more users joined its marketplace, the more data it collected. That data improved recommendations, which attracted more users and sellers. Each loop reinforced the next, forming a self-sustaining cycle. Netflix and Spotify operate on similar principles, turning user behavior into continuous refinement. Even foundational ecosystems like Linux show the same effect. The more developers contributed, the stronger the system became, which encouraged wider adoption and even more contributions. These loops are the heartbeat of platform health.

To measure a platform effectively, it helps to think in four dimensions. Imagine moving from the very top of the system down to the foundation that keeps it alive.

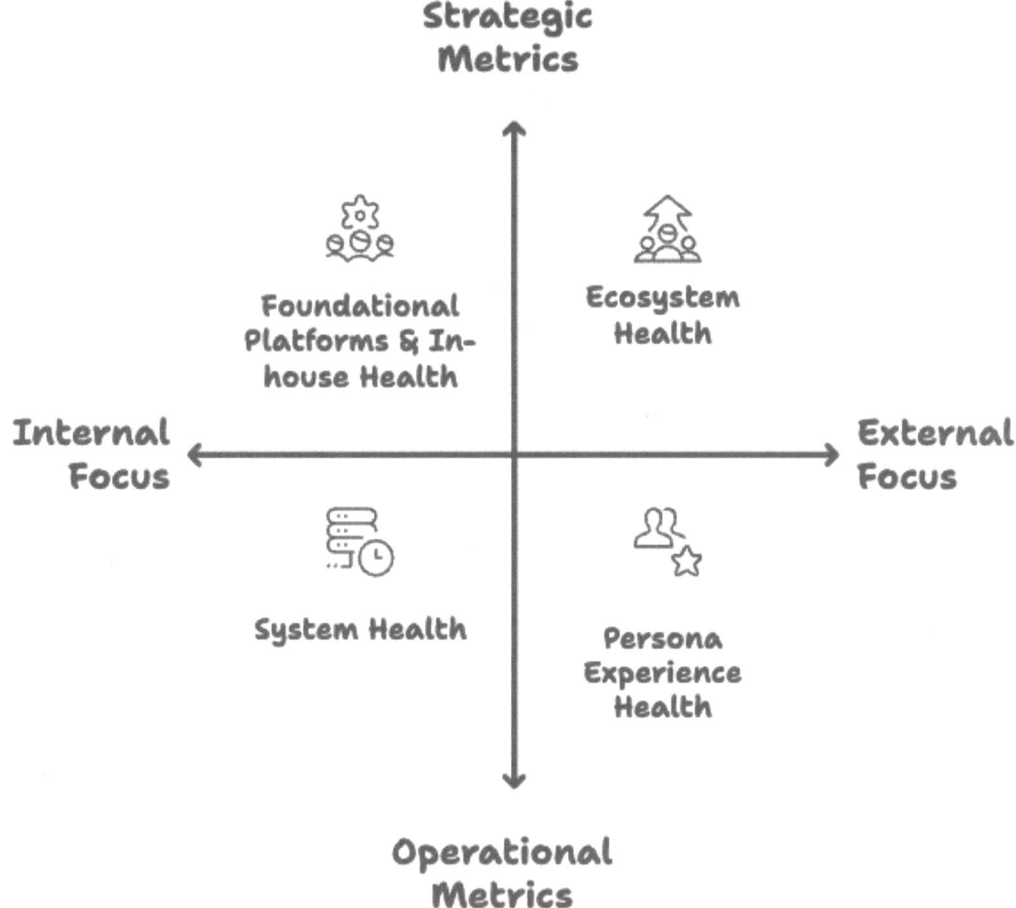

Figure 6-2. *Platform Health Measurement Framework*

Layer 1: System Health

This is the base layer. If your platform is unreliable, everything above it starts to wobble. System health measures reliability, performance, scalability, and security. It answers the most basic question: does the platform work consistently and under pressure.

Companies anchor their credibility on this layer.

AWS publicly shares its Service Health Dashboard to show customers that reliability is not negotiable.

Netflix continuously monitors playback latency and stream stability because even a few seconds of buffering damages user trust.

Stripe tracks latency and error rates in real time because a single failed payment can break customer confidence.

Common system-health metrics include uptime, latency, error rates, capacity usage, and recovery time. These aren't just technical indicators; they are the foundation of business trust. Every second of downtime costs revenue, reputation, and confidence.

Layer 2: Experience Health (for Personas)

Once the system is stable, the next layer is how people experience it. This measures adoption, satisfaction, ease of use, and engagement across all personas from consumers, users, and partners.

Different platforms emphasize different aspects of experience.

Google Cloud tracks how easily developers adopt new APIs and how quickly they can become productive.

Airbnb monitors both host and guest behavior to ensure its marketplace is balanced and fair.

Shopify tracks not only merchant sign-ups but also how many merchants become active sellers, renew subscriptions, and expand their stores.

Experience metrics move far beyond daily active users. They include activation rates, developer onboarding time, task success, usage depth, satisfaction surveys, and retention over time. This layer shows whether your platform is usable, enjoyable, and meaningful for real people.

Layer 3: Ecosystem Growth Health

This layer measures the platform's long-term contribution to its ecosystem. It reflects how value flows between participants and how strong the network effects really are.

When Apple launched the App Store, the measure of success was not downloads. It was how many developers could build sustainable businesses on top of it. That ecosystem strength pushed the App Store forward and reinforced the platform itself.

LinkedIn measures the number of job matches, recruiter engagement, and value created for businesses, not just profile views.Snowflake measures the volume of cross-organization data sharing on its platform, signaling the strength of its network of analysts, creators, and data producers.

Ecosystem metrics commonly include partner growth, third-party integrations, value created for participants, marketplace activity, and sustainability of revenue models. A strong ecosystem layer shows that the platform is not only valuable on its own but also makes others valuable too.

Layer 4: Foundation Health – Platform Engineering and In-house Vitality

This is the most overlooked yet most decisive layer. A platform's external success can never outpace the health of the team that builds it. Foundation health measures collaboration, culture, productivity, readiness, and the maturity of your internal developer experience.

Spotify built internal portals orchestrated through Backstage to streamline engineering flow, reduce friction, and support growth.

Atlassian measures developer satisfaction with internal APIs and tooling before measuring external partner satisfaction.

Netflix continuously reviews internal tooling adoption to ensure engineers spend their time building value, not managing complexity.

Useful metrics include engineering satisfaction, platform usability scores, deployment frequency, lead time for changes, onboarding time for engineers, automation maturity, and architecture review participation. This layer gives you a mirror to see how strongly your internal engine is functioning.

A platform becomes fragile when internal teams are burned out, processes are inconsistent, or workflows are unclear. Strong teams build strong platforms. Weak internal systems create fragile external experiences.

Inviting a Complete View

When these four layers are measured together, you see the whole truth. System health protects trust. User experience health protects relevance. Ecosystem health protects long-term value. Foundation health protects your ability to evolve.

Platforms that measure all four layers stay alive longer, adapt faster, and scale more responsibly. Platforms that measure one or two layers often grow quickly and collapse suddenly. The exact KPIs you choose will depend on your platform's type, context, and maturity. What you measure must serve your purpose, not someone else's checklist.

There will always be natural **tensions between metrics**. A system optimized for extreme global resilience may score high on reliability but may also increase your operational burden and cost. A platform engineered for rapid iteration might see faster delivery but may need stronger guardrails for security and compliance. These trade-offs are real, and acknowledging them openly helps you choose metrics that support your strategy instead of distracting from it.

The key is to choose wisely, review frequently, and adjust without hesitation when a metric stops serving your intent.

This is the essence of measuring what matters. A platform is not only what people see but also what people build, support, and sustain behind the scenes.

Platform Health Measurement Grid (Mapped to V-ARISE)

Let's look at some useful, common examples that should help you define your own. System Health System health measures reliability, performance, scalability, and security under real-world conditions. It reflects whether your platform can be trusted to operate consistently, even under pressure. This layer directly connects to *Repeatable*, ensuring consistent reliability, *Integratable*, ensuring stable interfaces under load, and *Ecosystem-enabling*, providing a dependable foundation others can build on. **Examples**: Availability through SLO or SLA targets, latency measured at p95 or p99 response times, and mean time to recovery for incidents. These are widely grounded in SRE practices and SLI and SLO frameworks.

Experience Health

Experience health focuses on how effectively your platform serves its users across different personas. It measures adoption, usability, and engagement, answering whether people can use your platform with ease and confidence. This layer aligns with *Adaptable*, as the platform fits diverse needs, and *Self-sufficient*, enabling users to operate with minimal friction or dependency. **Examples**: Time to onboard or activate a user or developer, task success rates, and retention or repeat usage. These are commonly guided by product analytics practices and frameworks like Google's HEART model.

Ecosystem Growth Health

Ecosystem growth health measures how value flows across participants and how strong your platform's network effects truly are. It reflects whether your platform enables others to create, integrate, and grow. This layer maps strongly to *Ecosystem-enabling*, where value is created beyond the platform itself, and *Integratable*, where partners can connect with ease. **Examples**: Growth in active partners or integrations, value or revenue generated per participant, and overall marketplace activity. These signals are often informed by platform economics and marketplace measurement and business models (more on this in next section).

Foundation Health

Foundation health reflects the strength of your internal engine, often popularized across industry as developer exerience (DX) and other similar terms. However this includes more such as team effectiveness, engineering flow, and platform maturity. It determines how well your platform can evolve over time. This layer aligns with *Adaptable*, enabling continuous evolution, *Repeatable*, ensuring consistent delivery patterns, and *Self-sufficient*, allowing teams to operate independently without bottlenecks.

Examples: Platform maturity score, Deployment frequency, lead time for changes, and change failure rate. Some of these are well established in DORA metrics and DevOps research.

Summing up – scale, security, and measurement form the invisible architecture of every enduring platform. Each tests a different aspect of maturity. Scale tests readiness. Security tests integrity. Measurement tests awareness. Together, they shape not just how platforms grow but how they evolve with resilience and purpose.

In a world where platform competition is accelerating, understanding these three essentials is no longer optional. They are the core of platform strength. From Netflix scaling its culture to Apple protecting privacy, from AWS earning trust through radical transparency to Spotify measuring internal engineering vitality, the same pattern emerges again and again. Platforms that last grow with intention because they secure and measure with intention.

"A platform is not judged by how much it does, but by how responsibly it does it."

Key Takeaways

- True platform scale is cultural as much as it is technical.

- Security is everyone's responsibility; trust is the reward for consistency.

- Regulations are not roadblocks but design constraints that promote discipline.

- Measuring what matters means balancing system health, experience, impact, and team vitality.

- The most successful platforms grow outward because they are strong inward.

As we close this chapter, we now step into Section 3: The Platform Success Blueprint (Strategy) is a proven way to bring clarity to complexity and turn platform ambition into a repeatable path to success.

The next chapter, "The Platform Success Blueprint," introduces the framework that binds everything together – helping you align strategy, design, and execution into one coherent platform vision.

SECTION III

The Platform Success Blueprint (Strategy)

Introduces the five-step Platform Success Blueprint and connects strategy, experience, and economics.

CHAPTER 7

The Platform Success Blueprint – Weaving Complexity into Clarity

"Platform paths are unwritten and tangled; an innovative blueprint is needed to weave them into success."

After exploring Section 1, where we uncovered platform challenges, innovation surges, and the myths that blur understanding, and Section 2, which explained how platform perspectives, patterns, and measures of scale can differ, it is now time to bring everything together.

We move from seeing platforms as many disconnected pieces to understanding them as one woven system of clarity. What does it truly take to build a successful, scalable platform? How can we shift from problem space to platform space, from endless experimentation to a proven path of success?

While we have seen that platforms involve many ecosystem contributors: providers, users, integrators, consumers, and maybe more. There are still certain traits that distinguish thriving, sustainable platforms from those that fade or fragment over time. These shared principles form the foundation of success, regardless of the platform's type, size, or domain.

This is where the **Platform Success Blueprint** comes in. It is an experiential model distilled from years of real-world practice, a practical map to structure complexity, connect perspectives, and build shared understanding across teams.

If you haven't read the earlier foundational chapters, I recommend revisiting them first. They provide the lens through which this blueprint becomes meaningful. Without that grounding, the cube you are about to explore may feel abstract, but with it, each side will come alive with purpose and connection. Let's dive in.

S. Vohra, *Decoding Platform Engineering Patterns*, https://doi.org/10.1007/979-8-8688-2555-2_7

Why a Blueprint and Why a Cube?

Platforms rarely fail because of technology alone. They fail when the connections between things are missing, between business and engineering, strategy and delivery, and intent and execution.

That is why this framework takes the shape of a cube.

A cube is not simple, yet it is manageable. It holds multiple perspectives, from foundation elements to user experience, keeping every layer alive and connected. Each side represents a vital dimension of a platform, and just like in a cube, every side depends on the others. You cannot move one without influencing the rest.

Together, they form a three-dimensional model that mirrors the reality of modern platforms, where business, technology, experience, and operations are woven into one cohesive system.

Once you understand this model for a single platform, you can extend it to a network of platforms – what many organizations today call platform ecosystems. The simplicity lies in its structure; the power lies in its ability to be reused.

The Platform Cube: A Shared Vocabulary

Before we explore the six sides, let's establish a shared language for this model.

The **Cube** represents the complete view of a platform, its structure, principles, and evolution. It is not about layering in a strict architectural sense but about seeing how a platform develops, connects, and operates within an organization. At its core, it remains a human endeavor, built, refined, and sustained by people.

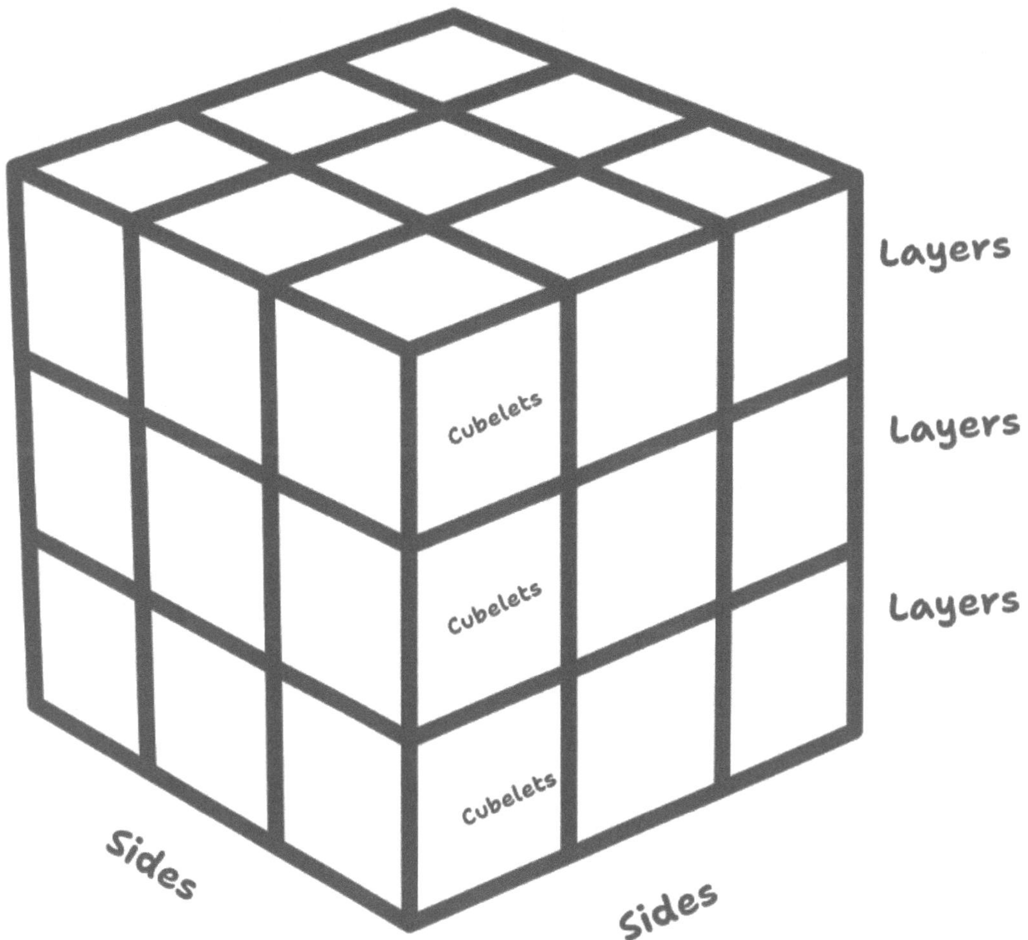

Figure 7-1. *The Platform Cube*

Sides (or Faces) are the six major dimensions that define platform success.

Cubies (or Cublets) are the smaller building blocks within each side, the components, modules, or decisions that bring the larger dimension to life.

Layers represent maturity. As one layer is stabilized, the next emerges, moving from alignment to automation to scale.

These shared terms create a common vocabulary that helps us navigate the framework consistently and clearly as we move forward.

The Six Sides of the Platform Success Blueprint

Each side of the cube represents a vital lens, a way of seeing the platform from a different yet connected perspective. Together, they ensure you do not just design technology but orchestrate a living, evolving system of value. I have provided industry examples at each stage and throughout this book to help you relate these ideas in practice and apply them in your context.

Core Business Domain

The core business domain is the reason your platform exists. It defines the products, services, or operations it powers. Clarity here ensures alignment between business outcomes and platform capabilities.

For example, in an e-commerce platform such as Amazon, the core business domain includes online retail, logistics, payment processing, and customer services. In the automotive industry, platforms by BMW or Ford focus on vehicles, parts, accessories, and related digital services that enhance customer engagement.

In a digital banking platform, the core domain may include mobile banking, transactions, and loan processing, all designed to manage sensitive data securely while delivering seamless experiences.When a platform is grounded in its core business domain, it strengthens focus, ensures scalability, and helps build a robust ecosystem that attracts and retains users.

Platform Strategy and Business Models

This side defines how value is created, delivered, and captured within the ecosystem. It aligns platform growth with economic logic, audience understanding, and incentives that encourage participation.

Effective strategies leverage network effects, such as Airbnb connecting hosts and guests or Samsung building on the Android platform to extend its Galaxy ecosystem. Both examples illustrate how thoughtful strategy and shared value creation drive adoption and scale.

Platform Experience and Economization

This dimension focuses on usability, operational efficiency, and financial sustainability. Platforms must be both enjoyable to use and efficient to operate.

For instance, Amazon combines exceptional user experience with strong cost discipline. Through its logistics, analytics, and cloud infrastructure, it maintains competitive pricing while sustaining profitability and customer trust.

The same principle applies internally: intuitive interfaces, streamlined workflows, and data-driven insights make platforms more adoptable and effective across teams.

Platform Technology Strategy and Ecosystem

This side covers the technical decisions and ecosystem participation that make a platform durable and extensible. It includes architectural principles, technology choices, and contributions to the wider technology community.

Apple's iOS ecosystem illustrates this well. By tightly integrating hardware and software, Apple ensures a seamless experience for users and developers alike. Strategic control over its ecosystem has fostered innovation, consistency, and resilience across devices and services.

Platform Design and Architecture

This dimension translates strategy into structure. It defines the building blocks, interfaces, and scalability patterns that give the platform its technical backbone.

A well-architected platform balances functionality and nonfunctional qualities such as security, performance, and interoperability. It allows systems to evolve without breaking dependencies, keeping both internal and external integrations smooth and predictable.

Platform Engineering (Development to Operations)

This final side represents engineering execution. It is where design becomes reality through disciplined workflows, automation, and continuous improvement.

Platform engineering focuses on scalability, reliability, and resilience through iterative development, observability, and feedback loops.

For example, Microsoft Azure exemplifies this maturity: its robust cloud infrastructure supports computing, storage, and networking services that enable developers to build and deploy applications globally with confidence.

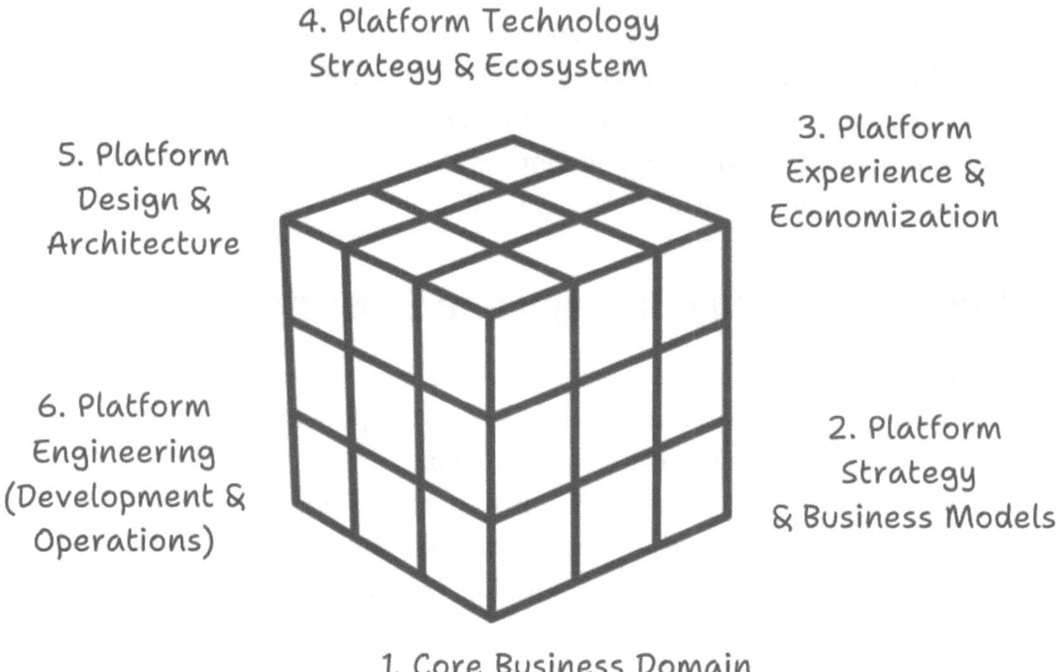

Figure 7-2. *Six Sides of Platform Success Blueprint*

When viewed together, these six sides form a complete, balanced system where design aligns with purpose, operations reinforce experience, and every part contributes to measurable business value.

This is what makes the Platform Success Blueprint more than just a framework. Once understood, it becomes a practical, repeatable map that helps leaders, architects, and engineers design, govern, and evolve platforms with intention and clarity.

The Power of Perspective and Patterns

Once you master this cube for a single platform, its versatility expands. The same model can guide

- A developer platform within a large enterprise

- A multisided marketplace connecting users and producers

- A platform of platforms that integrates multiple internal systems under one strategy

By learning to interpret the cube from any angle, you build a mental model that scales seamlessly from an individual team to an entire ecosystem. It helps you see interdependencies clearly, design with context, and act with coherence across technology, business, and operations.

Certain elements, however, apply universally across every side of the cube. Whether you are building, managing, or scaling a platform, three principles remain constant: **security, scale (innovation), and measurement**. These dimensions thread through the entire blueprint, ensuring every platform remains trustworthy, adaptive, and accountable.

We explored these three pillars in detail in Section 2, where we examined how they influence platform success, growth, and resilience. With that foundation already established, let's now begin unfolding each face of the **Platform Success Blueprint**, starting with the **Core Business Domain** – the foundation upon which every successful platform is built. This is where strategy meets purpose, where the "why" of the platform aligns with the "what" it enables. Understanding your core domain is not just about identifying the services or products your platform supports; it's about defining the unique value it creates and how that value connects across your ecosystem.

When this foundation is clear, every other aspect of the blueprint, from technology and experience to operations, finds direction and coherence. So, let's start where all strong platforms begin: with clarity of purpose.

Key Takeaways

- The Platform Success Blueprint turns complexity into clarity by bringing every perspective of platform success into one unified model capable of weaving success for any platform.

- The cube metaphor reminds us that platforms are intricate, multidimensional systems that are complex to align but never impossible. They demand a balance between business, technology, and user experience.

- Mastering the cube for one platform builds clarity that can be applied to many, whether developer platforms, specialized business platforms, or interconnected ecosystems.

- The goal is not to memorize the cube but to internalize its mindset so that your platform drives the business forward while technology remains manageable, purpose-driven, and adaptable at scale.

CHAPTER 8

Connect the Core – Align Business Domains and Platform Value Flow Mapping

"Think of platforms as canvases; without a core business, they remain blank – lacking purpose and direction."

In today's digital world, platforms and core businesses are inseparable. Your core business gives the platform its purpose; your platform gives the business its reach, speed, and scale. When these two align, value flows naturally; however, when they drift apart, even the most advanced technology struggles to deliver impact.

The core business domain is the anchor that defines why a platform exists and what value it creates. It encompasses the company's primary operations, offerings, and the value network that connects customers, partners, and employees. In essence, it's what the business *sells, serves, or enables* and what the platform must *amplify*.

For large enterprises, the core business domain often spans multiple platforms working together to power a vast ecosystem. For smaller firms, it may be a single, tightly integrated platform that defines the entire business. Regardless of scale, the relationship remains constant – **clarity in your core business determines clarity in your platform needs**.

The domain represents the essential functions, processes, and services that drive a platform's success. Take Amazon: its core business domain encompasses the full commerce lifecycle, from online retail and logistics to payment processing and customer service. Every platform Amazon builds, whether AWS or Prime, ultimately reinforces this value flow.

© Shweta Vohra 2026
S. Vohra, *Decoding Platform Engineering Patterns*, https://doi.org/10.1007/979-8-8688-2555-2_8

If your platform is your business (like Netflix or Spotify), this cube's foundation becomes your entire model. If your business *uses* platforms to scale, its effectiveness still depends on how well those platforms align with your domain's priorities and realities.

It sounds like common sense, but it often isn't. Organizations of every size, from startups to scale-ups to global enterprises, struggle to maintain this alignment. Complexity, legacy systems, and competing priorities make it easy to lose sight of the core.

Some confuse the need for internal platforms (to improve developer or operational efficiency) with external platforms (to serve customers or partners). You may need both or you may need neither. Many businesses still operate effectively with well-integrated tools and portals rather than building a full-fledged platform.

I have been asked this question repeatedly so let me address it here. When you do not need a platform? or How do you decide if you need a platform?

The distinction lies in repetition and scale. If your business repeatedly needs to roll out features, manage multiple tenants, or support diverse user and partner types, a platform becomes essential. But if your needs are simpler, for instance, you don't require multiple compute options just because they exist, then restraint is wisdom. Avoiding unnecessary complexity is still progress. Sometimes, *not building* a platform is the most strategic platform decision you can make.

With that perspective, let's now look at how different industries translate their core business domains into platforms and what lessons their journeys hold for us.

Example 1: Online Education Platforms

Online education ecosystems such as **Udemy** (now merged with another company equally popular named **Coursera**) connect educators and learners, offering a wide array of courses and credentials.

Key Business Services

- **Course marketplace:** Where instructors create and sell courses while learners browse and buy

- **Learning Management System (LMS):** Tools for course creation, content management, and assessment

- **Certification and credentials:** Verified specializations to enhance learner credibility

- **Corporate learning solutions:** Tailored programs with tracking and analytics for businesses

- **Community and support:** Forums and mentorship channels for peer-to-peer engagement

Core Lesson: The platform amplifies the education domain by creating scalable access, personalization, and a feedback loop between learners and instructors.

Example 2: Cloud Ecosystem Platforms and Services

Cloud ecosystem providers such as **AWS**, **Google Cloud**, and **Microsoft Azure** deliver infrastructure, application, and other service platforms that fuel digital transformation.

Key Business Services

- **Infrastructure as a Service (IaaS):** On-demand compute, storage, and network capabilities

- **Platform as a Service (PaaS):** User/Developer environments for building and deploying applications

- **Software as a Service (SaaS):** Managed software for productivity, analytics, and operations

- **Data, AI, and machine learning services:** Tools for insight generation and predictive capabilities

- **Security and compliance:** Embedded trust through encryption, IAM, and certifications

Core Lesson Explained:

These ecosystems go far beyond simply providing infrastructure. They serve as innovation foundations on which thousands of other businesses, products, and services are built.

For instance, cloud ecosystem platforms such as AWS, Azure, or Google Cloud are not pure platform businesses in themselves, and their primary function isn't to connect producers and consumers directly like a marketplace would. Instead, they provide the enabling environment where other platforms can emerge and thrive.

They supply the building blocks, such as compute, data, identity, AI, and integration services, that allow enterprises, startups, and developers to build their own unique platforms or applications on top. Over time, this creates a layered ecosystem that fuels the growth of countless other platforms that, in turn, serve new users, markets, and innovations.

In essence, cloud ecosystems show how platform thinking scales upward. They may not serve consumers directly, but they function as foundational services, products, or enabling platforms – nurturing innovation, accelerating time-to-market, and expanding what other businesses can build. However, not everything a cloud provider offers qualifies as a true platform; each must still pass the V-ARISE platform test (we learned in Chapter 4).

Example 3: Media and Entertainment Platforms

Streaming platforms like Netflix, Spotify, and YouTube illustrate how content delivery becomes a platform business.

Key Business Services

- **Streaming and discovery:** Seamless, on-demand access to content

- **Subscription and monetization:** Tiered plans and ad-based models

- **Content creation tools:** Enable creators to publish and scale globally

- **Recommendation systems:** Personalized algorithms driving engagement

Core Lesson: Success here depends on blending user experience, analytics, and creator enablement – forming a flywheel between consumption and creation.

Example 4: Digital Banking Platforms

Digital-first banks combine technology, compliance, and customer trust into their core domain.

Key Business Services

- **Digital account management:** Real-time deposits, loans, and payments.

- **Risk and compliance systems:** Automated controls for fraud and regulation.

- **Mobile experience:** Accessible, secure apps that redefine financial convenience.

Core Lesson: When a bank's platform mirrors its domain with trust, reliability, and simplicity, then adoption accelerates naturally.

Example 5: Hybrid Telecom Platforms

Telecom ecosystems demonstrate hybrid complexity by combining hardware, networks, and digital services.

Key Business Services

- **Network provisioning and management:** Rapid setup, monitoring, and optimization

- **Billing and payments:** Streamlined processes for recurring services

- **Customer support:** Always-on service channels for consumers and enterprises

- **Interoperability:** Ensures multi-device compatibility and smooth connectivity

Core Lesson: Telecom platforms thrive when they turn operational efficiency into user empowerment and expose seamless connectivity.

These examples reveal how diverse core business domains translate their strengths into platform value, whether through scale, connectivity, or customer reach. Each succeeds by aligning operational efficiency with ecosystem enablement. As you reflect on them, notice the recurring structures and principles that underpin their success. Let's now uncover some common learnings and patterns that emerge.

Common Patterns That Emerge

Across these domains, one insight stands out if you have noticed carefully:

Every service within a domain can become a platform of its own if designed with reusability, integration, and scalability in mind.

This is the beginning of Platform Convergence, where the boundary between business function and technology platform fades. Understanding this intersection is critical for creating long-term resilience and adaptability.

Core Business and Platform Adoption Challenges

The greatest platform challenges emerge not from technology, but from **misalignment between business intent and platform execution**. Integration succeeds when both sides speak the same language.

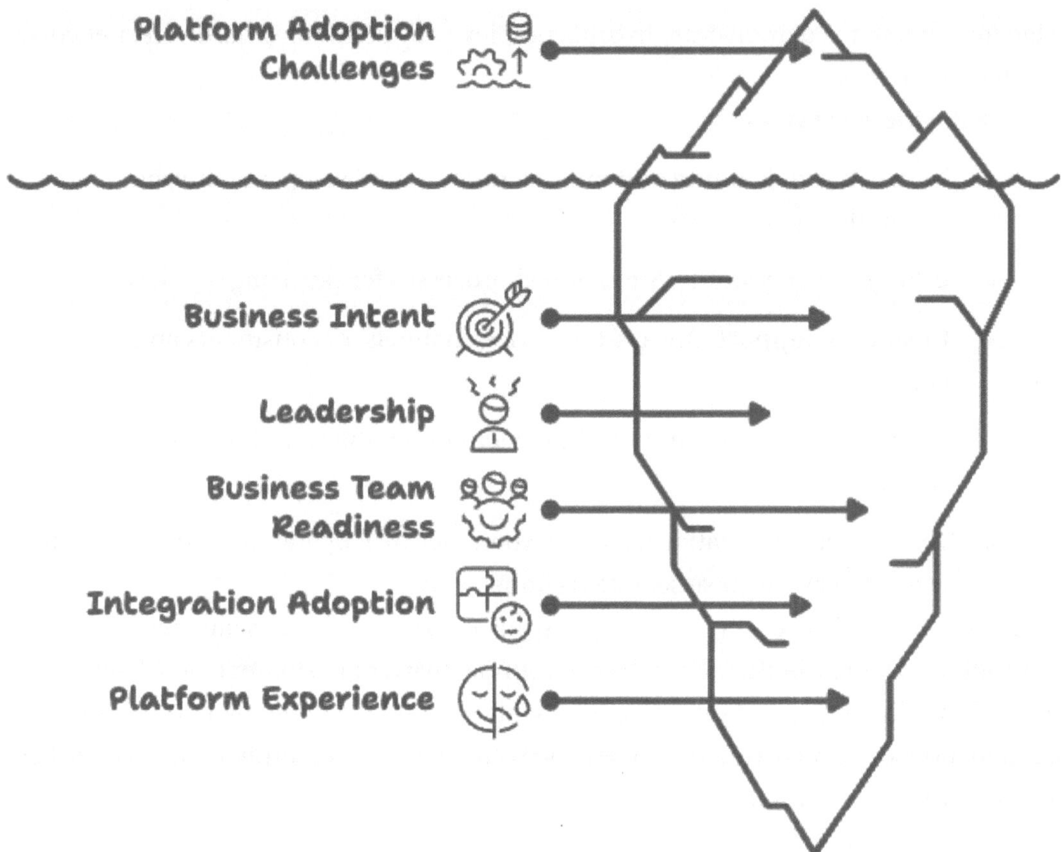

Figure 8-1. *Core Business and Platform Adoption Challenges*

1. **Leadership and Strategic Planning**

Platforms often falter when leaders focus on technical delivery without securing business clarity, vision, and translation. In my experience, the most common failure pattern isn't poor engineering – it's neglecting to define the *why* behind the platform.

Never build a platform that doesn't solve a problem.

Platform economics, ecosystem incentives, and business readiness are just as vital as features and APIs. Platforms succeed when leadership unites strategy and storytelling, making adoption a shared mission rather than an afterthought.

2. **Business Team Readiness and Platform Understanding**

A platform is only as effective as the teams who use it.

Training, communication, and transparency are essential to create what I call platform literacy, ensuring everyone understands not just how the platform works but how it adds value.

Communities of practice, platform demos, and internal showcases can dramatically improve confidence and adoption. And this is not a one-time effort. It must continue for as long as the platform evolves – and it will.

3. **Integration and Business-Level Adoption**

Sustainable integration happens when three conditions align:

- **Interoperability standards:** Clearly defined data, service, and interface contracts that prevent fragmentation.

- **Encapsulation of platform changes:** Use robust API ecosystems to shield users from constant underlying changes.

- **Continuous innovation and feedback:** Keep a visible roadmap, gather business input early, and iterate with agility.

Strong feedback loops between platform teams and business domains ensure the platform evolves in sync with real needs, not assumptions.

4. **Platform Experience and Adoption**

No matter how strong your technology, experience defines loyalty.

Smooth onboarding, intuitive workflows, and transparent feedback reduce friction and encourage adoption. When platforms *feel* coherent and empowering, both internal teams and external users naturally align with their purpose.

Checklist for Core Business Integration

Use this checklist as a reflection tool to assess your platform's alignment with your core business. Prioritize one platform at a time and revisit regularly.

Leadership and Strategic Planning

- How clearly are platform goals linked to business outcomes?

- Do leaders communicate the platform's value beyond technical terms?

- Are monetization and ecosystem strategies defined and measurable?

- Is cost management tied to value creation, not just expense reduction?

Platform Experience and Adoption

- Is user onboarding efficient and frictionless?

- Are UX principles integrated into design and updates?

- How well does your content, data, or service quality sustain engagement?

- Is user feedback continuously incorporated into platform evolution?

Integration and Business-Level Adoption

- Are interoperability standards formalized and understood across teams?

- How frequently are APIs and contracts reviewed for consistency?

- Does your platform scale seamlessly with demand and new business models?

- Are regulatory and compliance frameworks embedded, not bolted on?

Business Team Enablement and Learning

- Are platform roadmaps transparent to all stakeholders?

- Do business teams receive regular training and change management support?

- Is there a culture of co-ownership between platform and business leaders?

As you reflect on these strategies and insights, take a moment to examine how they apply to your own organization's platform journey. Every platform operates within a unique business context and its core domain, challenges, and opportunities. By tailoring these principles to your environment, you can design a platform that not only aligns with your business objectives but also sustains growth, adaptability, and long-term success.

What distinguishes great platforms from good ones is not their technology, but their ability to evolve with the business they serve. When business and platform strategy move in sync, innovation feels natural, and every iteration adds measurable value.

In the chapters ahead, we'll move from alignment to scale and translating purpose into performance. The next chapter dives deeper into platform strategy and business models, where we'll make the invisible visible through explicit value flow mapping. You'll learn how platforms not only connect business and technology but also create, capture, and expand value through clear streams of exchange, ecosystem incentives, and network effects. The journey from understanding *why* your platform exists to mastering *how* it grows begins here.

Key Takeaways

- Every platform is only as strong as the business domain it serves.

- Alignment between core business and platform strategy transforms technology into an advantage.

- Platform success depends on business participation, not just technical excellence.

Integration and feedback are continuous – the true signs of a living, learning platform.

CHAPTER 9

Craft the Platform Strategy – From Vision to Execution

"Hope and progress builds prototypes. Strategy builds platforms."

Let's begin this chapter by breaking patterns to make new ones and by questioning a comforting myth – that progress, meetings, or a flood of decisions automatically equal strategy. The truth is, in the world of platforms, progress without direction is simply drift. Platforms rarely fail because of a lack of ambition or technology; they fail because their choices lack an anchor. Teams build, scale, and integrate without an enduring design for purpose.

Studies show that platform ventures fail almost five times[1] more often than they succeed, and the common reason is strikingly consistent: a misalignment between business objectives and platform strategy. The problem isn't too few ideas, but too little structure to connect intent, design, and execution. To build new patterns, we first need to unlearn the old. Let's look at a few well-known examples and the lessons they leave behind.

Learning from Platform Failures

Let's look at a few familiar names.

---

[1] https://www.hfsresearch.com/research/your-cloud-transformation-will-fail-if-it-is-not-grounded-in-business-objectives/

eBay – Core Domain Misalignment[2]

In the early 2000s, eBay's acquisition of Skype and StumbleUpon stretched it far from its core mission of connecting buyers and sellers. The misalignment between marketplace DNA and new ventures diluted focus, forcing divestments later.

Lesson: Strategy without domain focus leads to fragmentation.

MySpace – Ignoring User Experience[3]

MySpace, once dominant, stopped listening to its users. Its design and privacy experience stagnated while Facebook evolved daily through feedback and iteration.

Lesson: Strategy must adapt faster than user expectations.

GE Predix – Missing Ecosystem Momentum[4]

Predix sought to be the "iOS for factories." Yet GE failed to attract external developers, creating a self-contained system that never gained a pulse beyond its internal users.

Lesson: Platforms that fail to attract external energy stagnate. Without an active ecosystem, adoption fades and decline begins.

BlackBerry – Closed Culture Impacts Innovation

BlackBerry's proprietary OS and restrictive app ecosystem couldn't compete with iOS and Android's open developer communities.

Lesson: Control is useful, but openness drives evolution.[5]

Friendster – Scaling Without Structure[6]

Friendster couldn't sustain its growing user base. Load times spiked, outages mounted, and frustrated users fled.

Lesson: Growth without architectural readiness of platform is self-sabotage.

Azure ChaosDB – When Trust Breaks[7]

A 2021 vulnerability in Azure Cosmos DB exposed cross-tenant risks, shaking enterprise confidence.

Lesson: Security isn't a feature; it's a pillar of credibility.

---

[2] https://hbr.org/podcast/2011/01/ebays-ceo-on-growth-acquisitio

[3] https://hbr.org/2009/12/lessons-from-myspace

[4] https://www.applicoinc.com/blog/ge-digital-failed/

[5] https://www.theguardian.com/technology/2015/nov/12/blackberry-ceo-john-chen-security-priv#:~:text=The%20CEO%20of%20troubled%20smartphone,from%20the%20edge%20of%20death%E2%80%9D

[6] https://techcrunch.com/2021/10/19/automattic-tc1-acquisitions/

[7] https://www.theverge.com/2020/6/22/21299032/microsoft-mixer-closing-facebook-gaming-partnership-xcloud-features

Each story echoes a shared truth: platforms fail not from lack of activity but from lack of coherence. Let's decipher that more clearly.

What These Failures Teach Us

Across industries, the pattern is consistent. Platforms hold huge power for the economy and business; however, they stumble and eventually fail due to common industry-wide concerns that includes

1. Lose sight of the core business they serve

2. Confuse innovation with expansion

3. Fail to attract or incentivize an ecosystem

4. Underestimate experience, trust, or governance

5. Scale without structural readiness

These are not separate problems; they are symptoms of a missing **Platform Strategy Stack**, which is the invisible architecture that links vision to execution.

The Platform Strategy Stack

Your platform strategy isn't a document or slide deck; it's a stack of interdependent choices. If any layer weakens, the entire system loses balance. Those choices are following:

1. **Platform functions**: The core capabilities derived from your business domain that the platform must enable.

2. **Platform business model**: The economic logic that defines how value is created, captured, and shared.

3. **Ecosystem approach**: How partners, producers, and consumers interact and are incentivized to participate.

4. **Technology decisions**: The technical foundations, interoperability, and adaptability required to sustain the platform.

5. **Organizational structure and governance**: The model of ownership, accountability, and decision-making.

6. **Metrics and feedback**: How success, reliability, and value are measured, validated, and evolved.

Figure 9-1. *Platform Strategy Stack*

The stack is not sequential; it is cyclical. Each layer informs and strengthens the others. Over time, this stack matures into a living framework for adaptability, shaping an V-ARISE-aligned platform strategy. Before we explore the platform strategy stack in detail, let us first understand how it connects with V-ARISE.

The V-ARISE Connection

In Chapter 4, we introduced the **V-ARISE platform model** – Adaptable, Repeatable, Integratable, Self-sufficient, and Ecosystem-enabling. These five attributes define whether your platform is a platform and is strategy-ready or simply activity-heavy.

V-ARISE Attributes	Strategic Alignment Example
Adaptable	The platform evolves as business models and technologies change. Adaptability keeps the platform relevant and future-ready. This is a core ingredient of lasting strategy.
Repeatable	Processes, patterns, and foundations are reusable across teams and products. Strategic decisions in platform design should support this repeatability to scale efficiently.
Integratable	APIs, data flows, and workflows connect seamlessly across domains. The strategy should clearly define how integration best serves users and consumers.
Self-sufficient	Platform should serve at least one core capability completely to build upon. Can integrate more, but the key is to do so without losing focus on the core domain. Each layer of the platform can operate independently when needed.
Ecosystem-enabling	A thriving platform empowers users, consumers, and partners to innovate around it. Strategy should create the space and incentives for this external growth.

A strong platform strategy ensures that every decision made in the strategy stack strengthens one or more V-ARISE attributes. That's how a strategy moves from paper to practice. Let's now look at all layers of platform strategy one by one.

Layer 1: Platform Functions

This layer begins where we left off in the previous chapter: your core business domain.

Every platform must serve a clearly defined business purpose. Its primary functions should mirror the activities that genuinely create value for your business and your users. This is why some platforms feel effortless and coherent, while others feel like a scattered collection of tools.

Platforms become powerful when they take one complete flow that matters to the business and make it repeatable, reliable, and self-sufficient. Anything outside that purpose creates noise, friction, or confusion.

Look at Tesla. Its over-the-air updates and autonomous driving capabilities are not random innovations. They extend Tesla's core strength: a fusion of manufacturing, software, and real-world telemetry. The platform functions reinforce the company's mission of continuous improvement and vehicle intelligence. Google's acquisition of Android is another example. Android extended Google's core business of search, data, and engagement. It became a platform that amplified everything Google already did well.

This is why clarity matters. If your platform's core function does not reinforce your business mission, you should pause before investing in it. Platforms fail not because they lack features but because they lack functional coherence.

Now, let's make this real with two examples from different worlds.

Example 1: Internal Developer Platforms and the Myth of "Providing Compute"
Many organizations assume that exposing infrastructure, Kubernetes clusters, or cloud accounts is enough to call something a platform. It is not. Exposing raw cloud access only shifts complexity to developers. It is the operational equivalent of handing someone a toolkit without instructions, safety rails, or a workflow.

A true internal developer platform provides an end-to-end experience for a complete engineering function. It abstracts infrastructure into a cohesive journey: provisioning, configuration, deployment, monitoring, security, logging, and ongoing operations. Each of these is a full lifecycle and can be shaped as a self-contained platform function.

For example, the infrastructure function can be elevated into a platform only when the developer journey is unified. A developer should be able to request an environment, deploy a service, observe behavior, roll back safely, and comply with policies without navigating dozens of tools and consoles. The platform team decides the maturity level based on business needs and developer personas. Some organizations need a light abstraction. Others need complete automation of the full flow.

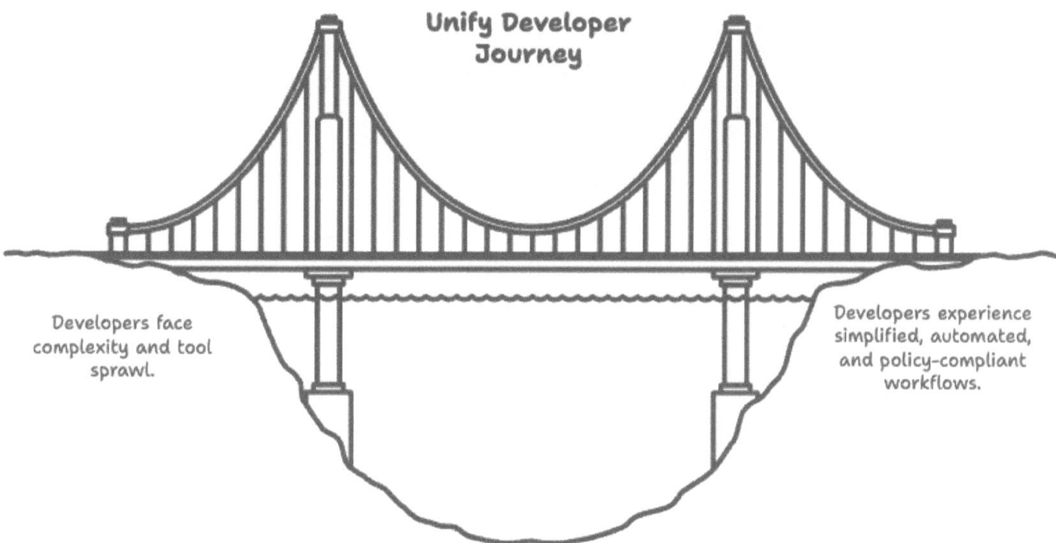

Figure 9-2. *Transitioning from Raw Infrastructure to Unified Developer Platform*

This is the difference between gluing tools together and shaping a complete platform function. Tools can be bought. Platform functions must be designed.

Example 2: Canva and Its Creator-Centric Functional Focus

Canva offers another perspective on platform functions. It is one of the most successful creator platforms because it nailed a single function early: simple, accessible visual creation. Everything else grew from that foundation.

Canva serves creators by giving them an end-to-end creation flow. Templates, editing tools, asset libraries, collaboration modes, brand kits, and publishing capabilities are all part of a coherent function. This is why the platform works for individuals, teams, educators, and marketers alike. Canva did not become a platform by offering a catalog of features. It became one by turning the entire creation flow into a guided, intuitive, repeatable experience.

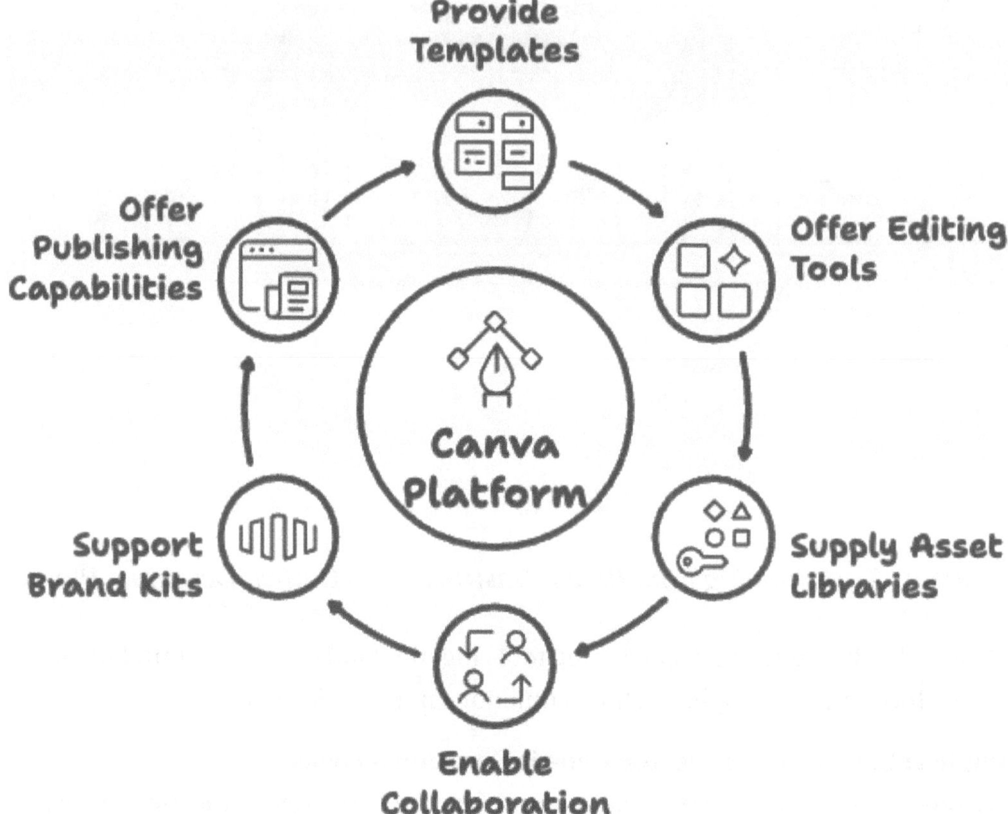

Figure 9-3. *Canva's Creator-Centric Functional Focus*

This shows how platform functions, when aligned to a mission and executed end-to-end, create both value and differentiation.

Rule of thumb: Know exactly what the platform does for the business and what it must never attempt to do.

Without this clarity, strategy becomes reaction.

A platform begins where purpose can be refined and called out in the form of functions. The rest of the strategy only works if this foundation is set.

Layer 2: Platform Business Model

A platform's business model defines the logic of its existence. It explains how the platform creates value, how that value flows across participants, and how the platform captures enough value to sustain and evolve. While we introduced business models earlier, their strategic relevance becomes practical here. A platform cannot rely on transactions alone. It must intentionally design the value exchange between consumers, users, providers, and partners.

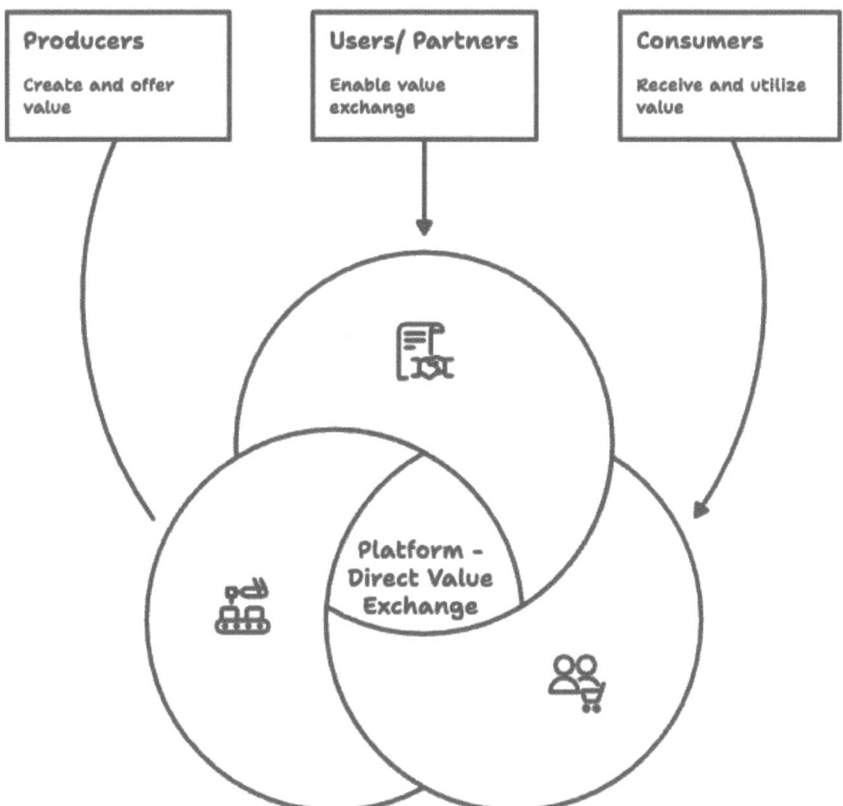

Figure 9-4. *Platform Value Exchange and Flow Mapping*

A strong value flow map clarifies three things:

Value creation: Where the contribution, service, or product originates
Value capture: Who benefits and in what form
Value leakage: Where inefficiencies or misaligned incentives weaken the system

In multisided ecosystems, mapping these flows exposes how tightly or loosely the platform connects its stakeholders. When the flow is explicit, platforms grow predictably. When the flow is vague or unbalanced, platforms stagnate, no matter how strong the technology is.

Airbnb is a good example. Hosts create supply. Guests create demand. The platform orchestrates pricing, trust, discovery, and dispute resolution. Its model succeeds because each participant has a clear role and receives clear value. When supply and demand slip out of balance, Airbnb adjusts incentives, pricing signals, and search logic to restore equilibrium.

Contrast this with GE Predix (GE's ambitious industrial IoT and cloud platform initiative). Predix struggled because the value flow remained mostly internal. It did not create compelling incentives for internal or external developers, partners, or industrial specialists. Without a clear multisided value exchange, it could not become a true ecosystem despite strong technical ambition.

The purpose of a platform business model is not just revenue. It is sustainability through shared value creation.

Reference Models: Five Distinct Platform Business Models

While there are many variations, most platform strategies draw from a small set of foundational business model structures. Below is a simplified table of the five most relevant platform business models, aligned with modern digital ecosystems.

Model	Description	Examples
B2B Platforms	Platforms where businesses transact with or build on services offered by other businesses. Often driven by scale, automation, and integration.	Salesforce, Alibaba Cloud
B2C Platforms	Platforms where businesses reach consumers directly through digital experiences.	Amazon, Netflix
C2C or P2P Platforms	Individuals exchange value directly with each other while the platform handles trust, discovery, or payment.	Airbnb, Uber
B2D Platforms	Platforms that target developers as primary users, enabling them to build, integrate, or extend capabilities.	GitHub, Heroku
B2B2C Platforms	Platforms enabling businesses to reach end consumers through another business layer, creating shared value across the chain.	Shopify, Instacart

While there are many business models, these five are intentionally chosen because they appear most frequently in platform strategy conversations and reflect modern digital ecosystems. They also help you identify how value is exchanged, which personas participate, and how to design incentives for sustainable use.

Competitive and Market Positioning

Even the strongest strategy cannot succeed without alignment with the surrounding market. Every platform must answer a single, decisive question:

Why would anyone build on your platform, buy from your platform, or integrate with your platform instead of alternatives?

This applies equally to internal platforms used by your engineering teams. If your internal developers find another tool faster or simpler, your platform will not scale.

Competitive positioning is about ecosystem advantage. Leading platforms mastered this through clarity and consistency.

PayPal differentiated through global trust and frictionless financial flows.

Snowflake differentiated through performance, elasticity, and multicloud compatibility.

Shopify differentiated through small business enablement, profit-sharing, and a developer-friendly marketplace.

To define your own position, map your Value Streams against your Differentiators. Reflect on:

What friction do you uniquely remove?
What shared value do you create across participants?
What do you enable others to build that competitors cannot?

When your platform strategy answers these three questions clearly, the market listens and aligns.

Layer 3: Ecosystem Approach

The third layer determines how open or closed your platform should be, how value is shared, and how your ecosystem will grow.

An open ecosystem invites innovation from the outside, while a closed ecosystem ensures consistency, control, and trust. Most successful platforms sit somewhere in the middle – a *selectively open model.*

Open Model Example:

Android's open source approach invited global innovation, creating an extensive app marketplace and rapid adoption.

Closed Model Example:

Apple's iOS ecosystem emphasizes security and a uniform experience. It was a closed system for a very long time. However, recently, Apple has gradually opened its ecosystem to creators and developers, and that's a sign of pragmatic evolution rather than philosophical change.

Middle Ground:

Salesforce enables an AppExchange marketplace but retains strong governance over integration standards.

When choosing your ecosystem approach, ask

- What kind of innovation do we want to enable?

- What level of control is necessary to preserve trust and performance?

- Which incentives will sustain both internal and external engagement?

Ecosystems thrive not by permission but by participation. Design the incentives that make participation natural and rewarding.

Core lesson: these ecosystems don't just deliver infrastructure; they *become* the enabling ground for countless others. They function as **services, products, or enabling ecosystems** where new platforms, features, and ventures are continuously born.

However, not everything offered by an AWS cloud provider qualifies as a platform. Each must be tested against the **V-ARISE attributes**: is it Adaptable, Repeatable, Integratable, Self-sufficient, and Ecosystem-enabling? Only then can it claim to be a true platform service. Same is true for any other platform that you want to access.

Layer 4: Technology Decisions

Every platform strategy is ultimately tested by the technical choices beneath it. Strategy defines intent, but technology determines whether that intent can survive scale, change, and real-world constraints.

At this stage of the book, we are not diving into a detailed technology strategy. Modern platforms require deep, low-level technology decisions, and that deserves its own structured treatment. Chapter 11 will walk through that in depth, including tools, principles, and patterns for mastering technology strategy. Here, at the platform strategy level, we focus only on the high-level technology decisions that shape the direction and boundaries of the platform.

Platform-level technology decisions typically revolve around four essential considerations.

Technology Stack and Direction

Every platform needs a stable toolbox: infrastructure choices, data architecture, integration patterns, ecosystem partnerships, and the core standards that shape how teams build. Selecting these intentionally – not reactively – is what gives a platform coherence.

Technology strategy itself is a discipline that requires granularity, trade-offs, and technical depth. That level of strategic work will be explored in Chapter 11. At the platform strategy level, the focus is on defining the high-level direction. What technologies will the platform rely on. What architectural posture it will take. What patterns it will prioritize. These decisions set the guardrails for everything that comes later.

Scalability and Adaptability

A platform must grow with usage, complexity, and business ambition. Scalability is not only about adding servers; it is about ensuring your systems can expand across user groups, geographies, and unpredictable future capabilities. Adaptability is the hidden multiplier that keeps a platform flexible even as it matures.

This is why Chapter 6 covers scale in detail. Different platform patterns experience scale differently – some scale through data, others through interactions, others through geography or internal teams. Your platform strategy must reflect the type of scale your platform expects.

Security, Compliance, and Observability

A platform becomes fragile when these elements are added late. Security is not a feature; it is a posture. Compliance is not a checklist; it is an operating model. Observability is not an add-on; it is the platform's nervous system.

These areas are deeply specific to every platform's domain and risk profile. That is why Chapter 6 treats security and regulation as one of the three pillars of platform strength. Your platform strategy must capture the security stance, compliance readiness, and observability expectations from day one, because these shape trust, governance, and market reach.

Innovation Readiness

A platform thrives when experimentation is easy and safe. This is where internal R&D, prototyping environments, and lightweight experimentation loops matter. Innovation readiness ensures that teams can explore new ideas without destabilizing the core.

It is not about chasing technology trends. It is about building a platform that learns, adapts, and evolves without friction.

Examples help illustrate this: Netflix built its identity by treating reliability as innovation. Microservices, chaos engineering, and automated resilience shaped a platform designed to handle global demand.

AWS chose a different path, turning its infrastructure capabilities into a foundation for thousands of other businesses. Their technology direction multiplied possibilities for others, which is the essence of platform thinking.

Finally, technology choices must acknowledge constraints. Many organizations collapse under over-engineering done in the name of "future-proofing." A platform should extend gracefully and intentionally. The right balance depends on your organization's culture, maturity, and governance structure – which is why the next layer focuses on organizational alignment.

Layer 5: Organizational Structure and Governance

I often return to Alfred Chandler's famous observation that structure follows strategy. In platform organizations, this is not a slogan – it is reality. A well-crafted platform strategy demands an equally thoughtful organizational structure. Governance is how your platform breathes. Too tight and innovation suffocates. Too loose and the platform drifts into chaos.

Teams often think governance is a rigid operating model. In practice, it exists on a continuum rather than a single choice.

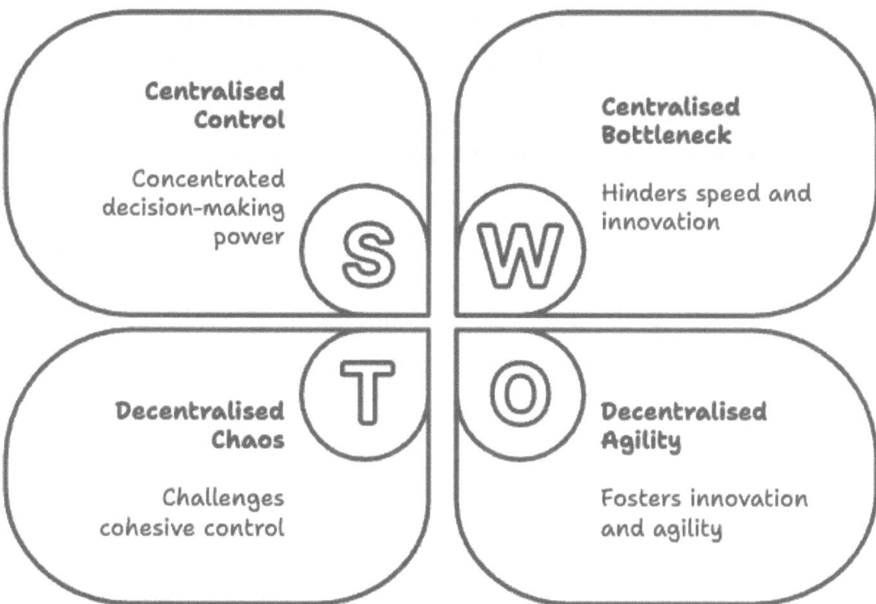

Figure 9-5. *Platform Governance Continuum Analysis*

Platform Governance Continuum

Each governance approach, whether centralized, decentralized, or shared, carries strengths and trade-offs.

Centralized governance offers control and consistency. Authority resides with a core team that enforces standards, compliance, and security. This model works well in regulated environments or when uniformity is essential. The trade-off is that decision cycles can slow and innovation can feel constrained.

Decentralized governance enables speed and creativity. Domain teams own their areas, make local decisions, and adapt quickly to business needs. But without alignment, this freedom can lead to fragmentation. Standards drift. Customer experience differs across teams. Integrations weaken.

Shared or federated governance sits between these extremes. It preserves alignment through a shared strategic compass while giving teams autonomy to innovate. In my experience, this model sustains long-term growth because it scales culture as much as code. It keeps everyone connected without over-controlling them.

Effective governance also requires clarity on decision rights: who defines standards, who approves budgets, who sets metrics, who manages risks, and how consensus emerges. There is no universal template. The right balance depends on your organization's existing culture, not its aspirational one. Apple is a good example. Historically, its governance leaned toward closed and highly controlled systems. Over time, it has adopted a more open orientation that is supporting open source efforts and integrations; however, they are always doing it in a deliberate and purpose-driven way.

Governance is not about control; it is about alignment. If teams cannot clearly explain how decisions are made, who makes them, and how they are reviewed, the organization is not practicing governance and systems clog many a time; it is improvising coordination.

Governance and Decision Rights Framework

Governance is not bureaucracy. It is the scaffolding that prevents collapse. Strong governance aligns technical choices, business priorities, and ecosystem expectations. Many large organizations struggle not because they lack talent but because they lack a clear decision rights framework.

An effective decision rights model answers three questions.

> Who decides (roles)

> How decisions are made (process and criteria)

> When decisions are reviewed (cadence)

Examples include

- Platform architecture and standards → Platform Council

- Budget and resource allocation → Business–Technology Steering Group

- Ecosystem and partner onboarding → Governance or Partner Working Group

- Platform-as-product roadmap → Product and engineering leadership jointly

This structure, or a customized version suited to your organization's culture, supports accountability without stifling innovation. It creates rhythm and clarity where work would otherwise slip into confusion or conflict.

Many voices in the industry strongly advocate for treating the platform as a product. Before adopting that mindset, it is important to understand when it genuinely helps and when it does not. Let's explore this next.

Platform as a Product: When It Helps and When It Doesn't

Platform-as-product is one of the most popular narratives in the industry today. It can be powerful when done intentionally, but much of the hype masks a more nuanced reality.

Product thinking and platform thinking are not the same. Product thinking gives you a vehicle to manage priorities, user feedback, and a roadmap. Platform thinking gives you a way to design value, scale, and enablement. You need both, but you need them at the right time.

I validated this through industry research and community surveys: many organizations rush into platform-as-product because it sounds modern, only to discover that their company culture is not ready for product rhythms or decision-making frameworks. Without cultural maturity in product thinking, even the best product manager cannot convert a platform into a cohesive product.

The opportunity to build meaningful platforms is still wide open. The world does not have enough well-designed internal or external platforms. A platform is not simply the assembly of services. It requires direction, discipline, and deliberate evolution.

The real shift happens when your platform's roadmap becomes demand-shaped instead of supply-shaped. When internal teams begin to request capabilities, when adoption starts to influence direction, and when the platform begins to support outcomes beyond its original design, that is the point at which you transition toward a product approach.

Figure 9-6. *Platform as Product Evolution*

When you do embrace platform-as-product, make sure the fundamentals are in place. Product thinking enforces essential questions such as:

- Who are the defined users and what problems do they experience?

- How much standardization is just enough for internal developers?

- What does the product roadmap look like and who influences it?

- How do feedback loops operate and how quickly can decisions adapt?

- What is the support and enablement model for teams adopting the platform?

- How do business and technology metrics connect to platform outcomes?

These questions protect your teams, align your organization, and ensure the platform evolves in a stable and intentional way over time.

Layer 6: Metrics and Feedback

If strategy provides vision and principles, metrics provide the mirror. They reveal whether the platform is moving in the direction it claims to be going.

A platform cannot be measured only by uptime, release velocity, or the number of features shipped. True performance lives in a wider space that includes adoption quality, trust, cost efficiency, developer experience, and ecosystem participation. Numbers without context create an illusion of health.

This is why in Chapter 6, we explored a holistic platform health model, covering four vital layers: system health, experience health, ecosystem growth, and in-house engineering health. Together, they paint a complete picture that no single metric ever can.

Many organizations fall into the trap of measuring what is easiest, not what is meaningful. Vanity metrics surface everywhere. Counting API calls without understanding their business purpose. Reporting developer satisfaction as the sole indicator of platform maturity. Celebrating uptime while ignoring architectural fragility beneath it.

A European bank I once worked with is a good example of this tension. They set "gold-tier" availability targets across every layer of their application and platform stack. The ambition was admirable but misaligned with architectural reality. Different components sat on different layers of the cloud stack, each with distinct limits and dependencies. By treating the entire system as one monolith with a single availability target, they created promises that could not be upheld and expectations that could not be met.

This is what happens when metrics are disconnected from architecture. They mislead more than they inform.

The remedy is simple but powerful. Measure both the system and its components. *Track reliability at the foundation, experience at the surface, ecosystem behavior at the edges, and engineering health behind the scenes.* This creates a complete loop of awareness so you can see not only *where* your platform is performing but also *why*.

Metrics, when grounded in architecture and strategy, stop being numbers on a dashboard. They become signals that guide decisions, trade-offs, and future direction. That is how strong platforms stay honest with themselves and stay aligned with the value they are meant to create.

Platform Strategy Evolution

A platform strategy is not static; it evolves through identifiable stages:

1. **Foundation:** Establish platform functions and align with the business domain.

2. **Adoption:** Engage first users, validate the model, and build trust loops.

3. **Expansion:** Introduce open interfaces, partnerships, and scaling patterns.

4. **Maturity:** Optimize operations, governance, and measurement.

5. **Renewal:** Revisit assumptions, sunset obsolete modules, and refocus innovation.

Figure 9-7. *Platform Strategy Evolution*

Each stage demands a recalibration of your V-ARISE readiness.

For example: In the *Foundation* stage, Adaptability and Self-sufficiency matter most; in *Expansion*, Integrability and Ecosystem enablement take center stage.

Strategy doesn't end once launched; it loops through renewal, just like code refactoring, but for business logic.

Bringing It All Together

A strong platform strategy is the thread that connects every layer of your platform with your unique purpose, value, and long-term viability. It does not exist in isolation; it builds on what you clarified in earlier chapters and what you will bring to life in the next ones.

It rests on three anchors:

Vision, grounded in the clarity of your core business domain.

Value, shaped by your business model, incentives, and ecosystem dynamics.

Viability, strengthened by governance, metrics, and the ability to adapt responsibly.

Platforms are not static systems. They are socio-technical ecosystems. The more interconnected they become, the more intentional your strategy must be. Technology alone cannot carry a platform; strategy ties together people, structure, incentives, and long-term direction.

When each layer of your strategy stack aligns with the V-ARISE traits, your platform gains the resilience to evolve instead of just growing. It becomes adaptable rather than rigid, integratable rather than isolated, and ecosystem-enabling rather than internally constrained.

From Strategy to Experience

A strategy only earns its place when people experience it.

The real test begins when users interact with your platform. That is when design meets friction, when trust is tested by performance, and when business goals confront real-world usability. A beautiful strategy without an experience proof collapses quickly.

In the next chapter, we shift to Platform Experience and Economization. You will see how usability, operational efficiency, and cost-awareness turn strategy into visible, measurable, lived value. This is where your platform truly comes alive and begins earning trust from every persona in your ecosystem.

Key Takeaways

- Clarity precedes strategy. Define what your platform will and will not do.

- The V-ARISE platform model characteristics sharpen strategic decisions by making them adaptable, repeatable, integratable, self-sufficient, and ecosystem-enabling.

- Mapping value flow exposes how producers, consumers, and partners create and exchange value across your platform.

- Ecosystem design and governance must be intentional. Participation does not happen by default; it must be enabled and earned.

- Organizational structure should evolve with strategy. Teams, governance, and metrics mature together; they cannot be isolated.

- Metrics must connect directly to business outcomes and platform health, not vanity numbers.

- Platforms evolve in stages – foundation, adoption, expansion, maturity, and renewal – each stage requiring its own strategic focus.

CHAPTER 10

Design the Golden Path – Experience, Efficiency, and Economies

"Master the art of platform experience, and you'll hold all the cards."

Every platform, regardless of its type, delivers some form of user experience. This experience can manifest through interfaces, integrations, support, or operations. The way these experiences are delivered can make or break a platform's success. As platforms are designed to scale and offer repeatable, adaptable experiences, it's crucial to think beyond traditional customer-facing or UX/UI interactions. It's about optimizing every aspect of the experience, including how efficiently these interactions are delivered. This is the key point this chapter will explore in detail.

Take Netflix. On one side, it delivers a seamless experience to users, whether they are watching a movie, a series, or newly released content. On the other, it provides internal platform capabilities that allow creators and partners to integrate and release content quickly, without worrying about underlying complexity. Over time, it has scaled from a content library to a broad ecosystem, yet the focus remains on experience and capability, not the tools behind it.

Platform experience is about seamlessly addressing user needs. When combined with resource optimization – ensuring efficiency at every level – you create platforms that become indispensable to users' lives. This principle applies not only to giants like Amazon, Netflix, and Apple but also to any tech-driven platform. For example, Slack leverages cloud-native technologies to deliver seamless communication while optimizing resources through scalable, flexible services. Similarly, Zoom has optimized its platform for high-quality video conferencing with minimal latency, efficiently managing infrastructure through cloud services to support millions of users.

© Shweta Vohra 2026

S. Vohra, *Decoding Platform Engineering Patterns*, https://doi.org/10.1007/979-8-8688-2555-2_10

Now consider Linux, one of the most foundational platforms. It provided a stable and consistent base that vendors could build on, from cloud providers to enterprise systems. Because integration was predictable, systems built on top of it simply worked. That is why even today, many platforms rely on it at their core. The experience here is not visual or interactive, but structural. It is the reliability and predictability that others depend on.

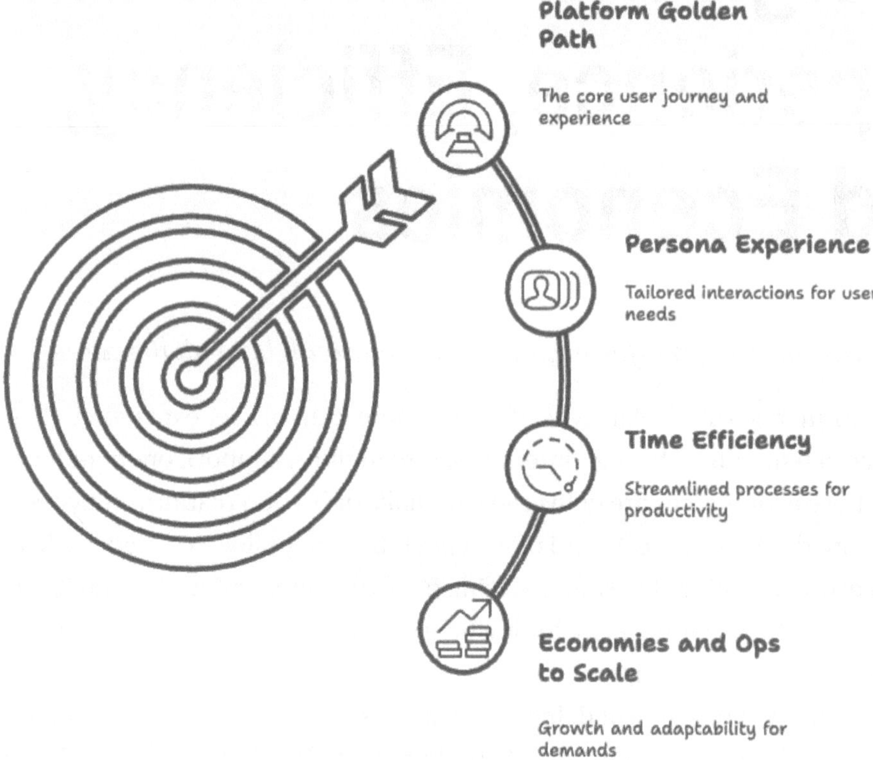

Figure 10-1. *Platform Golden Path Design*

Economizing the User Experience

Economizing the user experience reflects the strength of your core business and platform strategy. Efficiently managing user experience can be the difference between a sustainable, scalable platform and one that struggles to keep up with its operational demands.

It's not just about what you offer: whether a product, service, or documentation, but how efficiently you deliver it. By economizing resources like money, time, and effort, companies can streamline processes, reduce costs, and enhance operational efficiency.

Automation tools minimize manual intervention, while scalable cloud services reduce infrastructure demands. Without effective economizing, even the best user experience won't guarantee long-term success. Strategic economizing keeps your platform cost-effective while maintaining high-quality service delivery.

This aspect of the *Platform Success Blueprint* encapsulates your brand's identity and how it interfaces with users, applying equally to both customer-facing platforms and internal systems. For instance, a business platform, such as e-commerce, might showcase product listings and return policies, while Internal Developer Platforms (IDPs) integrate developer workflows and influence the growth and pace of the business. These internal platforms are essential to ensuring that developers can work efficiently, which ultimately impacts the user-facing experience.

The Importance of Platform Experience

The outward-facing element of the platform experience forms the first impression and the ongoing interaction point with customers, driving engagement and satisfaction. However, companies that excel in marketing and strategy but neglect their platform experience, particularly for their internal platforms and internal user experience, struggle with platform adoption and overall success as they scale.

This side of the blueprint covers user experience (UX), user interface (UI), financial models, financial operations (FinOps), technical operations (TechOps), customer operations, platform SLAs, and user satisfaction. While UX/UI ensures the platform is intuitive and engaging, operational aspects like FinOps and TechOps manage efficiency and growth. Customer operations focus on delivering excellent support and maintaining SLAs to ensure long-term user satisfaction and loyalty.

Let's explore these aspects of platform experience and economizing further.

Platform Experience: The Core of User Engagement

Platform experience is crucial for both internal and external users, encompassing everything from user interactions to platform operations and support channels. A seamless and intuitive experience is vital, whether it's customers interacting with the platform or developers building it.

To understand the importance of a cohesive platform experience, consider the difference between Digital Experience Platforms (DXPs) and traditional Content Management Systems (CMSs). DXPs go beyond just managing content – they unify data and content to create personalized customer journeys across multiple channels.

Other examples, platforms like Amazon or Netflix offer seamless journeys across devices, maintaining data integrity and providing continuity, whether users are completing a transaction or resuming a movie.

Many firms are rethinking their roles, envisioning themselves not just as providers of products and services but as enablers of platforms that allow customers to create their own experiences and value. This shift helps companies meet the ideal of delivering what customers want, when and how they want it.[1]

Successful companies like Pinterest and Salesforce exemplify this model by allowing users to craft their own experiences within clearly defined and governed interfaces.

A strong brand sets clear customer expectations and delivers on its promises. Consider BMW's *"The Ultimate Driving Machine"* or Lego's *"Endless Play."* These slogans encapsulate the brand's essence and promise. Unfortunately, this branding aspect is often overlooked in platform development. Organizations should integrate their brand's identity into the platform's design and experience. If a platform promises simplicity, every aspect of its interface and user experience should reflect that simplicity.

Take another powerful example, Canva's tagline is *"Empowering the world to design,"* which encapsulates its brand promise to make design accessible and easy for everyone, regardless of their skill level. This promise is delivered through an online platform filled with templates, images, and other tools that simplify the creation of professional-looking graphics for various purposes.

The platform experience must also cater to all platform ecosystem types – be it consumers, users, or internal developers. Each role is vital, contributing to the network effects that help platforms scale. A developer ecosystem that finds a platform easy to work with will create more tools and integrations, enhancing the experience for end-users and creating a virtuous cycle of growth and engagement.

UX/UI design should reflect the business purpose, brand identity, and user roles. Since your customers interact through this layer, the platform must be user-friendly and aligned with your brand. Effective UX/UI design boosts usability and satisfaction, such as with e-commerce platforms that offer easy navigation, quick checkout, and

---

[1] https://hbr.org/2012/05/turn-your-company-into-a-custo

personalized recommendations. Companies like Shopify, WordPress, and Squarespace provide customizable UX/UI templates that businesses can adapt to match their brand and functional requirements.

At the same time, meet the user where they are; for example, if a developer's workflow lies in code editors or Git, then meet them there, because, as I popularly say:

> A real platform disappears into the developer's (or user's) flow. A bad one interrupts it – daily.

By focusing on seamless user experience, unified content management, strong brand integration, and catering to all platform personas, organizations can create platforms that exceed user expectations, driving satisfaction and loyalty.

Platform Operations and Support: Extending the Experience

Customer operations and support can vary in scope depending on the complexity of your offerings. Effective support includes multiple touchpoints like live chat, email, phone support, and social media interactions. Platforms like Adobe Experience Cloud, Zendesk, Freshdesk, and Intercom offer integrated solutions to manage customer inquiries, track support tickets, and provide comprehensive analytics, ensuring timely and effective resolution of customer issues, which enhances satisfaction and loyalty.

Typically, Level 1 and Level 2 support are handled through this pillar of the platform strategy. More complex technical issues are escalated to the platform engineering teams, ensuring that deeper problems are debugged and resolved by experts. Simplest example of relatability can be if you use a website development platform from a third party, the initial support stages are handled by the business, while technical issues or advanced integrations are managed by the platform engineers/teams.

Economization: Optimizing Resources for Efficiency

Economizing – what does it mean? At its core, it's about optimizing every aspect of your platform to save on costs, time, effort, and resources, without compromising quality, performance, or user experience.

This involves making strategic decisions that streamline operations, reduce waste, and enhance productivity, ensuring resources are used as efficiently and sustainably as possible.

Automation plays a crucial role in economizing, driving scalability, efficiency, and innovation. By integrating automation with cost awareness into your economizing plan, you create a system that not only operates efficiently today but is also prepared to scale and adapt to future demands.

Let's explore the three key aspects of economizing: time, cost, and effort.

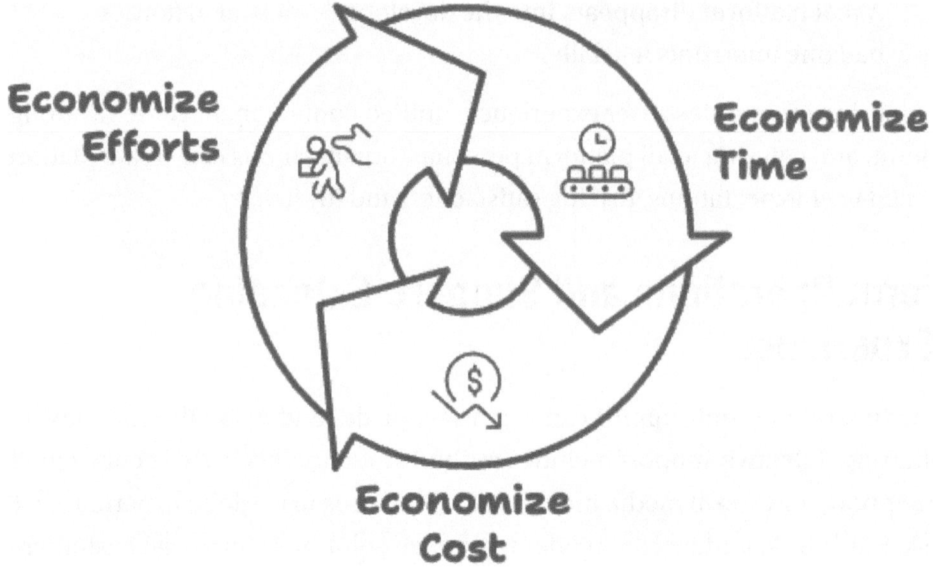

Figure 10-2. Economization: Optimizing Resources for Efficiency

Economization of Time

The pace at which you innovate and scale is directly tied to the time invested in your platform. Time is a crucial resource that often determines the success or failure of a platform. Efficient time management varies depending on whether you are a platform user or a platform provider. For platform users, time translates to experience and engagement. The more streamlined and intuitive a platform is, the less time users spend struggling with it, allowing them to focus on maximizing their experience.

For platform providers, economizing time involves investing in automation and creating easily integratable interfaces that reduce friction in the development process. Automating repetitive tasks, streamlining workflows, and minimizing deployment cycles are essential strategies. Tools like Jenkins or GitHub Actions, for example, can automate the build, test, and deployment phases, significantly reducing the manual effort required. This not only speeds up the development process but also ensures consistency and reliability in the platform's output.

To fully capitalize on this potential, organizations must develop a robust platform strategy that prioritizes the pace and depth of time investment. This includes both technical implementation and human aspects – investing in skilled professionals who can effectively manage and optimize time-saving technologies.

Economization of Cost

The cost of platforms is often overlooked in the early stages due to their complexity and variability. Typically, challenges such as assembling teams and navigating the nuances of the technology take priority, leaving platform cost considerations on the back burner. Platforms are inherently a composition of features, tools, technologies, and the experiences they aim to create, leading to a wide range of potential costs.

For platform users, the total cost of ownership (TCO) can be elusive, particularly when considering the platform's features. Users may overlook the additional expenses required for necessary integrations, time, and effort, leading to unanticipated costs. For instance, using a third-party platform might seem cost-effective at first, but hidden costs related to scaling, feature add-ons, or specialized integrations can dramatically increase the TCO over time.

Similarly, for platform providers, economizing costs revolves around strategically reducing expenses while maximizing value. Cloud providers like AWS (Amazon Web Services) or Microsoft Azure offer pay-as-you-go models and a broad range of services, which can help reduce upfront infrastructure costs. However, the TCO is often underestimated due to the additional expenses associated with utilizing these services.

To effectively economize costs, businesses need to implement robust cost management practices. This includes continuous monitoring of cloud usage, setting up automated alerts for cost thresholds, and leveraging governance.

Formula for Success with Cost Management

Operational management today appears under many different banners: *FinOps, MLOps, CloudOps, AIOps,* and more. While each focuses on its own domain, they share a common goal – to create visibility, accountability and efficiency across systems at scale. The terminology may differ, but the underlying discipline remains the same: understanding where value is created, where waste occurs, and how to optimize without slowing teams down.

There is no one-size-fits-all formula for managing costs in complex and large multi-platform scenarios. However, successful patterns do exist, and platform companies can develop effective strategies for achieving cost efficiency and sustainability. Here are some key approaches:

Focused Ninjas: Expecting everyone in the organization to naturally assume cost responsibility and frugality is a common mistake. Instead, platform companies should establish a core group – referred to as "Focused Ninjas" here – who specialize in cost management. These individuals quickly develop the skills to optimize costs and are responsible for educating the rest of the organization on cost-saving measures. The focus should extend beyond cost planning and visibility to fostering a cost-conscious culture throughout the company.

Implement predictive analytics: Leverage data-driven insights to forecast demand, optimize resource allocation, and anticipate potential cost overruns. Predictive analytics can identify underutilized resources or areas where costs are likely to spike, enabling timely adjustments to keep spending in check. By automating the detection of high-cost mistakes or potential errors through predictive analysis, you can proactively prevent issues and maintain efficiency. This is a highly effective approach that benefits everyone involved.

Automate cost management: Adopt a consumption-driven approach from the outset by incorporating automation to manage costs effectively. Automate tasks such as resource scaling, budget tracking, and alerting for cost anomalies, reducing the burden on human resources while ensuring accurate and timely cost control, whether for platform users or internal cost attribution.

Invest in security and compliance: While it may seem like an added expense, investing in robust security protocols and ensuring compliance with industry standards can prevent costly breaches and fines. Regularly updating these measures will protect your platform and save money in the long run by avoiding the financial repercussions of security incidents.

Prioritize high-ROI R&D projects: Focus on research and development projects that offer the highest potential return on investment (ROI) and significant market impact. By channeling resources into these high-value projects, platform companies can maximize their financial returns while minimizing waste on less impactful initiatives.

Make compatible choices: Choose tools and vendors that seamlessly integrate with your existing ecosystem and provide transparent cost visibility (more on this in the next chapter on Technology Strategy and Ecosystem). Ensuring compatibility can streamline operations and improve cost management.

Economization of Efforts

Effort economizing focuses on maximizing productivity by automating platform management tasks. Technologies like Kubernetes reduce manual intervention in areas such as scaling and load balancing. However, the complexity of Kubernetes can limit these benefits if not managed by skilled professionals. This topic will be explored in depth in Chapter 11.

So far, we have explored platform experience and economization. Now, let's look at some opportunities to learn from a few real-world examples:

Enhancing User Experience: Key Opportunities

Opportunity 1 – Enhancing cost visibility and control: Implementing advanced cost tracking and management tools helps maintain financial discipline and optimize spending. Example: Netflix's efficient cost management strategies allowed it to streamline operations and outperform competitors like Blockbuster, which struggled with higher operational costs.

Opportunity 2 – Embracing new experiences and technologies: Adopting innovative technologies and practices enables continuous improvement and cost efficiency. Example: Companies that embraced digital photography, such as Canon and Sony, successfully transitioned and thrived, in contrast to Kodak's challenges. Nokia's resurgence with new technology adoption showcases how embracing change can lead to renewed market relevance.

Opportunity 3 – Strategic scaling for growth: Effective planning and execution in scaling infrastructure ensures smooth performance and user satisfaction. Example: Facebook's robust scaling strategies allowed it to accommodate rapid growth, positioning it ahead of competitors like MySpace, which faced challenges in scaling effectively.

Opportunity 4 – Economizing through robust security investments: Investing in strong security measures is not just a safeguard but a strategic way to economize. By proactively protecting against breaches, companies can avoid the substantial costs associated with data loss, fines, and damage control. This approach ensures that resources are allocated efficiently, thereby reducing the long-term financial impact of potential security incidents. Example: Companies like Google and Microsoft, which prioritize cybersecurity (despite occasional challenges), have not only protected their reputation and finances but also economized by preventing the expensive repercussions that befell companies like Equifax,[2] which suffered a massive breach in 2017 due to inadequate security measures, resulting in severe financial and reputational damage.

Opportunity 5 – Optimizing customer support management: Efficient customer support processes reduce costs and enhance satisfaction. Example: Companies like Amazon and Zappos (a subsidiary of Amazon, known for its outstanding customer service) are renowned for their exceptional customer service, which not only reduces operational costs but also drives customer loyalty and market leadership.

Experience and Economizing: The Platform Reflection

Your platform reflects your business strategy, influencing both your ecosystem and company culture. Clear documentation, seamless user interfaces, and efficient operations enhance user satisfaction while optimizing resources.

By focusing on experience and economizing time, money, and effort, you can create and maintain platforms that are not only efficient and scalable but also cost-effective, driving business success.

Key Takeaways

- Deliberately design and detail the user experience to ensure it aligns with your platform's goals and user expectations. Provide a seamless experience for both external and internal users.

- Wherever possible, allow users to personalize their experience, fostering creativity and engagement.

- Develop your platform with scalability in mind, while economizing time, resources, and effort from the outset to ensure long-term efficiency and sustainability.

- Never economize on something that fails you; user experience and operations reflect your stability with platform technology. This includes the financial model and operational model. Sharpen your saw.

---

[2] https://www.ftc.gov/enforcement/refunds/equifax-data-breach-settlement

SECTION IV

Building and Scaling the Platform (Build)

Focuses on technical, architectural, and operational mastery for platform providers.

CHAPTER 11

Mastering Technology Strategy and Ecosystem

"When a business dreams big, technology builds the ladder. The trick is balancing the climb!"

Technology strategy defines how you select, build, and nurture the technical foundations that bring your platform strategy to life. It shapes how you grow, innovate, and participate in the ecosystem. While platform strategy defines *what* value to create and *for whom*, technology strategy defines *how* to build, operate, and evolve it with purpose and discipline.

Both are interlinked but not identical. Platform strategy focuses on business design, audience, and value capture. Technology strategy translates that vision into the tools, patterns, and operating practices that make it real. It sets the direction for architecture, team skills, governance, and innovation. A strong technology strategy aligns with current capabilities yet remains flexible enough to evolve with business growth and ecosystem change.

Platform Strategy vs. Technology Strategy

Platform strategy and technology strategy work in parallel but serve distinct purposes.

Platform strategy (covered in detail in Chapter 9) defines the platform functions, business model that it serves, its value stream, audiences, and participation rules. It determines whether the platform will be open or closed, internal or external, and what outcomes matter most. What business problem and market it serves? It represents the "why" and "what."

© Shweta Vohra 2026

S. Vohra, *Decoding Platform Engineering Patterns*, https://doi.org/10.1007/979-8-8688-2555-2_11

Technology strategy provides the "how." It chooses the tools, design standards, and operational methods that support platform success. It covers interoperability, security, data, observability, and cost governance. It also defines how teams will grow skills, manage change, and sustain innovation across the ecosystem.

A well-crafted technology strategy ensures that every platform decision connects to business outcomes and that technical complexity serves a clear purpose rather than becoming an end in itself.

Introduction to Platform Technology Strategy

Technology choices today are not single decisions; they are ongoing commitments. As innovation accelerates and markets globalize, the range of available tools and frameworks grows exponentially. This abundance makes focus essential.

Modern technology strategies extend beyond selecting tools. They balance stability with experimentation and integrate partner and open source ecosystems into the innovation process. The open ecosystem now generates more progress than any single vendor can, making community participation as strategic as internal development.

This chapter explores how platform providers and users can create robust technology strategies that balance business alignment, security, interoperability, and ecosystem growth. The goal is not to prescribe specific tools but to help you make decisions with clarity and purpose. For example, when launching a global e-commerce platform, it rarely makes sense to build a payment gateway from scratch when secure, established solutions like Stripe or PayPal can be integrated and extended. Similarly, if your strategy requires AI-driven analytics, leveraging proven frameworks from Google Cloud AI or Microsoft Azure AI is often wiser than building an entire AI platform in-house.

Technology Decision Framework

A good technology strategy stands on a few core principles that guide every decision.

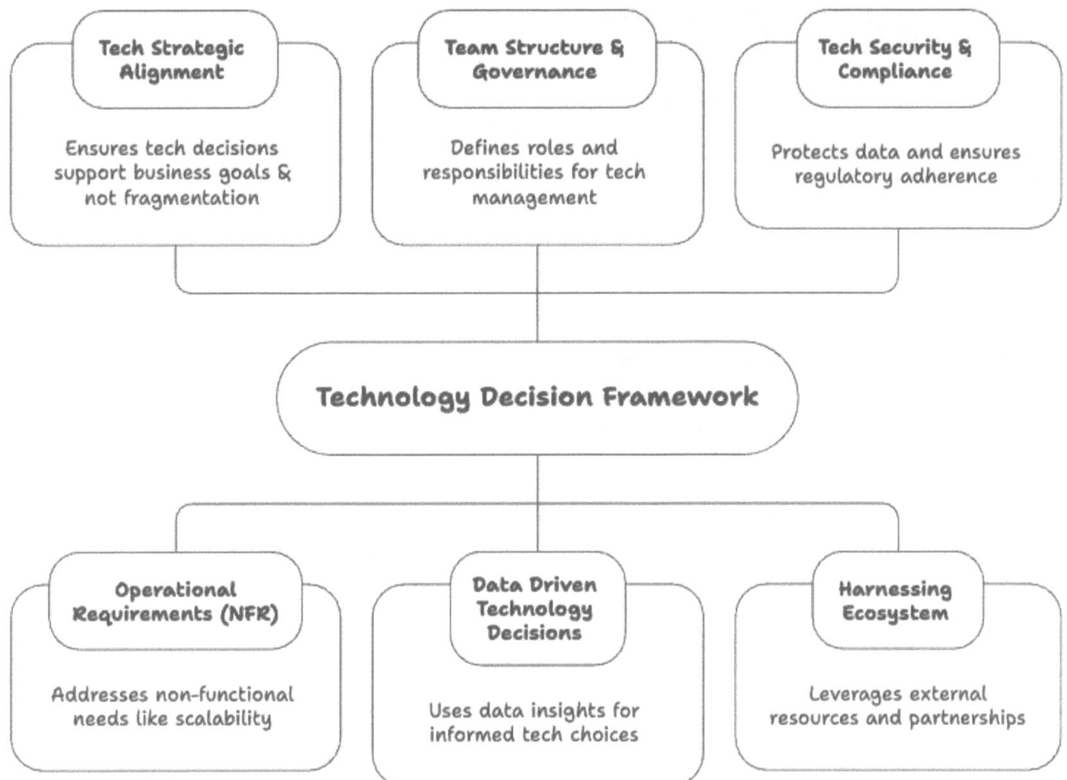

Figure 11-1. Comprehensive Technology Decision Framework

Strategic Alignment

Every technology choice must connect directly to the platform's objectives and, by extension, the organization's goals. Teams should ask whether a given technology supports the outcomes that matter most: scale, customer engagement, efficiency, or innovation. Many teams fail not due to lack of talent but because they make disconnected choices. Alignment ensures effort leads to impact.

Operational Requirements

Choosing technology based purely on functional fit creates blind spots. Nonfunctional aspects such as scalability, performance, reliability, and interoperability often determine long-term success. Evaluating these early helps prevent future bottlenecks. For example, scalable architecture choices, reliable uptime, and strong integration capabilities enable consistent operations and user trust.

Financial Considerations

Technology is an investment, not an experiment. Total cost of ownership includes not just licenses but also maintenance, upgrades, training, and support. Measuring return on investment by outcomes such as speed, reliability, or reduced manual effort ensures every expense links to value.

Security and Compliance

Security and compliance must be embedded into design, not retrofitted after launch. As cyber risks increase, platforms must ensure encryption, access controls, and compliance with regulations such as GDPR, HIPAA, or PCI. Apple's layered approach to device and ecosystem security is an example of security by design – where integration never compromises protection. Organizations that ignore this early often face costly rework, technical debt, or loss of trust later.

Data and AI Readiness

The way data flows across your technology stack determines how effectively you can analyze, automate, or innovate later. Structured governance, data contracts, and visibility into data lineage build confidence in decisions. As Generative AI becomes more pervasive, these foundations will matter even more, ensuring technology remains transparent and explainable.

Structure and Governance

The technology strategy must define how decisions are made, who owns standards, and how accountability is distributed. Centralized models favor consistency and compliance. Decentralized models give domain teams autonomy and speed. Shared governance combines both offering local innovation within a common compass.

Effective governance also demands clarity on decision rights: who approves budgets, who defines metrics, who manages risk, and how consensus is reached. There is no universal formula; it depends on the culture you already have, not the one you aspire to. For example, Apple began with closed governance to maintain quality and control but gradually opened selected frameworks to external developers and open source projects when it benefited end-users.

Ecosystem Leverage

Strong technology ecosystems multiply innovation. Choosing partners and vendors with stable roadmaps, active communities, and strong integration support ensures your platform evolves safely. Cloud providers such as AWS, Azure, and Google Cloud thrive because they offer not only tools but entire ecosystems that other businesses can build upon.

V-ARISE Alignment for Technology Strategy

Every technology choice should strengthen one or more traits of the V-ARISE model:

- **Adaptable:** Can this technology in context or view evolve with minimal disruption?
- **Repeatable:** Can teams reuse patterns and practices across products?
- **Integratable:** Can systems connect easily through APIs and contracts?
- **Self-sufficient:** Can each layer operate reliably without manual intervention?
- **Ecosystem-enabling:** Can external partners and teams extend or innovate safely?

Each architecture decision record (ADR) should clearly state which V-ARISE traits it supports and how success will be measured.

Building Blocks of a Modern Technology Strategy

A practical technology strategy involves more than intentions. It relies on a small set of living artifacts that guide consistency across the organization.

Figure 11-2. *Modern Technology Strategy Pyramid*

Reference architectures: Maintain two to four well-defined architectural patterns that teams can reuse. Each should include tested templates, diagrams, and sample configurations.

Technology radar: A quarterly review of technologies across four categories: adopt, trial, assess, and hold. This ensures teams explore safely without drifting into chaos.

Architecture decision records (ADRs): Simple, one-page summaries that capture what was decided, why, and which platform outcomes it supports.

Migration roadmap: A structured view of current systems, migration paths, and planned retirements. It should include versioning policies, sunset dates, and compatibility notes.

Observability standards: Define how systems will log, trace, and measure performance. Include service-level objectives (SLOs) and error budgets as part of platform contracts.

Security and supply chain management: Maintain software bills of materials (SBOMs), enforce dependency updates, and sign all artifacts. Security is both a discipline and an expectation.

Cost governance: Set tagging policies, automated alerts for cost anomalies, and transparent dashboards. Managing unit economics keeps teams accountable for sustainability.

Technical debt register: Record and track debt, cap its growth, and assign clear plans to reduce it. Neglected debt is one of the largest hidden risks in large platforms.

Data-Driven Decisions and Feedback Loops

Technology strategies must evolve through measurable learning. Every proof of concept or MVP should include clear success criteria: reliability targets, cost baselines, and V-ARISE trait coverage.

Feedback loops connect users, developers, and architects to real-world impact. By measuring usability, reliability, and cost efficiency continuously, teams ensure technology decisions stay grounded in business reality.

In one telecom platform project, delayed compatibility testing between vendors created months of rework and technical fixes. That experience reinforced a critical lesson: compatibility checks belong in the proof-of-concept phase, not after launch. Intentional validation early prevents costly detours later.

Harnessing Technology Ecosystems

Technology ecosystems define the environment where your platform grows. Selecting the right partners and contributors can amplify innovation and resilience.

Vendor Ecosystems

A strong vendor ecosystem provides support, scalability, and a steady roadmap. Partnering with established ecosystems such as AWS, Azure, or Google Cloud gives access to pre-built integrations and communities that accelerate development. Vendor selection should weigh reputation, reliability, and openness to collaboration, not just cost.

Open Ecosystems

"Community is the lifeblood of open source, and open source is the engine of software innovation"

said Priyanka Sharma, Executive Director of CNCF[1].

The open ecosystem is where much of modern platform innovation begins. Foundations such as Linux, CNCF, and Apache have produced technologies like Kubernetes, Kafka, and Linux itself, which are core components of most commercial platforms. Engaging with these communities keeps organizations connected to the latest developments and strengthens long-term resilience.

Contributing back is equally important. Companies that engage with open source shape the direction of innovation while building goodwill and reputation. Active participation also mitigates risk, as it allows earlier awareness of upstream changes that could affect your platform.

Using resources such as the Gartner Hype Cycle or McKinsey Technology Trends reports helps navigate emerging technologies responsibly. These insights ensure decisions stay informed, not reactive.

Technology Strategy in Practice

Technology strategy should be visible, reviewed, and owned collectively. Some organizations also call it by the name of Tech Radar. However, simplicity helps everyone adopt and use it; therefore, here are three immediate actions you can take.

1. **Examine your current technology stack**
   List all core technologies, their purposes, and responsible owners. Maintain this inventory openly for all architects, engineers, and product teams. Transparency reveals duplication, misalignment, and improvement opportunities.

2. **Follow an iterative decision process**
   Start with assessment and evaluation, conduct small-scale pilots, and involve the right stakeholders early. Perform cost-benefit analysis and document the rationale for each decision. Reassess technologies regularly using an adopt–trial–assess–hold model to stay current without chasing hype.

---

[1] https://www.forbes.com/sites/adrianbridgwater/2022/10/26/cncf-director-sharma-community-is-the-lifeblood-of-open-source/

3. **Measure and learn continuously**

   Establish checkpoints for reliability, cost, and adoption. Use data to guide renewals or replacements rather than opinions. Technology excellence depends on reflection as much as innovation.

At end result of the above exercise can be maintained in various forms such as tech stack or Tech Radar. Sample tech stack for the platform team, in its simplest form, can be represented like below and similar to this Vendor maturity should also be continuously assessed and risk assessed:

Sample tech stack (only for reference)		Maturity assessment of each	Company ADR or decision
Languages	Java, C++, Go, JavaScript, Python, Dart, Kotlin	Adopt (Java, Python), Assess (Go, Kotlin), Hold (Dart, C++)	Standardized on Java/Python; evaluating Go for specific services
Frameworks	Angular, Spark, Quarkus	Adopt (Angular, Spark), Assess (Quarkus)	Angular for front-end, Spark for data processing; exploring Quarkus for microservices
Middleware	Apache Kafka, Flutter	Adopt (Apache Kafka), Assess (Flutter)	Kafka for event streaming; Flutter for mobile app PoCs
DBS	PostgreSQL, DynamoDB, MongoDB, AWS RedShift, AWS EMR, ElasticSearch	Adopt (PostgreSQL, DynamoDB, ElasticSearch), Assess (MongoDB, AWS RedShift, AWS EMR)	PostgreSQL for relational, DynamoDB for key-value, ElasticSearch for search; considering others for specific use cases
Public Cloud Services	AWS, Azure, Google	Adopt (AWS), Assess (Azure, Google)	Primary cloud provider is AWS; exploring multicloud for resilience/specific services
Tools	GitHub, Terraform, Artifactory, Jenkins, Sonar, JIRA, Confluence	Adopt (All)	Standardized toolchain for CI/CD, IaC, code quality, project management

(*continued*)

Sample tech stack (only for reference)	Maturity assessment of each	Company ADR or decision
Observability/ Monitoring OpenTelemetry, Splunk, DataDog, Prometheus, Grafana, AppDynamics, Dynatrace	Adopt (Prometheus, Grafana), Assess (Splunk, DataDog, OpenTelemetry), Hold (AppDynamics, Dynatrace)	Open source for core monitoring; evaluating commercial tools for advanced features
Security SE Linux, eBPF, OPA, Cloud services	Adopt (Cloud services, OPA), Assess (SE Linux, eBPF)	Leveraging cloud-native security, OPA for policy enforcement, investigating eBPF for runtime security
Data Analytics Tableau, QlikView, Snowflake, Databricks	Adopt (Snowflake, Databricks), Assess (Tableau), Hold (QlikView)	Snowflake for data warehousing, Databricks for data engineering/ ML, Tableau for business intelligence
Machine Learning Services GenAI services, Open Models, ML services	Assess (All)	Actively exploring and piloting various ML services and models

V-ARISE Technology Checklist

Use this short checklist to ensure technology decisions align with platform success:

Does this technology (in context) align with the platform's strategic goals?

Does it scale reliably and integrate easily?

Does it strengthen one or more V-ARISE traits?

Is security, privacy, and compliance embedded from the start?

Are operational SLOs and observability standards defined?

Does it optimize cost per outcome and reduce manual effort?

Is vendor or open source dependency monitored and portable?

Are lifecycle and deprecation plans documented and shared?

Have teams been trained to operate and evolve it independently?

Key Takeaways

- Technology strategy translates vision into action and ensures the platform remains adaptable, repeatable, integratable, self-sufficient, and ecosystem-enabling.

- Every technology decision should have a clear link to business outcomes and V-ARISE traits.

- Security, compliance, and observability are not add-ons but foundational elements of design.

- Effective governance defines who decides, who approves, and how consensus is achieved.

- Engage with both vendor and open source ecosystems to stay current and resilient. Assess their maturity and risk exposure with pre-defined frequency.

- Build feedback loops to learn from usage, performance, and cost data continuously.

- Keep your technology radar, migration roadmap, and decision records alive and transparent.

- Portability and interoperability protect your long-term flexibility and prevent lock-in.

- The true measure of a technology strategy is not the number of tools used but the clarity with which each serves purpose, people, and progress.

CHAPTER 12

Designing Effective Platform Architecture

"If a well-designed platform is expensive. A poorly designed one is unaffordable."

Design and architecture are where strategy becomes real. If you want a platform that scales, performs, and endures, design it right the first time. This chapter translates platform strategy into a practical architectural foundation and prepares the ground for implementation in the next phase of your platform journey.

A well-architected platform is like a well-built structure – while one can survive in a poorly designed building, the consequences are inevitable and costly. Many teams rush the design phase, only to spend months patching, fixing, or rebuilding later. Building a platform demands effort, so the effort is best spent on designing it correctly from the start.

Design and architecture define how your platform will integrate technology, ensure security, manage performance, and enable innovation. They embed cost, compliance, and adaptability into the foundation rather than leaving them as afterthoughts. Ultimately, architecture shapes how easily your platform evolves and how consistently it delivers value to users and partners.

The Platform Purpose and Types

Platform patterns can vary hugely, and we discussed them in detail in Chapter 5. Here we are diving deep into platform design from the lens of a platform provider, designer, or architect. When it comes to designing, platform providers typically design platforms for three broad purposes, each tailored to specific user needs and exposure levels. These purposes balance **generative** capabilities (creating new opportunities) with **repetitive** ones (standardizing and scaling existing capabilities).

© Shweta Vohra 2026

S. Vohra, *Decoding Platform Engineering Patterns*, https://doi.org/10.1007/979-8-8688-2555-2_12

Business platform: Integrates and delivers business applications, domains, and features directly to consumers and users. Example: the customer-facing app of a food delivery platform that integrates ordering, payments, and tracking.

External enablement platform: Exposes and orchestrates platform features for external developers and systems, creating network effects by inviting others to build on your foundation. Example: an API platform that allows third parties to integrate payments, logistics, or analytics capabilities.

Internal enablement platform: Empowers internal developers and product teams to build, test, and deploy faster. Example: an internal observability or CI/CD platform that accelerates delivery and ensures system reliability.

Revisiting these three types form what we can think of as the **Platform Prism**:

- **Provider:** Builds and maintains the core

- **User:** Internal or external persona/developers who extend it

- **Integrator:** Connects it to other systems or products

- **Consumer:** The end-user or customer who benefits from it

Each platform type may demand a distinct architectural approach and governance model. Let's look at platform architecture essentials and choices:

Platform Design Principles

While architectures and patterns vary, certain design principles are universal. These serve as foundational guidelines for platform architects and engineers. Every principle should ultimately strengthen one or more V-ARISE traits.

Modularity and decoupling: Design modular components that operate independently yet integrate seamlessly. Each module should be buildable, testable, and scalable in isolation. Microservices exemplify this principle, enhancing flexibility and reducing systemic risk.

Interoperability and integration: Use standardized APIs, contracts, and protocols that allow systems to connect easily across environments. Kubernetes embodies this through its orchestration model, enabling interoperability across public and private clouds.

Security by design: Build security into every layer, not as an afterthought. Embed encryption, identity, and compliance early. Apple's design philosophy demonstrates how integrated security builds user trust and resilience.

Scalability and elasticity: Design for growth and change. Plan for increasing users, data, and workloads without re-platforming. Cloud services such as AWS Fargate enable dynamic resource scaling for consistent performance.

Resilience and fault tolerance: Expect failure and design for recovery. Platforms like Netflix validate resilience through Chaos Engineering, ensuring services stay available even when components fail.

User-centric design: Keep developers, partners, and end-users at the heart of every decision. A user-centric platform simplifies adoption and encourages loyalty. Shopify's architecture, serving multiple front ends from one backend, illustrates this well.

Ecosystem enablement: Build for participation. Allow third parties and partners to extend, enhance, and innovate. Samsung's Galaxy Store exemplifies how openness to collaboration increases platform value.

Operate by design: Bake in observability, automation, cost controls, and operational readiness. When you design for operations, scale and performance follow naturally.

Clarity of boundaries and contracts: Clear domain boundaries, API contracts, and ownership rules reduce ambiguity and enable predictable scaling. This is especially important in large organizations where ambiguity weakens platform cohesion.

Collaboration and co-creation: Foster shared ownership between platform providers, orchestrators, and complementors. Airbnb's model of cocreating value with hosts, service providers, and users reflects the power of collaborative design.

V-ARISE Attributes Mapping with Platform Design Principles

V-ARISE Attribute	Mapped Platform Design Principles
Adaptable	• Modularity and Decoupling • Scalability and Elasticity • Resilience and Fault Tolerance • Security by Design

(continued)

V-ARISE Attribute	Mapped Platform Design Principles
Repeatable	• Modularity and Decoupling • Resilience and Fault Tolerance • User-centric Design • Operate by Design • Clarity of Boundaries and Contracts
Integratable	• Interoperability and Integration • Ecosystem Enablement • Collaboration and Co-Creation • Clarity of Boundaries and Contracts
Self-sufficient	• Security by Design • Scalability and Elasticity • Operate by Design • Clarity of Boundaries and Contracts
Ecosystem-enabling	• Ecosystem Enablement • Interoperability and Integration • Collaboration and Co-Creation • User-centric Design

The more your design aligns with these principles, the stronger and more sustainable your platform will become.

Platform Design Approach

Choosing between open and closed design approaches defines how innovation flows in your ecosystem.

Open or community-driven platforms (e.g., Kubernetes, Kafka) encourage collaboration and external innovation. They thrive on openness but demand governance and vigilance to maintain quality and security. That's also the reason sometime they act as anchor and industry then heavily relies on licensed secured vendor platforms or companies bringing their own practices to turn the open source implementations into platform implementations.

Closed or vendor-controlled platforms (e.g., Apple iOS or AWS ECS Fargate) prioritize consistency and control. They offer security and predictability but limit external innovation.

Your design approach should reflect your platform's intent, industry context, and user expectations, not ideology. The right level of openness should create energy, not chaos.

Platform Design Elements

No matter what type of platform you build or how open you choose to make it, a set of core design elements always form the architectural backbone. These elements are foundational, but they are **never** one-time design exercises. In today's cloud-native and configuration-driven world, they require **ongoing iteration, refinement, and adaptation** as technologies evolve and patterns mature.

In the words of Dr. Werner Vogels from Amazon Web Services, *"Be a frugal architect."* [1]

This mindset is crucial. It reminds us that platform design is not about adding endless complexity but about making deliberate, sustainable choices that strengthen the platform over time.

Infrastructure: Choose the right mix of managed and self-managed cloud services to ensure scalability and integration.

Outcome: Reliable foundations for scaling without constant rework.

Services and applications design: Structure services around clear business capabilities and align with domain boundaries.

Outcome: Reusable and maintainable service models.

DevOps and release management: Adopt CI/CD practices that automate build, test, and deployment cycles.

Outcome: Faster, safer releases and reduced operational overhead.

---

[1] https://frugalarchitect.com/

Containerization and orchestration: Use Docker, Kubernetes, or similar tools for portability and efficient scaling.

Outcome: Portable workloads and automated resource optimization.

API management: Secure, versioned, and documented APIs connect internal and external users.

Outcome: Safe, predictable integration that accelerates innovation.

Packaging and interfaces: Design intuitive interfaces and developer toolkits for seamless onboarding.

Outcome: Lower friction for both internal and external users.

Integration and interoperability: Ensure data and feature-level integration across systems and platforms.

Outcome: Connected ecosystems that eliminate silos and duplication.

Security, regulation, and access management: Embed security and regulatory compliance in design. Define clear access boundaries and verify supply chains.

Outcome: Trusted and compliant platforms by design.

Data management and governance: Establish clear ownership, contracts, and quality rules for data. Apply domain-driven design to align with business intent.

Outcome: Trusted, explainable, and AI-ready data foundations.

Measurement: Track key metrics such as change failure rate, mean time to recover, and time to first value for new consumers.

Outcome: Insight-driven improvement and accountability.

Workflows, standards, and governance: Define clear workflows, coding standards, and operational guidelines.

Outcome: Consistency, compliance, and smoother collaboration.

Innovate and iterate: Decide with expiry in mind. Test new ideas early and retire what no longer serves your strategy.

Outcome: Sustainable innovation through deliberate experimentation.

Figure 12-1. *Platform Design Elements & Iterative Cycle*

Platform Reference Blueprint

A platform can be visualized as a layered blueprint. At the very top sit channels and edge interfaces, followed by the API gateway that governs access. Beneath that lies the heart of the system: services, domains, and workflows that deliver core business behavior. Below them are the data and event layers that hold state and enable communication. Supporting all of this are the essential cross-cutting concerns such as security, observability, and FinOps. And at the very bottom sits the infrastructure and orchestration foundation that keeps everything running.

This layered view becomes the backbone of platform architecture. It clarifies boundaries, prevents accidental complexity, and acts as a guide for both developers and architects.

In the next chapter, we will explore full platform blueprints, examples of layered architectures, and detailed Internal Developer Platform patterns. Before we go there, this chapter focuses on the architectural patterns and principles that make those platforms easier to design, develop, evolve, and operate. These principles form the difference between a system that merely runs and a platform that endures.

Popular Platform Design Patterns

Each platform type can be realized through different architectural patterns. Many platforms blend several to achieve balance and scalability. Here are popular architecture patterns that suit most platform architectures and long-term designs:

Figure 12-2. *Platform Architecture Patterns*

Headless architecture: Decouples back end from front end. Example: Shopify uses a single backend serving multiple interfaces like web and mobile.

Ecosystem architecture: Integrates external partners and third-party APIs to form an innovation network. Example: application stores that enable thousands of developers to extend platform value.

Composable architecture: Builds systems from reusable modules that can be assembled to create tailored solutions. Example: Adobe Experience Manager.

Repository architecture: Simplifies data access and persistence. Example: GitHub's model for managing and versioning large-scale repositories.

Layered architecture: Separates user interface, business logic, and data access layers. Example: Amazon's e-commerce architecture.

Event-driven architecture: Enables responsiveness and real-time processing. Example: IoT or streaming platforms where user actions trigger immediate events.

Microservices architecture: Divides platform capabilities into independent, deployable services. Example: Netflix's platform, where each service scales independently.

Hexagonal (ports and adapters) architecture: Decouples business logic from external systems. Example: Payment platforms like Adyen use it to plug in new gateways easily.

API gateway architecture: Provides a unified entry point for services. Example: AWS API Gateway managing multi-tenant traffic and authentication.

Platform as a Service (PaaS): Offers complete environments for building and deploying applications. Example: Google App Engine or AWS Elastic Beanstalk.

Multi-tenant architecture: Allows multiple users or organizations to share one instance while keeping data isolated. Example: Salesforce's cloud model.

Choosing Patterns

Start with the change you want to accelerate. Here are a few need-based selection patterns of platform architectures:

- Need independent releases across domains → Microservices.

- Need multiple front ends on one core → Headless.

- Need third-party extension at scale → Ecosystem or API-first architecture.

- Need high control and audit → Layered or Hexagonal.

Common Design and Architecture Pitfalls

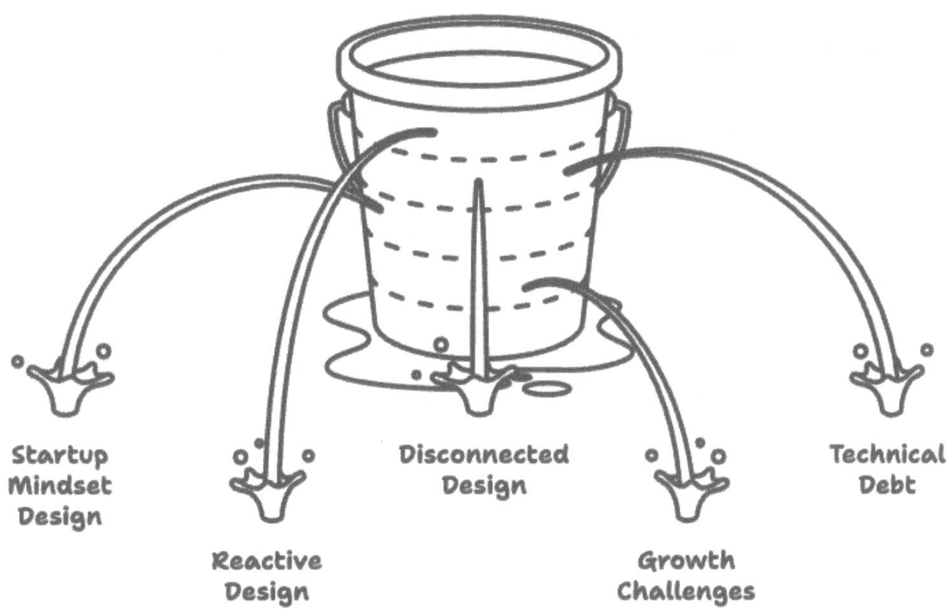

Figure 12-3. *Common Design and Architecture Pitfalls*

Startup Mindset Design

Teams overfocus on prototypes without foundational design.

Fix: Establish a minimal reference architecture and guardrails before coding.

Reactive Design

Lack of planning causes rework and inconsistency.

Fix: Create an architectural runway with quarterly reviews and automation guardrails.

Disconnected Design and Implementation

Great designs fail when poorly communicated.

Fix: Tie design acceptance to tested reference implementations.

Growth and Sustainability Challenges

Designs that work in the early stage often collapse at scale.

Fix: Regularly rehearse scale scenarios and invest in load testing and chaos drills.

Technical Debt and Governance Gaps

Ignoring documentation, debt, or security limits agility.

Fix: Empower architects with decision rights and maintain a debt reduction plan.

Technology Strategy Evolution

Whether you are starting or scaling, design intentionally.

1. List your platforms and assess their criticality.

2. Begin with the most critical and involve an architect from the outset.

3. Document the "As-Is" design or create one if missing.

4. Choose architectural patterns aligned with your platform's purpose.

5. Identify gaps in scalability, cost, or compliance.

6. Create an iterative "To-Be" plan and embed it in your roadmap.

7. Maintain a **one-page platform map** and a **platform contract pack** (API and event schemas with versioning and deprecation rules).

8. Communicate regularly with platform engineers, developers (who might be users of your platform) and other required stakeholders.

9. Measure progress using defined metrics.

10. Revisit architecture decisions with expiry in mind and frequency defined.

Proactive design prevents reactive firefighting. It builds coherence across teams and creates platforms that are reliable, adaptable, and aligned with business evolution.

Key Takeaways

- Architecture is where strategy meets execution.

- Align platform and technology strategies to drive purposeful design.

- Understand your platform type and design accordingly.

- Apply V-ARISE traits to test design strength.

- Choose architecture patterns that complement your context, not the trend.

- Empower platform architects with decision rights and clear accountability.

- Measure design success through performance, adoption, and cost efficiency.

- Revisit and refine design decisions regularly to keep architecture alive.

- Design once, evolve always. The effort invested early saves countless hours later.

CHAPTER 13

Platform Engineering – From Development to Operations

"Never wrestle with a technology problem; break it into manageable pieces and conquer it step by step."

Building a platform is the first step. Making it run, change, and recover every day is where its true value emerges. This chapter explores the journey from development to operations – the bridge between architectural intent and business outcomes. It covers the path from a developer's change to real value in production: environments, delivery, reliability, support, and continuous feedback loops that improve performance and user experience.

A well-designed transition from development to operations is visible and measurable. The most effective platforms track lead time for changes, deployment frequency, change failure rate, time to restore service, and developer satisfaction. When these indicators consistently improve, you know the platform is doing its job: delivering both speed and stability at scale.

Before we go deeper, it is important to clear a common misconception. Platform engineering is often reduced to a narrow focus on internal developer platforms or similar implementations. This view is shaped by vendor-driven narratives and a limited understanding of its broader scope.

Platform engineering should not be evaluated through market hype; it must be understood through its actual role in building a strong, reliable platform. And to appreciate that role properly, we must first distinguish platform development from software development – two disciplines that appear similar but serve very different purposes.

Platform Development vs. Software Development

If software development is like building an app to solve one focused problem, platform development is like creating the operating system that supports thousands of such apps over time. A software developer thinks in terms of features and short-term user needs. A platform developer thinks in terms of ecosystems, contracts, and how many different teams or products will rely on the foundations being built.

> *"Software development optimises for delivery; Platform development optimises for enablement."*

The platform exists so others can build with confidence. It provides consistency, scalability, and reliability – the V-ARISE way. The qualities that make ongoing innovation possible. As defined earlier in Chapter 4, a platform comes to life when it offers stable contracts, predictable interfaces, and the flexibility to evolve without breaking what already works.

Whether you are building a business-facing platform, an external enablement platform for partners, or an internal enablement platform for developers, the development mindset must shift accordingly. Platforms demand deeper automation, stronger guardrails, clearer governance, and long-term reliability and not just feature delivery.

From Development to Operations – The Right Way

Platform development leverages tools to build, test, deploy, and monitor capabilities so that users can interact effectively and consistently. This journey becomes seamless only when rooted in earlier artifacts from the Platform Success Blueprint – particularly platform design and architecture. With a strong foundation, development becomes smoother because strategy, technology choices, personas, and constraints are already aligned.

Having clarity on which features to build, which tools to use, how integrations work, and which security and regulatory standards apply makes development a guided process rather than a guessing game. This chapter assumes Chapters 11 and 12 on platform technology strategy and architecture have already set that groundwork.

At the same time, it is crucial to avoid the industry's most persistent mistake: placing everything on engineers under the banner of "developer productivity" or "platform engineering." This overburdens teams and creates the illusion that engineering alone can fix gaps in strategy, governance, and business alignment. True platform progress requires balance across strategy, design, architecture, business clarity, and technology readiness – all of which we have deep dived in earlier chapters.

Engineers accelerate a platform; they do not replace the foundational thinking that makes it viable.

Platform Engineering and Its Core Architectural Layers

Platform engineering is not a bundle of tools; it is an architectural discipline that organizes cloud, automation, governance, and developer experience into a coherent system. A well-designed platform abstracts complexity, standardizes workflows, and gives teams a predictable path from idea to production.

The layered model below describes the core components of modern platform engineering.

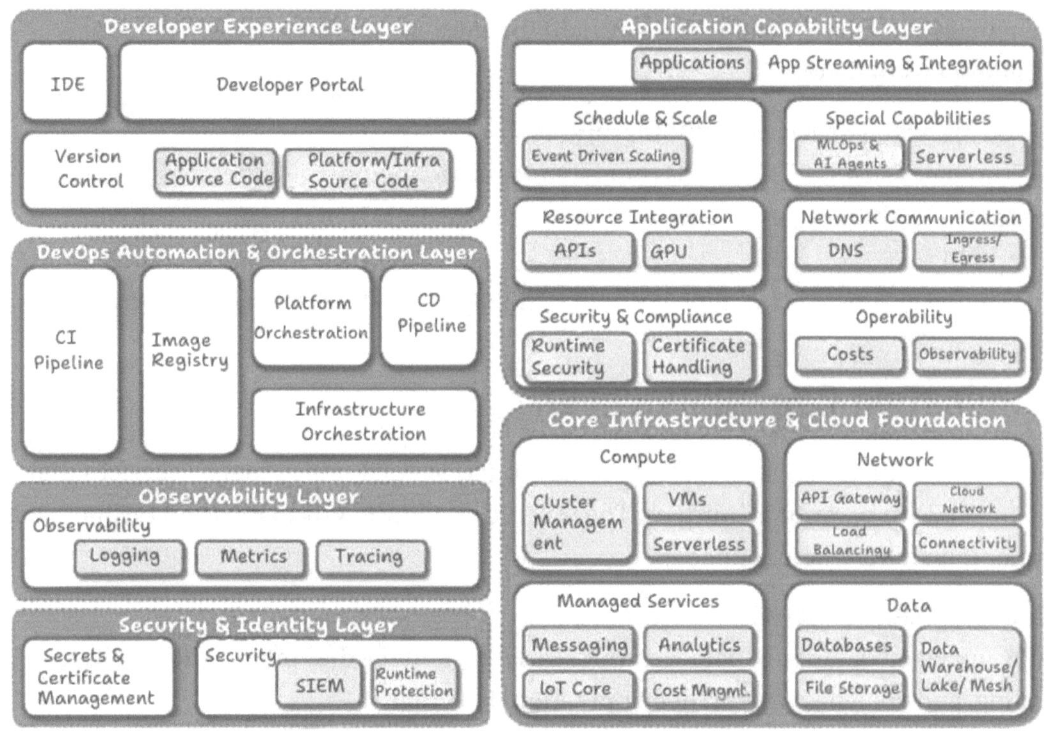

Figure 13-1. *Platform Engineering and Its Core Architectural Layers*

Core Infrastructure and Services Layer

This is the bedrock of the platform. It includes the raw or minimally managed compute, network, and storage primitives on which everything else is constructed. Whether provided through hyperscalers or on-premises data centers, this layer is the closest to the hardware and demands careful design for reliability and scale.

Compute

Virtual machines, containers, serverless runtime environments, and cluster managers form the execution backbone. Their job is simple: provide compute elasticity and isolation.

Network

Core networking includes connectivity across VPCs, DNS, load balancers, API gateways, and CDNs. These ensure secure communication pathways and global delivery of content and services.

Data

Foundational storage systems span block storage, object stores, shared file systems, and unmanaged database instances. They hold the raw data and state on which higher-level services depend.

Cloud Managed Services and Integrations

Technologies such as GPUs, TPUs, and CXL-enabled memory architectures extend compute capabilities for specialized workloads like AI, ML, and high-performance computing.

This layer provides stability. Without it, no higher abstraction can operate effectively.

Application Capability Layer

Once the foundation is stable, organizations build or consume managed services that abstract away operational burdens. These services allow teams to focus on business logic rather than infrastructure upkeep.

Managed Data Services

Fully managed databases, data warehouses, lakes, and meshes provide durability, scaling, and analytics without deep operational overhead.

Managed Application Services

Messaging systems, event streams, analytics engines, and IoT cores power asynchronous communication and large-scale data flows.

Network Communication

Platform-level ingress controllers, service meshes, and routing components handle east-west and north-south traffic reliably.

Security and Compliance

Certificate automation, runtime monitoring, policy engines, and compliance automation enforce safety, consistency, and regulatory alignment across systems.

Special Platform Services

ML workbenches, managed serverless/FaaS offerings, and event-driven scaling provide advanced capabilities for modern workloads.

This layer defines the "building blocks" platform engineers rely on to create internal products.

DevOps Automation and Orchestration Layer

This is where raw infrastructure and managed services become *usable* at scale. Automation, orchestration, and continuous delivery turn the platform into an operational engine.

Platform Orchestration

Infrastructure orchestration uses IaC to provision and manage resources repeatably. Platform orchestration manages upgrades, configuration drift, lifecycle operations, and cross-service coordination.

Application Delivery

Container image registries, CI pipelines for build and test automation, and CD pipelines for safe rollouts form the engine that moves software from source to production.

This layer provides the repeatability and reliability needed for consistent delivery.

Observability and Security Layer

These cross-cutting layers provide visibility, protection, and operational insight across the entire system. Without them, everything above becomes guesswork.

Observability

Centralized logs, metric aggregators, distributed tracing, and real-time alerting give teams the ability to diagnose, tune, and improve the platform.

Security and Identity

Secrets management, certificate stores, runtime threat detection, WAFs, SIEM systems, and zero-trust identity architecture protect the platform from misuse and compromise.

This layer ensures the platform is trustworthy and maintainable at all scales.

Developer Experience Layer

This is the layer users see first – and judge most harshly. It is the interface that brings together all the underlying components into a frictionless workflow.

Developer Portal

A unified experience for service discovery, golden paths, scaffolding, documentation, self-service actions, and operational context. Tools like Backstage embody this philosophy.

Development Tools

IDEs, linters, local testing frameworks, and toolchains that align developers with platform workflows.

Version Control

Repositories for application code and platform/IaC code ensure consistency, governance, and traceability.

Developer experience is the multiplier of platform value. ***When this layer is intuitive, the rest of the stack becomes invisible, which is the ultimate goal.***

Addressing Challenges in Cloud-Native Development

Even the best-designed architectures encounter turbulence. Tool sprawl, fast-changing technologies, fragmented cloud ecosystems, compliance demands, and the learning curve of distributed systems all create friction for teams.

Kubernetes is a prime example. It solves orchestration but is not a platform on its own. To turn Kubernetes into a usable, scalable platform, you must layer networking, service meshes, observability, registries, policy enforcement, CI/CD automation, and more – each evolving at its own pace and introducing its own integration challenges.

This layered complexity is exactly why platform engineering requires strong architectural governance, not just strong engineering. The diagram below illustrates the multiple layers teams must integrate and climb, almost like a ladder, before Kubernetes becomes a coherent platform. It shows how today's fragmented tooling landscape increases cognitive load and demands disciplined design for stability and scale.

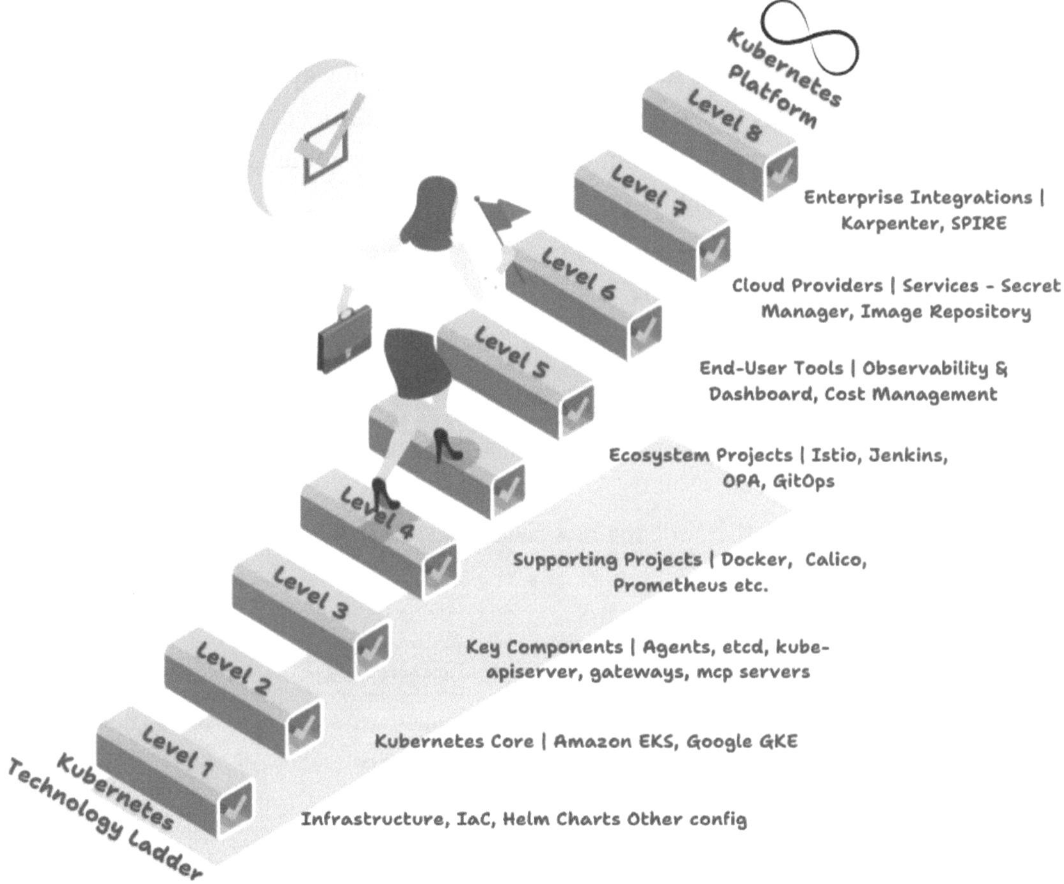

Figure 13-2. *Kubernetes Technology Ladder With Various Levels Integration*

Internal Developer Platforms Explained

Internal platforms have existed for decades in different forms. What has changed today is the scale, complexity, and pace at which modern organizations operate. As teams grow, architectures expand, and cloud services multiply, the development experience becomes fragmented. This is the context in which Internal Developer Platforms (IDPs) have gained attention, and not because they are trendy, but because they help organizations organize the growing sprawl of tools, processes, and environments into something coherent.

At their core, IDPs bundle the common components that almost every digital organization needs: infrastructure provisioning, deployment workflows, environment management, observability, and standardized templates. This bundling reduces friction for engineering teams and gives platform teams a structured way to deliver consistency, safety, and speed. It is easy to see why IDPs are being popularized: they promise a unified path from idea to production in organizations where toolchains have grown organically and often chaotically.

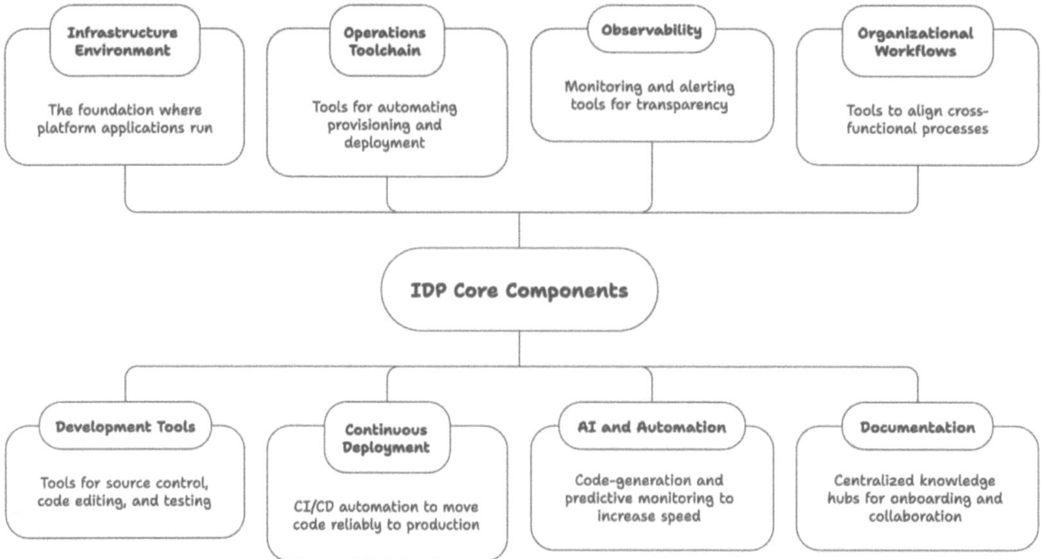

Figure 13-3. *Components of an Effective IDP*

But it is equally important to recognize that **not every organization needs a full-fledged IDP**, and not every collection of tools must be transformed into a "platform." Many companies simply need clarity, standardization, and visibility – not another heavy abstraction layer. In some cases, an internal engineering portal is enough: a lightweight interface that aggregates documentation, golden paths, service catalogs, and onboarding guides without enforcing deep automation behind the scenes. These portals improve discoverability, reduce cognitive load, and make it easier for teams to self-service common tasks without building an entire IDP from scratch.

A good internal platform, whether a simple portal or a sophisticated IDP, has one purpose: reduce friction and empower engineers. It should feel like a well-lit path, not a maze of tools stitched together. And as we will explore in the next sections, its effectiveness depends far more on the clarity of platform strategy, design, and architecture than on how many tools it integrates.

System Models – The Connective Tissue of Large Platforms

As organizations grow, simple diagrams stop being enough. Architecture charts, flow sketches, and service maps become outdated almost instantly. What large platforms need instead is **system modeling** – a structured way to represent how every layer of the platform fits together: domains, workflows, dependencies, cloud components, identity boundaries, policies, environments, and personas.

System models turn complexity into something navigable. They provide

- **Clear boundaries** that prevent capability creep

- **Predictable contracts** between teams and services

- **Traceability across layers** from business flow to domain to service and infrastructure

- **A shared, organization-wide language** for engineering, product, security, governance, and architecture

Example that reflects real-world platform complexity
Consider a digital bank building an enterprise-wide system model for its payments platform.

A high-quality model would show

The **domain boundaries** across payments, accounts, identity, fraud, and customer support

The **workflow** connecting a user's payment initiation to authorization, ledger updates, reconciliation, and notifications

The **cloud components** that support the flow: compute clusters, VPCs, API gateways, event buses, and encrypted storage

The **identity and policy boundaries**, such as which services require step-up authentication, which operate under PCI-DSS, and where data residency rules apply

The **dependency graph**, showing which microservices must be available for settlement, fraud scoring, or transaction history retrieval

The **environment mapping**, illustrating differences between development, staging, and production

The **personas**, from backend engineers to fraud analysts to customer ops teams, each using different slices of the model

When the bank later exposes services through its **developer portal**, the same system model becomes the foundation: every service, capability, and golden path maps cleanly back to the underlying model, making the portal trustworthy and coherent.

Why System Models Matter

In large organizations, system models become the connective tissue that holds the platform together. They prevent accidental complexity, reduce troubleshooting time, improve cross-team alignment, and act as the backbone for your internal developer platform or portal.

A strong system model makes your entire platform supply chain – from idea to production. Things become visible, trackable, governable, and safe to evolve.

Backstage – What, Why, How

Backstage, originally developed by Spotify and now a thriving CNCF open source project, has become one of the most widely adopted internal developer portal frameworks in the industry. Over the last few years, organizations of all sizes have embraced Backstage because it provides a structured, extensible way to bring order to sprawling developer ecosystems.

What Backstage Is[1]

A unified, central portal that brings together

- Service catalogs

- Documentation and API references

---

[1] https://backstage.io/

- Golden paths and templates

- Self-service operations

- Plugins for CI/CD, monitoring, security, and more

It becomes the front door to the platform – one place where developers discover, build, ship, and operate.

Why Organizations Use It

Backstage reduces cognitive load by giving developers a single, predictable interface across tools, environments, and workflows. It improves discoverability, standardization, and onboarding. In large organizations with dozens of tech stacks and hundreds of services, this eliminates the invisible tax of context switching and accelerates delivery.

How Backstage Works

Backstage is a plugin-based open source project. Each plugin brings a capability:

- CI/CD visibility

- API browsing

- Infrastructure provisioning

- Security and compliance checks

- Dependency maps

- Cost insights

- Golden path scaffolding

This modular design lets organizations adopt Backstage at their own pace, adding capabilities as their maturity grows.

Why System Models Matter Here

The real power of Backstage emerges when an organization has a solid system model. A well-defined model lets Backstage represent

- Accurate service dependencies

- Domain boundaries

- Ownership and lifecycle metadata

- Environment mapping

- Architecture guardrails

- Platform golden paths

Backstage plugins then operate cleanly because they are built on top of a consistent, shared representation of the system.

If your system model is weak or undocumented, Backstage becomes "just another dashboard." But when the system model is strong, Backstage becomes the living interface to the entire organization – a discoverable, navigable, and governable map of your engineering universe.

Open Source Momentum and Plugin Ecosystem

Backstage's adoption has grown massively because it is open source and community-driven. Hundreds of organizations contribute plugins that extend the platform responsibly: observability, Kubernetes operations, cost controls, site reliability engineering (SRE) tools, security scanners, cloud management, and more.

These plugins help organizations adopt features progressively – based on their architecture maturity, developer needs, and system model clarity rather than forcing a "big bang" implementation.

In summary, whether used lightly as an internal engineering portal or deeply as the core of an Internal Developer Platform, Backstage supports clarity, consistency, and discoverability. It aligns teams around shared standards and becomes the connective interface between system models and platform engineering workflows.

APIs and Composability – The Backbone of Modern Platforms

APIs remain the most durable and universally adopted pattern in platform development. While tools, frameworks, and clouds evolve constantly, clear APIs outlive them all.

APIs enable composable systems by

- Abstracting implementation details

- Enforcing stable contracts

- Allowing internal and external services to evolve independently

- Enabling marketplace and partner ecosystems

- Reducing duplication by reusing shared capabilities

Deep-Tech Example

At a European bank I worked with, APIs enabled consistent risk scoring across dozens of applications. Without API-driven contracts (versioning, schema validation, policy enforcement), every change in a downstream model would have broken upstream systems. APIs acted as the stability layer that allowed innovation without destabilizing the core.

> ***"Good APIs behave like Lego bricks*** *– predictable, interchangeable, and extensible.*
>
> ***Poor APIs behave like glued puzzles*** *– impossible to modify without breaking something."*

API governance, discoverability, and observability therefore become essential parts of platform engineering.

Capabilities and Golden Paths – Predictability Without Stifling Innovation

A golden path or standard paths are the fastest, safest, and most supported ways to build on a platform. It includes templates, CI/CD workflows, quality gates, default SLOs, dashboards, runbooks, and rollback strategies.

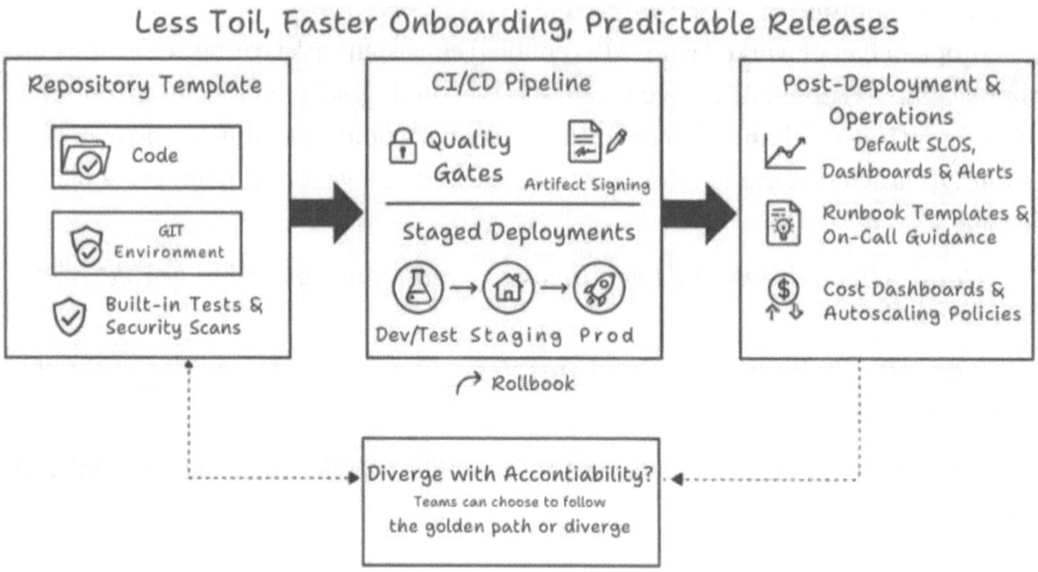

Figure 13-4. *Golden Path Templates*

A standard golden path provides the following and more:

1. A repository template with built-in tests and security scans

2. CI/CD pipelines with quality gates and artifact signing

3. Staged deployments with rollback and monitoring

4. Default SLOs, dashboards, and alerts

5. Runbook templates and on-call guidance

6. Cost dashboards and autoscaling policies

Teams can choose to follow the golden path or diverge with accountability. The result is less toil, faster onboarding, and more predictable releases. I am attaching the diagram here so teams can clearly understand the strengths and limitations of this approach. In organizations where teams prefer high flexibility and minimal standardization, the golden path may feel restrictive. This tension is common.

The responsibility of the platform engineering function is to secure early agreement on these expectations during the platform strategy phase, not later when teams are already debating whether automation, templates, or standard workflows should even exist. Early alignment prevents conflict and ensures that the golden path becomes a shared commitment rather than a source of friction.

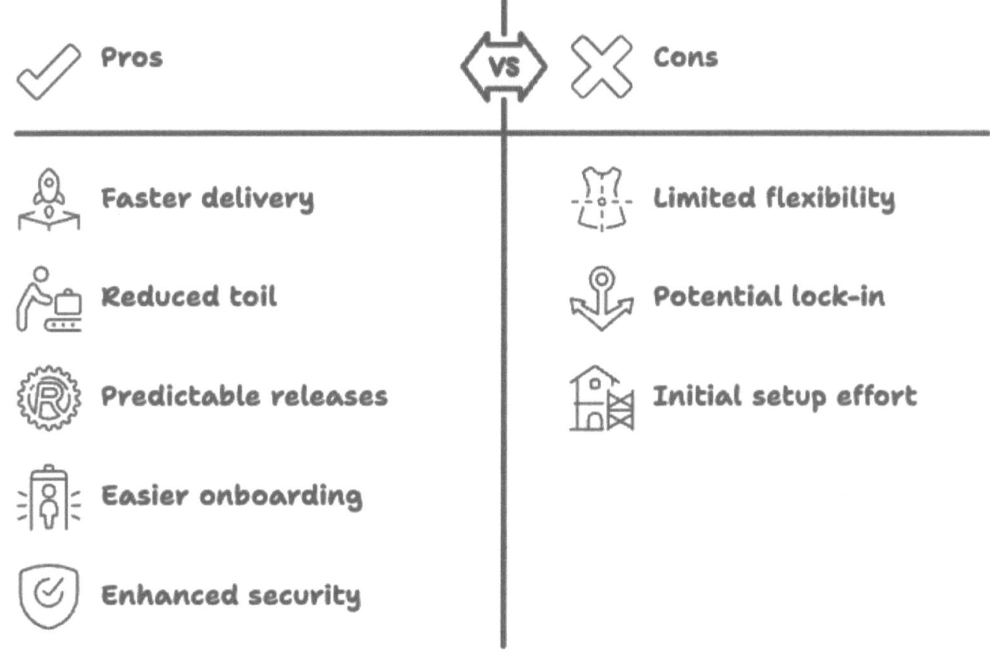

Figure 13-5. *Golden Paths - Pros & Cons*

Responsibilities and Ownership

Effective platform operation requires shared responsibility.

Platform engineering teams: Own the internal platform, CI/CD systems, templates, and guardrails.

Product teams: Own their service health, reliability, and user experience.

Site reliability engineering (SRE) teams: Enable and enforce reliability practices, SLOs, and incident management.

Together, they ensure that every change has a safe path to production.

Environments and Releases

Maintain clear and limited environment tiers – development, staging, and production – with traceable promotion rules. Progressive delivery reduces risk using feature flags, canary deployments, and blue-green strategies.

Approvals should reflect risk, not rank. Low-risk changes move automatically; high-risk ones follow reinforced checks. This ensures speed without sacrificing stability.

Operational Readiness

Before any production release, a readiness review ensures stability and compliance. This includes

- Documented runbooks and on-call rotation

- Defined SLOs, alerts, and dashboards

- Tested rollback and backup procedures

- Security scans and software bill of materials (SBOM)

- Data migration and restoration rehearsals

- Cost and scaling thresholds established

A platform that passes this checklist is resilient by design.

Reliability and Observability

Reliability should be defined in terms users understand. For example:

SLI – Successful checkout within two seconds

SLO – 99.5% of checkouts meet this SLI per week

Error Budget – 0.5%

If the budget is exhausted, teams pause feature rollouts and focus on recovery. Reliability is a business choice, not just a technical metric.

Observability ensures every service is visible and understandable. The standard telemetry pack includes metrics, traces, logs, and events – all correlated to deployments and incidents. Dashboards are templated for consistent analysis across teams.

Secure Delivery and Supply Chain

Security cannot wait for post-release fixes. Secure the build pipeline through signed artifacts, dependency scans, secret management, and least-privilege access. Regular vulnerability scans and release attestations ensure supply-chain integrity.

FinOps in Platform Operations

Cost management is part of reliability. Each team should have a visible budget, cost dashboard, and alerts for anomalies. Autoscaling policies must include upper limits, and periodic reviews should link cost efficiency to performance goals.

Incident Management and Learning

Every incident is an opportunity to strengthen resilience. Define clear severity levels, incident commanders, escalation paths, and communication protocols. Follow up with a blameless post-incident review, identify lessons, and close actions visibly.

Developer Experience and Empowerment

Two moments define developer satisfaction: time to first commit and time to first successful deploy. The IDP should be made both quick and intuitive. Provide self-service onboarding, one-click environment setup, and lightweight documentation to reduce friction.

Where to Start and How to Stay on Track?

Platform development and operations thrive on intentionality, not accident. When you look at the value chain in the diagram, most organizations progress through strategy, design and architecture, implementation, and finally operations. At that point, the cycle often stops. The remaining stages that drive learning and maturity, feedback collection, refinement, and the return to strategy tend to happen in an unstructured or reactive manner.

Feedback is gathered inconsistently. Refinement becomes a secondary task carried out only when deadlines allow. Strategic adjustments are initiated only after significant issues emerge. This is the point where products begin to lose coherence and where teams unintentionally step into a difficult platform learning curve.

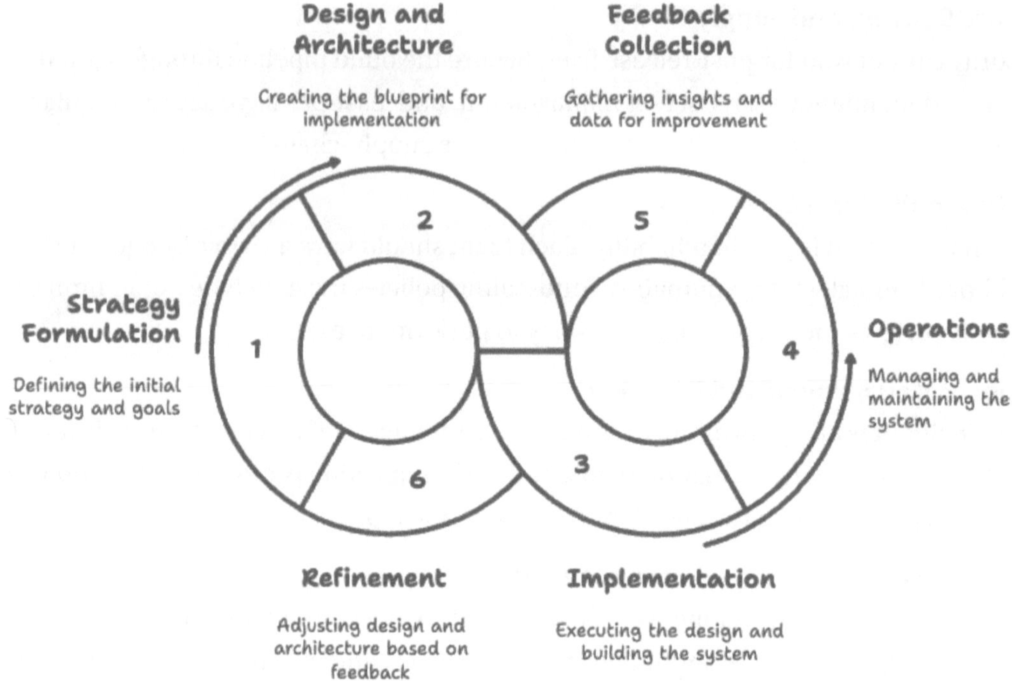

Figure 13-6. *Development to Operations Value Chain Cycle*

To shift this pattern, begin with a clear technology strategy that is fully aligned with business objectives. Build on rigorous design and sound architectural foundations. Automate wherever possible and evolve that automation into reusable platform capabilities.

The essential shift comes from completing the entire loop with discipline. Treat feedback as a formal input to the platform. Use refinement cycles to improve architecture intentionally instead of responding under pressure. Revisit strategy proactively, not as a response to disruption.

Measure success continuously. Ensure teams understand the platform's design principles and operational model. Maintain open communication about changes. Acknowledge progress. Every enhancement in developer experience leads to broader improvements in reliability, delivery speed, and innovation.

This is how an organization moves from building isolated solutions to becoming a platform-driven organization. The transformation is not about tools but about committing to the complete lifecycle.

Key Takeaways

- Platform engineering succeeds only when grounded in clear strategy, strong architecture, and stable contracts and not just tooling.

- A platform is an ecosystem. Development and operations must work as one continuous flow, not disconnected functions.

- The five platform engineering layers – infrastructure, managed services, automation, observability, and developer experience – form a logical, dependable backbone.

- APIs, system models, and golden paths create the consistency and predictability that large organizations depend on.

- Internal developer platforms and engineering portals reduce friction by giving teams a clear, unified way to build and deliver.

- Reliability is a business decision. SLOs, error budgets, and observability bring accountability and confidence.

- Secure delivery, cost awareness, and supply-chain integrity must be baked in, not retrofitted.

- Developer experience is the multiplier of platform value – fast onboarding and predictable workflows accelerate everything.

- Continuous learning, refinement, and feedback create the long-term momentum that transforms a platform into an organizational advantage.

Transition to the Next Section

With this chapter, you now hold the full **Platform Success Blueprint** – a practical, repeatable way to design, scale, secure, measure, and operate platforms that endure. It is a blueprint meant to be used, reused, and revisited with your teams: a shared discipline that helps you build platforms the right way, grow responsibly, and create the next generation of change.

In the next section, we shift from blueprint to lived experience.

We will follow the journeys of platform users and providers, explore how real organizations apply these principles, and trace how platforms evolve in the world around us with a case study.

In the next section, we explore how platforms become a source of lasting legacy. Let's dive in.

SECTION V

Leaving a Legacy Through Platforms (Execute and Evolve)

Humanises the platform journey through user, provider, and industry examples.

CHAPTER 14

Mapping the User Journey – Seeing Through the Consumer's Lens

"Platform user's journey shines through platform experience; keep it relevant."

In the previous chapters, we explored platform strategy, architecture, design, and development – the foundational layers that make a platform possible. Now we shift our lens to those who bring it to life every day: the users. This chapter focuses on the journey of platform users, while the next will focus on providers. Together, these journeys complete the human side of the Platform Success Blueprint introduced in Chapter 5.

The experience of a platform user is a story of discovery, familiarity, and connection. It begins when curiosity meets opportunity and evolves into trust and long-term engagement. From a user's perspective, this journey can be divided into three phases: **Introduction**, **Navigation**, and **Retention**. Each phase represents a shift in relationship – from trying to trusting, and finally to thriving.

Every platform's success depends on how well it manages this journey. Users decide whether to stay, upgrade, or move on based on how meaningful and effortless their experience feels. Understanding this journey helps both users and providers reflect on what strengthens engagement and what weakens it.

© Shweta Vohra 2026
S. Vohra, *Decoding Platform Engineering Patterns*, https://doi.org/10.1007/979-8-8688-2555-2_14

Introduction Phase

The introduction phase is the first handshake between a user and a platform. It begins when interest sparks and ends when the user either signs up or walks away. First impressions are powerful here. A clear, accessible experience helps users form early trust and decide whether to explore further.

This phase consists of three moments of truth: **Interest and Need Alignment**, **Evaluation**, and **Onboarding**.

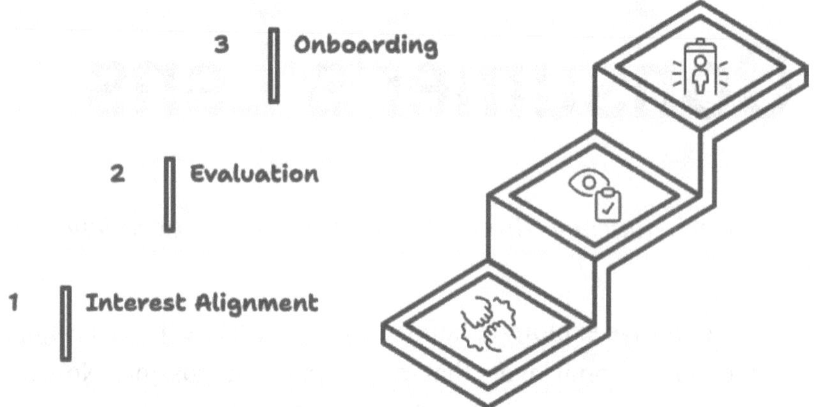

Figure 14-4. Introductory Phase Stages

Interest and Need Alignment

This is the moment where curiosity meets relevance. A user or developer encounters your platform and thinks, *This might actually solve something for me.* It is also the moment where many platforms lose people. If the promise feels vague, exaggerated, or disconnected from their real need, interest disappears before adoption begins.

Core Insight

Clarity is your strongest asset. Users must instantly understand what your platform does, for whom, and why it matters. When the value is crisp, people continue exploring. When it is fuzzy, they quietly walk away.

Example

Notion cut through a crowded market with one line: "One workspace. Every team."

Stripe did the same with "Payments for developers."

Common Challenges

- Mismatched features that don't reflect what personas actually need

- Potential users being unaware of the platform's existence or purpose

- Targeting attracting the wrong personas

- Messaging that promises too much or nothing concrete

Practical Guidance

Focus your promise on two or three core jobs-to-be-done. Anchor your narrative in relatable scenarios for each persona. Practical relevance builds early trust.

Evaluation

Once interest forms, users move into assessment. They compare, verify, and test. They look for alignment with their goals, constraints, and expectations. This is where they decide whether your platform stands on real substance or just strong words.

Core Insight

The easier you make the evaluation, the faster confidence builds. Transparency reduces risk. Clear comparisons reduce friction. A platform that is simple to assess feels trustworthy.

Example

AWS Free Tier excels at this. It lets developers test real services before committing. That small, hands-on experience reduces anxiety and builds conviction.

Common Challenges

- Information overload that leads to decision fatigue

- Users unable to clearly compare your platform with alternatives

- Inadequate or outdated documentation

- Hidden constraints or unclear pricing models

- Persona-specific needs not addressed in evaluation materials

Practical Guidance

Offer clear evaluation paths. Provide concise comparisons, transparent pricing, and scenario-based documentation. Let people test meaningfully without hurdles.

Onboarding

Onboarding is the moment potential turns into participation. This is where users either feel a sense of momentum or hit frustration that derails everything. Early success is often the strongest predictor of long-term engagement.

Core Insight

People remember their first initial time far more than their future roadmap. If they achieve a credible early win, they stay. If they struggle, they leave silently.

Example

Canva shines here. A new user can create a design within minutes. That early achievement creates confidence, curiosity, and emotional investment.Another platform parallel: Shopify lets new merchants publish a basic storefront quickly, even before configuring the full stack.

Common Challenges

- Complex onboarding flows that demand too much setup

- Confusing interfaces or scattered guidance

- Friction around integrations, identity, or data import

- Lack of simple, progressive learning paths

- Support that reacts slowly or not at all

Practical Guidance

Design onboarding as guided acceleration, not instruction overload. Provide simple workflows, clear prompts, and small, achievable guidance.

Navigation Phase

Once a user completes onboarding, they begin navigating the platform's daily realities. This is where experience replaces curiosity. The user integrates the platform into routines, tests its boundaries, and decides whether it feels reliable enough to stay.

The navigation phase has three natural progressions: **Integrate**, **Run**, and **Drop**.

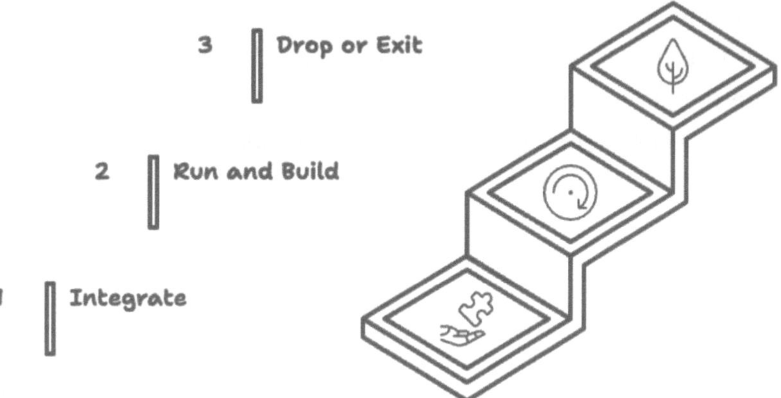

Figure 14-2. *Navigation Phase Stages*

Integrate

Integration is the stage where the user stops *trying* your platform and starts *living with it*. This is when the platform stops feeling like an external tool and becomes part of their daily rhythm. At this stage, adoption deepens because the platform fits naturally into the user's existing ecosystem, not because the user adapts to the platform.

Core Insight

Integration succeeds when your platform bends to the user's world, not when the user bends to yours. The more your platform respects existing workflows, data flows, and tools, the faster it becomes indispensable.

Example

Slack became essential because it connected seamlessly with everything people were already using – email, calendars, CI pipelines, monitoring tools, ticketing systems, and countless third-party apps. It reduced cognitive load instead of creating more work, becoming the connective tissue of team collaboration.

Common Challenges

- Integration friction with existing systems or tools

- Limited customization or configuration patterns

- Data sync inconsistencies or duplication

- Security or compliance blockers during setup

- Incompatible identity or access management flows

Practical Guidance

Treat integrations as first-class platform features. Validate integration points early, design with interoperability in mind, and ensure the platform behaves like a cooperative citizen in the user's ecosystem. Friction here can stall adoption; smoothness accelerates it.

Run

The Run stage reflects the quiet phase of sustained, habitual use. By now, users rely on your platform enough to build routines around it. What keeps them here is not novelty, but stability, performance, and trust. At this point, the platform's invisible decisions matter more than the visible ones.

Core Insight

Reliability is retention. Transparency is reassurance. When users depend on your platform daily, they must trust that it will work without surprises.

Example

Zoom's rise was not driven by features alone. It became the default video platform because it *worked* – consistently, even under poor network conditions. Its reliability under pressure became its brand and the reason organizations standardized on it.

Common Challenges

- Learning curves that slow deeper adoption

- Recurring bugs or fragile features

- Cluttered or unintuitive interfaces

- Performance bottlenecks, latency, or scaling issues

- Poor role management or identity complexity

- Gaps in monitoring, alerting, or on-call practices

Practical Guidance

Strengthen operational discipline. Support must be responsive. Feedback loops must be active. Release cycles must demonstrate improvement, not instability. Sustained use comes from consistent dependability, not constant reinvention.

Drop

Every platform will see disengagement. Some users fade gradually; others leave abruptly. The reasons are almost always predictable: unmet expectations, friction, lack of progress, or discovering something that simply does the job better. If the earlier stages shape adoption, this one reveals whether you've earned loyalty.

Core Insight

Retention is not the opposite of churn; understanding is. You must uncover why users leave before the departure becomes irreversible.

Example

Early photo-sharing apps died quickly once Instagram offered a more integrated, delightful, and low-friction experience. People did not leave because they disliked the old apps; they left because Instagram unified creation, sharing, discovery, and community into one coherent place.

Common Challenges

Gradual Parting

- Users lose patience with recurring glitches or slow improvements

- A clearly superior competitor emerges

- Vendor lock-in makes them feel trapped rather than supported

Decisive Parting

- Major technical failures

- Regulatory or compliance roadblocks

- Pricing or policy changes that break trust

- Security lapses or data concerns

- Compatibility issues after upgrades

Practical Guidance

Monitor sentiment continuously. Watch early warning signals: declining engagement, reduced integration activity, and support tickets rising in specific themes. Respond before dissatisfaction becomes departure. Maintain an adaptable platform and balanced vendor strategy to stay future-proof.

Retention Phase

The retention phase represents a mature, stable relationship between user and platform. At this point, users have built routines around the platform and derive consistent value. Retained users often evolve into advocates, contributing feedback and inviting others to join.

Retention is not passive loyalty; it is active renewal. Users stay because the platform continues to meet changing needs. When this balance is lost, even the most loyal user begins to drift.

This phase unfolds through three key experiences: **Maintain**, **Upgrade or Grow**, and **Replace or Retire**.

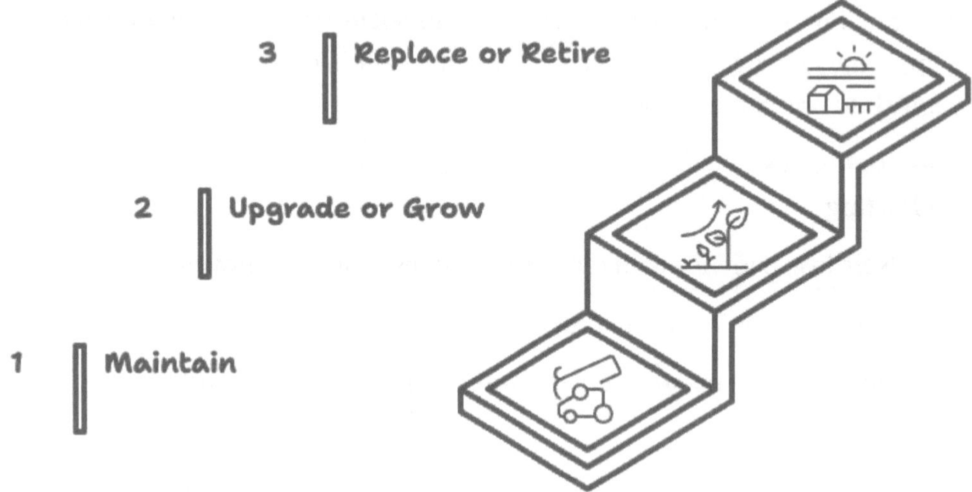

Figure 14-3. *Retention Phase Evolution*

Maintain

Maintenance is the phase where long-term users stay engaged because the platform continues to feel alive and thoughtfully improved. This is not just about patches and fixes; it is about signaling that the platform is evolving with purpose. When updates bring clarity, stability, or delight, users feel their investment is validated.

Core Insight

Maintenance becomes meaningful when updates demonstrate real, visible progress – improving reliability, adding practical value, and strengthening trust without overwhelming users.

Example

Apple's iOS cadence exemplifies this. Users anticipate updates because they consistently refine performance, introduce well-considered features, and maintain a sense of continuity. It is improvement without disruption, evolution without friction.

Common Challenges

- Frequent update requirements that fatigue users

- Risk of stagnation or outdated capabilities

- Rising security responsibilities

- Increasing complexity as features expand

- Dependence on third-party components with unclear longevity

Practical Guidance

Treat maintenance as an ongoing relationship, not a reactive chore. Keep updates intentional, security-current, and considerate of legacy integrations. Retire or replace aging dependencies proactively so they never become bottlenecks.

Upgrade or Grow

In this stage, users deepen their commitment. They begin exploring advanced features, broader capabilities, or higher tiers. This is where the platform either grows with them or quietly loses them. Platform maturity is tested here because expansion must feel empowering, not exhausting.

Core Insight

True growth happens when the platform expands at the user's pace. Upgrades should feel like natural next steps – not pressure, not complexity, but capability unlocked.

Example

Shopify excels at this rhythm. Sellers often start with a simple storefront and expand organically into automations, analytics, and premium integrations. Shopify never forces acceleration; it simply meets users wherever their business evolves.

Common Challenges

- Difficulty scaling features as needs expand

- High pricing jumps between tiers

- Complexity introduced by new workflows or integrations

- Data integrity issues during expansion

- Lack of architectural readiness for growth cycles

- Absence of meaningful feedback loops to guide evolution

Practical Guidance

Design upgrades with architectural foresight. Test transitions thoroughly. Communicate future changes clearly and early. Growth should feel guided rather than risky, predictable rather than disruptive.

Replace or Retire

Eventually, every platform reaches a point where it no longer fits a user's needs. This is natural. It is not a failure; it is a sign of a healthy lifecycle. The aim here is to support departure with dignity. A graceful exit preserves trust even in the moment of separation.

Core Insight

The most responsible platforms design for exit. Clear migration paths, transparent data portability, and predictable decommissioning protect users and reflect organizational maturity.

Example

Google Workspace offers friction-light export tools that allow organizations to leave on their own terms. This confidence reinforces trust, because a platform that helps you exit is a platform you're more likely to return to.

Common Challenges

- Complex or painful data migration

- Operational stress during transition

- Uncertainty about replacement tools

- Ensuring continuity of service while winding down

- Secure decommissioning of environments

- Compliance and legal considerations for data transfers

Practical Guidance

Create a structured transition plan. Include migration steps, communication touchpoints, and user education. Support during departure should be as thoughtful as support during onboarding. A platform's legacy is shaped not only by how it begins but also by how it ends.

Mapping the User's Journey to the Platform Success Blueprint

The Platform Success Blueprint from Chapter 5 provides a powerful way to analyze each phase of the user journey. Every phase interacts with a different aspect of the Blueprint.

During the **Introduction phase**, the **Platform Experience and Design** pillars are most active. They define first impressions, clarity, and ease of use.

In the **Navigation phase**, the **Platform Technology Strategy** and **Platform Development and Operations** pillars are tested. They determine whether the platform feels reliable, performant, and adaptable.

In the **Retention phase**, the **Platform Strategy and Business Models** pillar sustains long-term engagement by ensuring value alignment between user and platform.

Together, these interactions make the user's journey not just experiential but structural. They show how every touchpoint is rooted in one or more elements of the Blueprint.

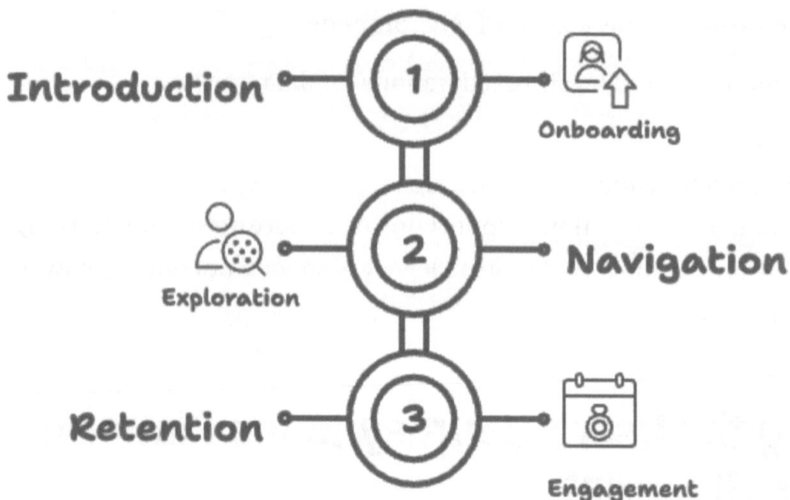

Figure 14-4. *User Journey Across the Platform Success Blueprint*

Reflection Points

Ask Yourself

How quickly can a new user reach value on your platform?

Where do users most often drop off, and what pattern do you observe there?

What feedback loops exist to capture early friction and resolve it before disengagement?

Every platform benefits from answering these questions honestly. The insights often reveal not just product gaps but cultural blind spots in how platforms listen and adapt.

A great platform does not just retain users; it evolves with them. Every click, complaint, and compliment reflects the quality of design and architecture beneath. When the user's journey and the platform's design move in rhythm, loyalty becomes a natural outcome rather than an incentive-driven one.

In the next chapter, we will look at the other side of this relationship – the journey of the platform provider. Understanding both perspectives completes the cycle of empathy that turns a functioning platform into a thriving ecosystem.

Key Takeaways

- The user journey unfolds through three essential phases: Introduction, Navigation, and Retention.

- Every phase presents opportunities for alignment, trust, and innovation.

- Clarity, reliability, and adaptability define long-term engagement.

- User loyalty is sustained through continuous learning, transparent communication, and genuine value delivery.

- The Platform Success Blueprint helps diagnose which part of the journey needs attention and why.

A platform that listens, adapts, and evolves with its users remains relevant – even as technology and expectations change.

CHAPTER 15

The Provider's Journey – What It Takes to Build One

"Platform providers' journeys shine through a strong foundation. Strive to grow stronger and clearer with each step."

In the previous chapter, we viewed the platform through the eyes of its users. We saw how curiosity turns into trust and how every experience leaves a mark. Now we shift perspective to those who build, nurture, and sustain these platforms – the platform providers. Their journey is far more complex, continuous, and layered. It involves managing technology, people, governance, and scale, often at the same time.

While users experience the surface, providers live the depth. They are responsible not just for making the platform work but also for making it evolve. This chapter maps that journey through the lens of the Platform Success Blueprint and helps providers identify where they must focus as they grow.

The Provider's Reality

The platform provider's world is filled with opportunities, but every opportunity brings new complexity. Unlike users, providers cannot opt out when things get hard. They must continuously build, measure, adapt, and balance what is already running while creating what is next.

A provider's journey involves constant motion – new features, evolving markets, changing technologies, and the pressure to innovate faster than the ecosystem around them. To illustrate this, let's look at one of the most studied examples in the technology world: Amazon Web Services.

© Shweta Vohra 2026

S. Vohra, *Decoding Platform Engineering Patterns*, https://doi.org/10.1007/979-8-8688-2555-2_15

AWS began with just two essential services – storage through S3 and compute through EC2. Over time, it evolved into a massive marketplace of more than 200 offerings that serve millions of developers, startups, and enterprises. This growth transformed AWS into a collection of technologies and platforms within a platform ecosystem – each with its own customers, integrations, and ecosystems. While this evolution reflects exceptional vision and scale, it also highlights a challenge many providers face today: maintaining coherence while growing fast. Even AWS, admired globally, occasionally faces friction where overlapping services, unclear naming, or complex pricing blur its once simple proposition.

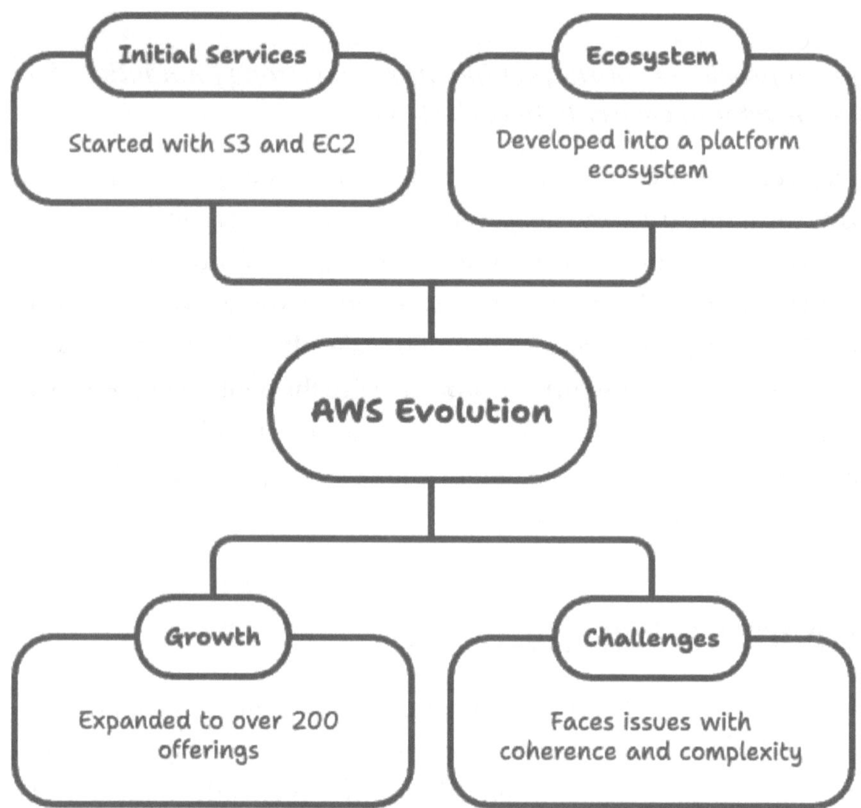

Figure 15-1. *AWS Evolution and Challenges*

This story is not unique to cloud platform providers. Similar transitions are happening across industries – in retail, e-commerce, automotive, healthcare, and pharmaceuticals, where companies that once offered standalone products are now building interconnected platforms. This shift demands new thinking, new structures, and new ways of managing growth.

The Balancing Act

The biggest challenge for any platform provider is the balance between speed and stability, openness and control, and growth and coherence. Without this balance, platforms fragment into disconnected products and lose their identity.

Figure 15-2. *Platform Provider's Balancing Act*

Think of a platform provider as the captain of a large ship. This ship is not just a vessel but a floating city that keeps expanding mid-journey. Every new passenger represents a user, partner, or service. The crew must add new rooms, upgrade engines, and improve facilities – all while sailing through unpredictable weather. The ship must keep moving smoothly even as new decks are added. That is what building a platform feels like: balancing progress with safety, innovation with order.

Growth without balance leads to chaos. Stability without innovation leads to stagnation. The best providers learn to sail and rebuild at the same time.

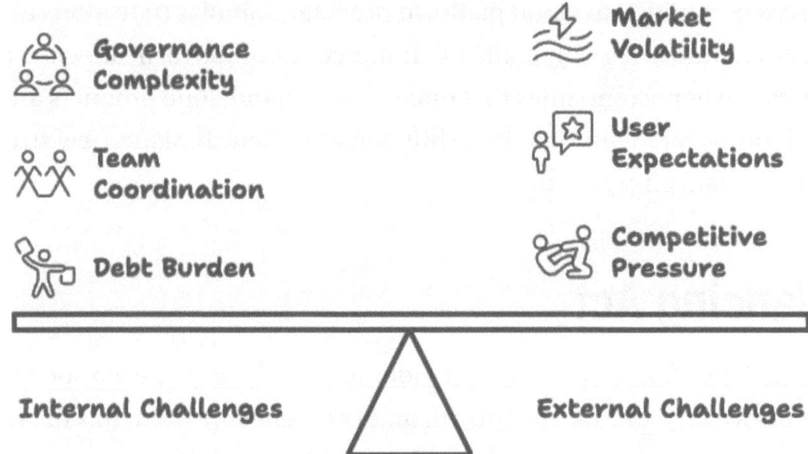

Figure 15-3. *Balancing Internal and External Challenges for Provider Success*

Internal and External Forces

Every provider faces two sets of challenges. The internal ones include team alignment, governance, security, and managing technical debt. The external ones include rapid technology shifts, changing customer expectations, and competition from emerging platforms.

A mature provider learns to harmonize both. Strong internal discipline creates resilience. This allows the organization to respond to external changes without losing direction. Internal coherence becomes the anchor that holds everything together when the waves get rough.

This is why platform engineering, internal developer platforms, and strong architectural foundations matter so deeply. They abstract complexity, automate repeatable work, and make scaling easier. But this balance is delicate. If the responsibility for design, governance, and operation shifts entirely onto developers, it creates long-term inefficiency. The goal is not to offload complexity, but to manage it with clarity.

The Provider's Journey Cycle

The provider's journey can be understood through five connected phases: Create, Assess, Change, Feedback, and Repeat. These phases are not linear; they form a continuous loop that strengthens over time.

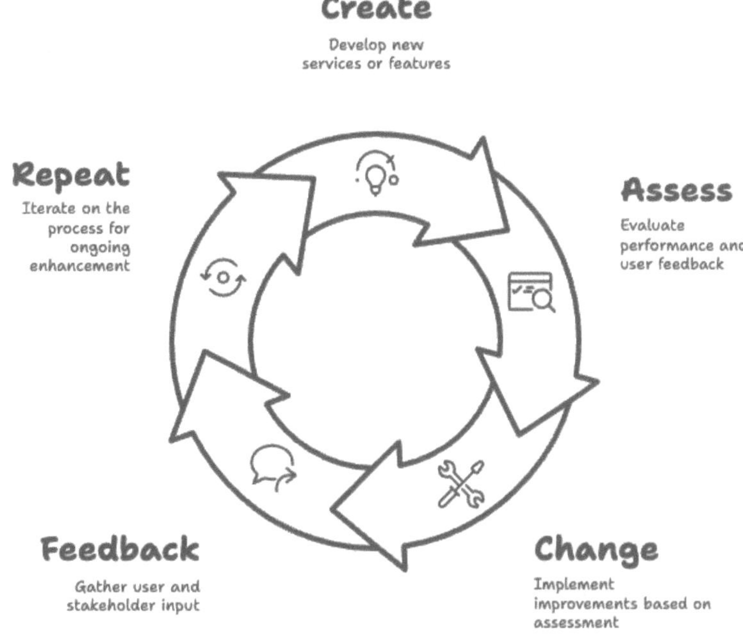

Figure 15-4. *Provider's Journey Cycle*

Create (or Update) Phase

This phase lays the foundation. Providers define their platform's purpose, align it with user needs, and create scalable systems that can evolve. The emphasis here is on clarity, not speed.

Common challenge: Teams rush into building without aligning on purpose or architecture.

Key lesson: Clarity before complexity. Design before delivery.

Example: Netflix's platform teams start by defining measurable developer outcomes before writing code. This ensures that technology choices reinforce strategic goals rather than reacting to them.

Assess Phase

The assessment phase involves evaluating how well the platform delivers on its promises. This includes reviewing performance, technology decisions, design, and user experience.

Common challenge: Assessments often happen too late, when issues are already visible to users.

Key lesson: Regular reviews prevent expensive recoveries.

Example: Spotify runs quarterly "health checks" across its internal platforms to assess usability, adoption, and technical debt. This rhythm keeps their engineering teams proactive rather than reactive.

Change Phase

The change phase focuses on evolution. Providers introduce new technologies or features while protecting the stability of what already exists.

Common challenge: Innovation can disrupt ongoing operations.

Key lesson: Manage change like an experiment, not an emergency.

Example: Google Cloud often releases new features through alpha and beta channels, allowing gradual adoption and user feedback before general availability. This controlled approach balances innovation with reliability.

Feedback Phase

Feedback turns experience into improvement. This phase involves capturing insights from both users and internal teams, then integrating them systematically.

Common challenge: Feedback is collected but rarely acted upon.

Key lesson: Listening is not enough; response builds trust.

Example: Atlassian actively gathers feedback from its developer community to improve the Confluence and Jira APIs. Each improvement cycle is documented publicly, creating transparency and credibility.

Repeat Phase

The repeat phase ensures continuity. Providers return to the Create stage with new insights, stronger metrics, and better alignment. This cycle keeps the platform relevant and ready for what's next.

Common challenge: Continuous improvement can slip into endless change without direction.

Key lesson: Repeat with purpose, not motion.

Example: Microsoft Azure runs structured retrospectives after every major service rollout to refine its internal playbooks and inform future decisions. This institutional memory accelerates innovation over time.

Using the Platform Success Blueprint

The Platform Success Blueprint acts as a compass throughout this journey. It provides structure without rigidity and ensures that every phase aligns with a shared vision. Each team member – from architect to engineer to product owner – should understand how their work connects to one or more pillars of the blueprint.

When everyone uses the same blueprint, alignment becomes easier. Teams know why certain decisions matter and how success will be measured. Shared understanding prevents fragmentation and builds collective ownership.

Innovation, security, and measurement run through every phase of the provider's journey. Innovation drives growth, security sustains trust, and measurement ensures accountability. Together, they form the continuous rhythm that defines platform excellence.

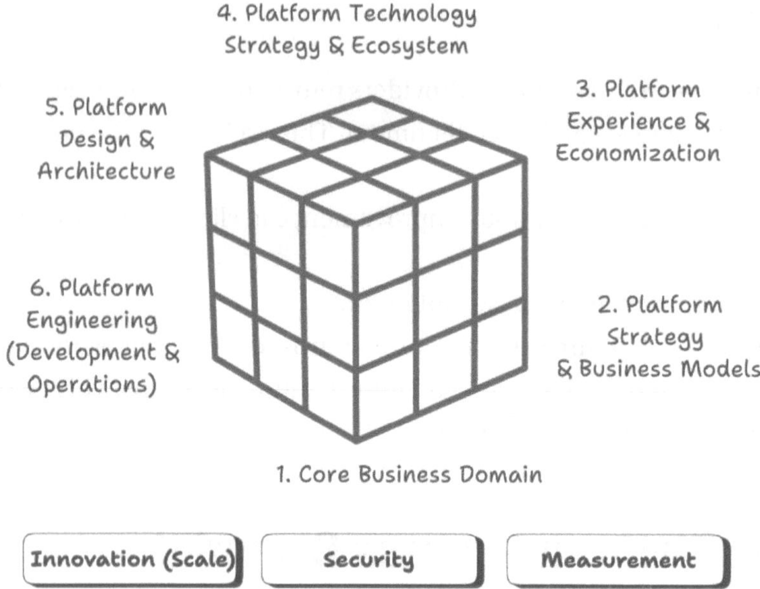

Figure 15-5. Six Sides of Platform Success Blueprint

In summary: Building a platform is not a one-time project. It is an ongoing act of care. Providers must constantly balance ambition with clarity, complexity with simplicity, and vision with execution.

The provider's journey mirrors the user's in one essential way: both seek relevance. Users stay when platforms evolve with them, and providers succeed when they evolve with purpose. Platforms that grow with clarity and humility earn loyalty that no marketing campaign can buy.

The next chapter explores Apple's platform patterns – a case study that demonstrates how these principles come to life in one of the most successful technology ecosystems ever built. Through Apple's journey, we will see how strategy, design, and experience merge to create lasting impact.

Key Takeaways

- Mastering the phases of Create, Assess, Change, Feedback, and Repeat is essential for sustainable platform success.

- Balance flexibility with standardization to preserve coherence while scaling.

- Use the Platform Success Blueprint as a shared compass across teams and functions.

- Prioritize innovation, security, and measurement throughout every phase.

- Remember that the provider's journey never truly ends. Each iteration builds clarity, strength, and resilience – the true markers of platform maturity.

CHAPTER 16

Case Study: Apple's Platform Patterns in Action

"Apple's platform journey is a masterclass; harness it from the lens of the Platform Success Blueprint."

Apple's platform journey is a masterclass in turning product excellence into a durable platform advantage. Through this case study, we will explore how Apple's growth, structure, and platform design map directly to the six sides of the Platform Success Blueprint, demonstrating how a clear platform vision, when executed consistently, can drive decades of success.

Apple Inc., a multinational technology leader, is synonymous with innovation in hardware, software, and scalable platforms. Over the past two decades, the company has become a global household name, with products like the iPhone, iPad, Mac, Apple Watch, and Apple TV becoming integral to modern life. Yet its success is not solely the result of remarkable design – it stems from decades of strategic alignment, careful integration, and platform thinking at scale.

In 2021, Apple sold about 24% of the 1.43 billion smartphones purchased globally, underscoring the company's massive reach.[1] It continued to dominate the list of top ten best-selling smartphones in Q2 2024, reinforcing its sustained leadership in an intensely competitive market.[2]

---

[1] https://seaopenresearch.eu/Journals/articles/NIS_21_7.pdf

[2] https://www.theguardian.com/technology/2015/nov/12/blackberry-ceo-john-chen-security-priv

© Shweta Vohra 2026
S. Vohra, *Decoding Platform Engineering Patterns*, https://doi.org/10.1007/979-8-8688-2555-2_16

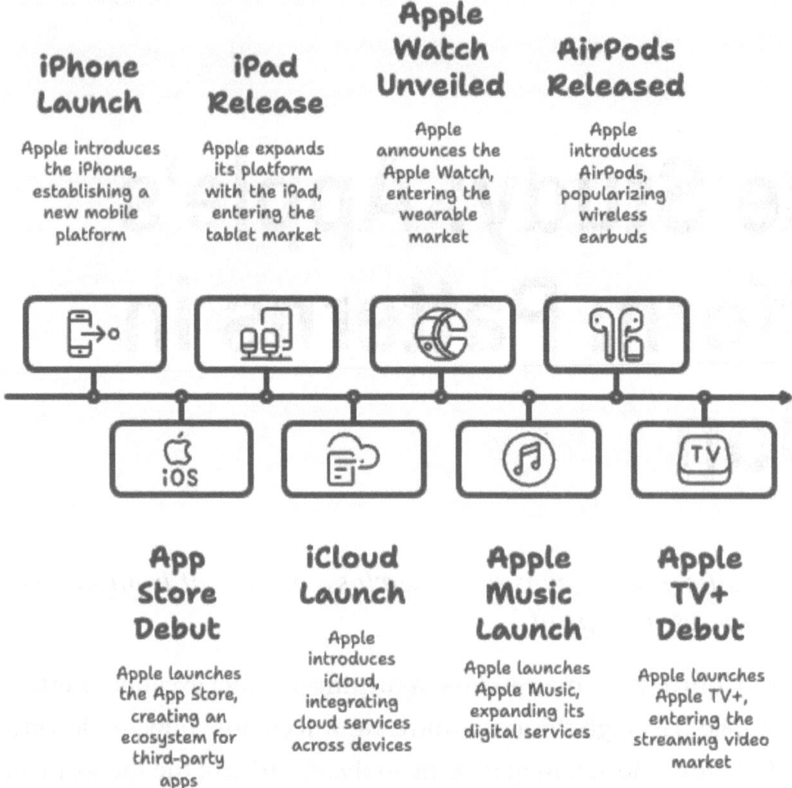

Figure 16-1. Apple's Platform and Ecosystem Evolution

This raises an important question: is Apple a product company or a platform company? The answer is both. Its strategy is built on a seamless integration of hardware, software, and services – an interdependent system that fuels one another. Unlike Google or Meta, which began as pure digital platforms, Apple built its platform strength from the ground up, aligning devices, operating systems, and ecosystems under one vision.

The Roots of a Platform Vision

Apple's modern platform story can be traced back to Steve Jobs' simple yet revolutionary promise: *"1,000 songs in your pocket."* That idea not only launched the iPod but defined the company's obsession with integrating experience and technology. From that moment, Apple evolved from product excellence into platform orchestration – where every device, service, and framework reinforced the other.

Between 1997 and 2017, Apple's market value grew more than 300 times.[3] This exponential rise would not have been possible without leveraging digital platforms, global ecosystems, and scalable design models. Apple's journey is one of the clearest real-world examples of how a platform-driven strategy, when executed deliberately, compounds both value and trust.

Platform Network Effects and Offerings

Apple's strength lies not only in creating beautiful products but also in crafting platforms that serve multiple audiences – users, partners, developers, and even other businesses. Its ecosystem is a tightly woven fabric of hardware, operating systems, development frameworks, and cross-device services that reinforce one another.

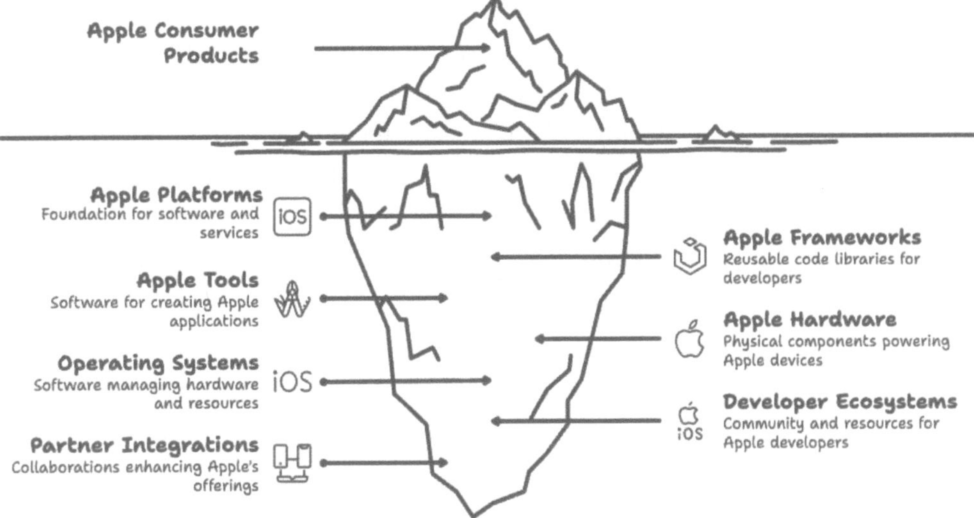

Figure 16-2. *Apple's Platform Landscape: Unveiling the Interconnected Layers*

Broadly, Apple's platforms fall into two categories:

Core Business Platforms include iOS, macOS, iCloud, and the App Store. These serve as the foundation for Apple's product experience and developer ecosystem.

---

[3] https://hbr.org/2020/11/how-apple-is-organized-for-innovation

Internal and Partner Platforms include Apple Business Manager, Apple School Manager, and AppleCare for Enterprise. These extend platform value into enterprise, education, and service ecosystems.

Apple's strategy exemplifies the Platform Success Blueprint, especially the sides of Core Business Domain and Platform Strategy. Each decision begins from its business purpose, aligns with the company's values, and then extends outward through technology, design, and experience.

Core Business Domain

Apple's every move reflects its core business intent: **to deliver security, stability, and quality through simplicity**. These attributes are not design choices; they are strategic.

Sustainability, for instance, is not an afterthought but a built-in part of Apple's operations. The company aims for net-zero carbon emissions across its entire footprint by 2030.[4] This goal is realized through platforms and technologies that support circular economy models such as the iPhone trade-in program, where devices are refurbished, resold, or recycled.

Apple's organizational design reinforces its platform mindset. After Steve Jobs' restructuring, the company moved away from traditional business units to a function-based leadership.[5] Leaders are chosen for expertise, decision ownership, and attention to detail. This has created a cohesive environment where platform decisions are debated and refined collaboratively, ensuring long-term alignment across product, design, and technology.

Apple's "walled garden" approach, closed enough to ensure safety and open enough to foster innovation, remains one of its most defining strategies. While Android and Linux ecosystems offer openness, Apple's model prioritizes trust and predictability, creating a user base that values experience consistency over customization freedom.

---

[4] https://www.apple.com/newsroom/2024/06/new-features-come-to-apple-services-this-fall/

[5] https://hbr.org/2020/11/how-apple-is-organized-for-innovation

Platform Strategy and Business Model

Apple's platform strategy is the cornerstone of its success. Its in-house operating systems act as both the foundation and differentiator for its entire ecosystem.

Each operating system – iOS, macOS, watchOS, tvOS, and visionOS – is custom built to meet the needs of specific devices while retaining a unified design language and shared frameworks. This enables a seamless experience for users and a consistent development model for creators.

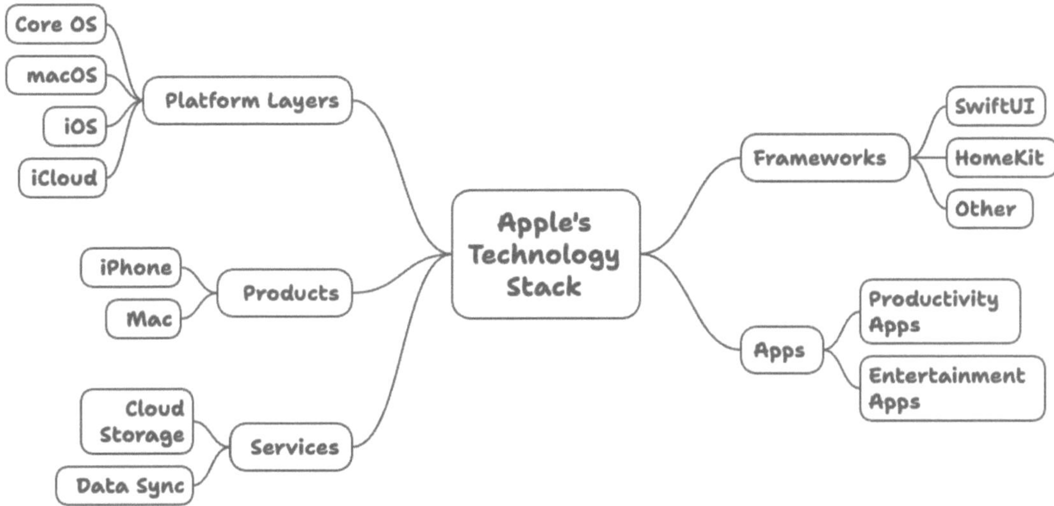

Figure 16-3. *Apple's Layers of Technology & Platform Stack*

The introduction of iCloud in 2011 transformed Apple from a product company to a platform company. iCloud synchronizes files, settings, and experiences across devices, turning continuity into a habit. It now serves hundreds of millions of users globally, embodying scalability, security, and reliability.

Security and privacy are integral to Apple's brand and platform. The Secure Enclave[6] is a dedicated subsystem within Apple devices that handles cryptographic functions and biometric data. This illustrates how architecture and trust can coexist when design and security teams collaborate from the beginning.

---

[6] https://www.counterpointresearch.com/insights/global-top-10-best-selling-smartphones-q2-2024/

Apple's platform business model spans every type of interaction:

- **B2B** through partnerships with IBM and Deloitte for enterprise solutions

- **B2C** through its global retail stores and App Store ecosystem

- **B2D** by empowering developers with tools like Xcode and Swift, distributing apps to millions

- **C2C** via the App Store and Apple Pay, enabling peer-to-peer transactions

- **B2G** by delivering tailored solutions for education and government

This multisided model demonstrates the repeatable and integratable sides of the V-ARISE framework, where value flows smoothly between producers and consumers across boundaries.

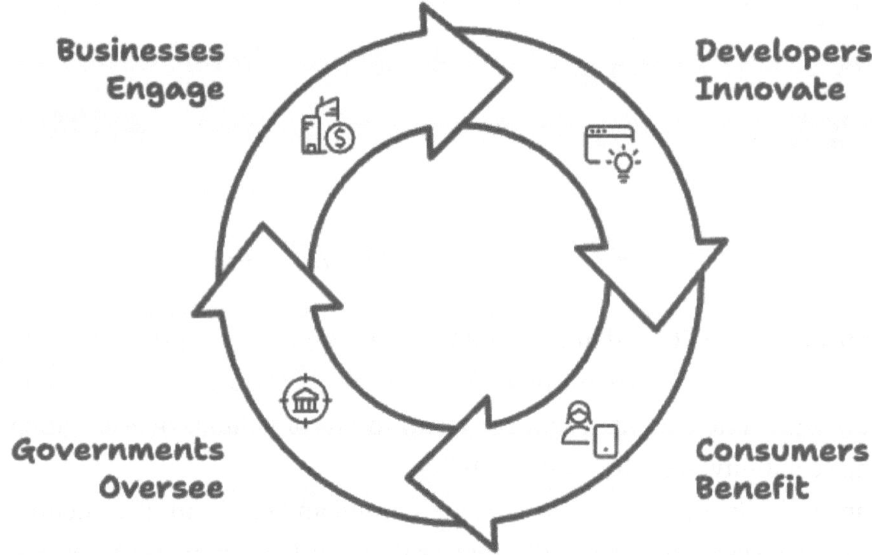

Figure 16-4. *Apple's Platform Ecosystem Cycle*

V-ARISE in Action

Apple embodies the V-ARISE traits in its platform approach:

- **Adaptable:** OS families evolve with devices while maintaining consistency.

- **Repeatable:** Design systems, SDKs, and review processes scale across products.

- **Integratable:** APIs and continuity services connect applications and devices.

- **Self-sufficient:** Vertical integration ensures reliability and end-to-end control.

- **Ecosystem-enabling:** The App Store, developer programs, and partner integrations drive continuous innovation and revenue.

Platform Experience and Economization

Apple's user experience is both design philosophy and economic engine. Every interaction, from the tactile feel of an iPhone to the flow of payments through Apple Pay that reinforces loyalty through simplicity and reliability.

As Jony Ive once said, **"It's very easy to be different, but very difficult to be better."**[7] Apple's design principle is not about novelty but continuous refinement.

The evolution of Apple Pay demonstrates this. When it launched in 2014, adoption was slow.[8] Over time, as more retailers adopted it and users became familiar, Apple refined the experience. Today, Apple Pay has become a trusted global payment layer integrated across the ecosystem. Its recent *Tap to Cash* feature in iOS 18[9] exemplifies adaptive innovation guided by user behavior.

---

[7] `https://learning.oreilly.com/library/view/platform-scaling-fast/53863MIT62303/`
[8] `https://www.globenewswire.com/news-release/2015/10/27/780466/37330/en/Phoenix-Marketing-International-Releases-New-Data-Revealing-the-Ongoing-Challenges-Surrounding-Apple-Pay.html`
[9] `https://www.apple.com/uk/environment/`

Apple has also learned to open parts of its ecosystem. The App Store allowed external developers to shape user experience, creating a two-sided market. Hundreds of thousands of developers now build applications that enhance the iPhone and iPad experience. In 2022, App Store developers generated $1.1 trillion in billings and sales.[10] This scale of value creation is the purest form of network effect.

Platform Technology Strategy and Ecosystem

Apple's technology strategy blends selective openness with deep vertical integration. It participates actively in the cloud-native and open source ecosystem while keeping its core infrastructure proprietary.

Its engagement with the Cloud Native Computing Foundation (CNCF) as a Platinum End-User Member[11] and its open sourcing of Swift under the Apache 2.0 license reflect pragmatic adoption of open technologies. These moves balance control with collaboration and show how even a tightly governed ecosystem can benefit from external innovation.

Apple invests heavily in developer experience, modern tooling, and internal automation. Practices such as Infrastructure as Code, CI/CD pipelines, and continuous monitoring underpin its platform operations. However, what sets Apple apart is its architectural discipline – security, scalability, and user privacy remain central to every technical decision.

---

[10] https://www.apple.com/newsroom/2023/05/developers-generated-one-point-one-trillion-in-the-app-store-ecosystem-in-2022/

[11] https://www.forbes.com/sites/adrianbridgwater/2022/10/26/cncf-director-sharma-community-is-the-lifeblood-of-open-source/

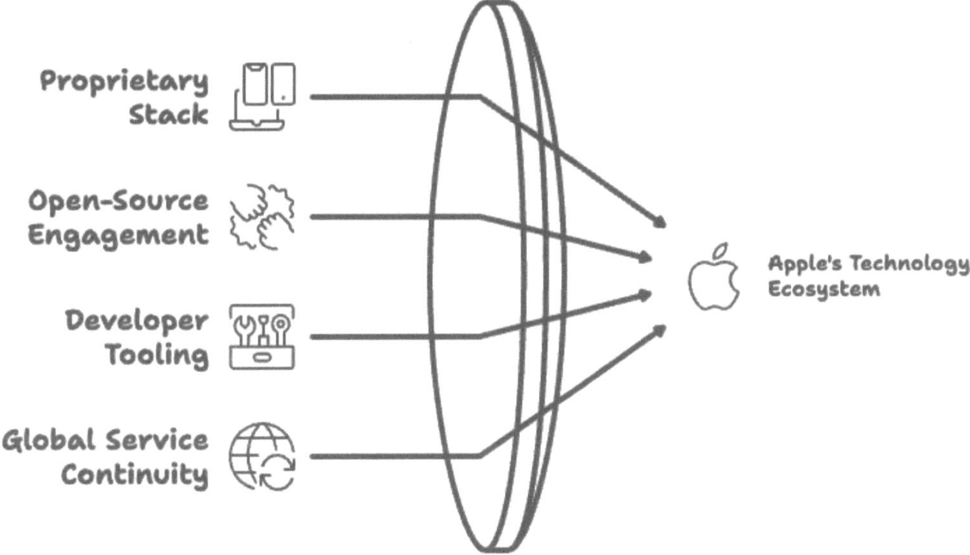

Figure 16-5. *Apple's Technology & Ecosystem Integration*

Platform Design and Architecture

Design and architecture are Apple's invisible power. From the earliest prototypes to product release, hardware and software teams collaborate seamlessly. The Face ID example illustrates this perfectly – its success depended on close cooperation between chip engineers, software developers, and designers to ensure security without friction.

Apple's design reviews still follow a tradition established decades ago: no design moves forward without executive review. Once approved, specifications flow downstream to align manufacturing, App Store integration, and iCloud support. This alignment between product and platform reflects a culture where architecture is a living discipline.

Figure 16-6. Apple's Platform Roles and Feedback Loop

Platform Development

Apple's development model is a careful blend of creativity, confidentiality, and continuous feedback. Cross-functional teams of engineers, designers, and product managers collaborate closely while maintaining tight information security.

This confidentiality protects innovation and brand integrity. Employees often "dogfood" unreleased products internally, identifying performance or usability issues before public release. Tools like Xcode, internal CI systems, and automated testing platforms support these workflows efficiently.

Vertical integration is a core advantage. By designing its chips, operating systems, and development environments together, Apple ensures performance and user experience remain predictable. However, this comes with trade-offs – tight control limits external contribution. Apple mitigates this by sharing clear SDKs, documentation, and regular updates at WWDC, maintaining ecosystem trust while protecting core IP.

Platform Journey

Apple's platform journey mirrors the five-phase provider cycle discussed in the previous chapter: **Create, Assess, Change, Feedback, and Repeat**. Each product generation begins with new ideas, refines them through user insight, and reinvests learning into the next release.

The continuity between iPhone generations, OS updates, and developer frameworks is no coincidence. It is the structured result of a disciplined, iterative platform approach that keeps Apple's ecosystem both stable and dynamic.

Lessons and Reflections

Apple's platform story offers lessons for every organization building modern technology ecosystems.

1. **Purpose before platform:** Every Apple platform begins with clarity about the problem it solves and the experience it must create.

2. **Governance is design:** The App Store's review policies, revenue models, and developer guidelines are not barriers but part of the experience design itself.

3. **Integration over imitation:** Apple's success lies not in inventing everything first but in connecting the right elements better than anyone else, be it platforms, frameworks, or ecosystem layers.

4. **Iteration builds trust:** Each product generation is a learning cycle that strengthens ecosystem stability and loyalty.

5. **Balance openness and control:** Selective collaboration with open source communities keeps innovation alive without compromising coherence.

In Summary

Apple's journey through the Platform Success Blueprint demonstrates how clarity, design, integration, and feedback turn platforms into enduring ecosystems. Its V-ARISE traits – Adaptable, Repeatable, Integratable, Self-sufficient, and Ecosystem-enabling – are visible across every layer of its operations.

By aligning platform vision with business purpose, Apple has built not just products but a living ecosystem that learns, scales, and endures. The company's approach shows that platforms succeed not because they are large, but because they are coherent, continuously improved, and relentlessly focused on purpose.

Disclaimer   The data and insights in this case study are based solely on publicly available information, including Apple's published resources, referenced links, books, and reputable online sources. No confidential or proprietary information has been used. The conclusions drawn belong to the author, based on the interpretation of this material.

CHAPTER 17

The Platform Maturity Model – Assess, Grow, and Sustain

"Every platform begins with an idea, but only those that mature rise with discipline, clarity, and ecosystem awareness."

Platforms do not succeed because they are ambitious. They succeed because they learn how to mature. Most platforms start exactly like good ideas do, scrappy, creative, hopeful, and full of possibility. In the early days, momentum feels like progress. Usage feels like adoption. And every new feature feels like growth.

But platforms do not grow the way products grow. A product matures when it satisfies its customers. A platform matures when it enables others to succeed, including developers, partners, contributors, and entire ecosystems. That is the shift most organizations underestimate.

You may build the strongest foundations, define the clearest strategy, and design an experience that delights. But unless your platform evolves in a disciplined, measurable way aligned to V-ARISE principles, it will eventually hit friction. Technical friction. Organizational friction. Ecosystem friction. And friction is where many platforms silently stall.

This chapter exists to prevent that.

Up to this point, we have explored how to design platforms with a holistic success blueprint and measure what truly matters. Now we turn to the question that every platform must eventually confront:

Where are we in our maturity?

And what must we do next to grow responsibly?

© Shweta Vohra 2026

S. Vohra, *Decoding Platform Engineering Patterns*, https://doi.org/10.1007/979-8-8688-2555-2_17

Why Platform Maturity Matters

V-ARISE gives you the behavioral compass for great platforms. It explains *how* a mature platform behaves: adaptable, repeatable, integratable, self-sufficient, and ecosystem-enabling. But organizations also need something more concrete. Something observable. Something that reveals strengths, gaps, and the silent areas where friction slowly accumulates.

That is the purpose of the Platform Maturity Model.

It is not a checklist or a badge. It is a mirror. It reflects the truth about your platform's readiness, cohesion, and evolution. Maturity tells you whether your platform can sustain growth, whether teams can rely on it, and whether your ecosystem can thrive on top of it.

Platforms rarely fail in dramatic ways. They fail quietly when maturity stagnates, when learning slows, and when gaps widen unnoticed. The maturity model helps you see these cracks long before they spread, so your platform grows not only bigger but also more adoptable, more aligned, and more influential.

Maturity in the platform world is not about age or size. It is about balance.

Balance between innovation and stability, autonomy and governance, and creativity and consistency.

A platform that is technically brilliant but disconnected from business goals will struggle to survive.

A platform that scales quickly without clear architecture or cost discipline eventually collapses under its own momentum.

A platform that thrills consumers but frustrates developers loses its internal heartbeat.

Mature platforms strike the balance that lets them evolve without losing direction. They grow without breaking. They adapt without losing coherence. They sustain value long after the early excitement fades.

That is why maturity matters. It is the difference between a platform that works today and one that endures tomorrow.

The Six Sides of Platform Maturity

To assess this balance, the Platform Maturity Model is built around six interconnected quadrants. Each side captures a different dimension of platform health, and together they mirror the six sides of the **Platform Success Blueprint** discussed in earlier sections.

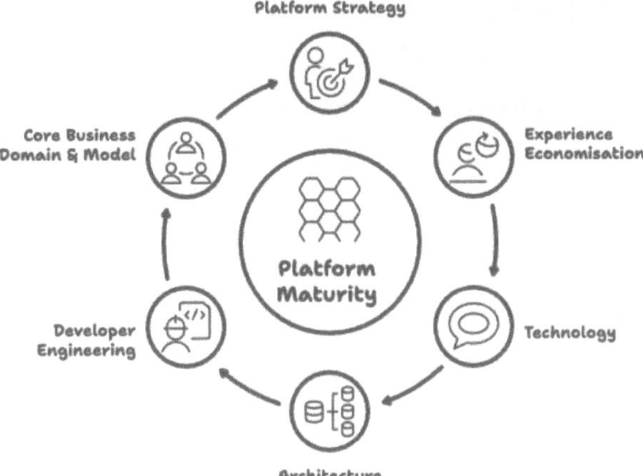

Figure 17-1. *Platform Maturity Cycle*

1. **Core Business Maturity**

   How clearly the platform aligns with the organization's goals, revenue streams, and ecosystem value. Mature platforms don't just support the business; they *are* the business model.

2. **Platform Strategy and Team Maturity**

   How strong the shared vision, leadership alignment, and team capabilities are. Mature platforms have clearly defined ownership and well-orchestrated collaboration between architects, product leaders, and engineers.

3. **Experience and Economization Maturity**

   How well the platform delivers a seamless user and developer experience while remaining cost-efficient. Mature platforms continuously refine experience, measure operational performance, and economize intelligently without cutting corners.

4. **Technology Maturity**

   How resilient, scalable, and modern the technology foundation is. Mature platforms integrate observability, security, and adaptability as part of their DNA and not as afterthoughts.

5. **Architectural Maturity**

   How structured and evolvable the architecture is. Mature platforms have modular boundaries, well-defined contracts, and the flexibility to evolve as the system grows.

6. **Developer and Engineering Maturity**

   How frictionless the building and maintaining experience is for developers. Mature platforms invest in documentation, automation, and self-service capabilities that empower developers to innovate confidently.

The Platform Maturity Matrix

To understand maturity in action, imagine it as a progression through three levels, **Nascent, Scaling, and Mature**, for each of the six quadrants.

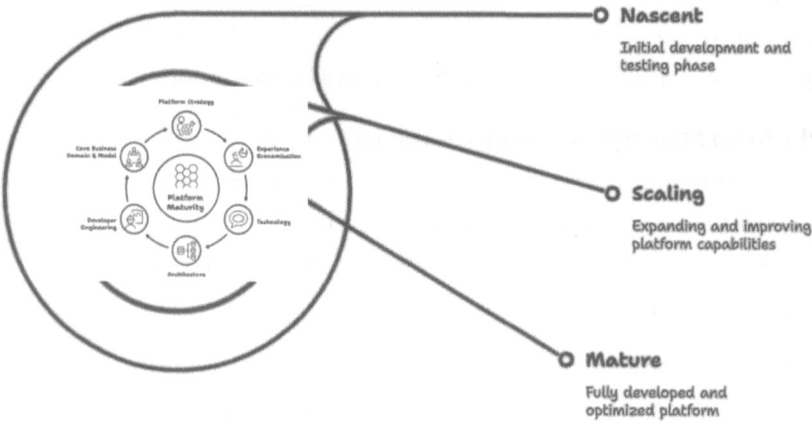

Figure 17-2. Platform Maturity Assessment

Quadrant	Nascent	Scaling	Mature
Core **Business Maturity**	Platform value is unclear. Goals are disconnected from the business strategy.	Platform KPIs and business metrics begin aligning. Ecosystem adoption is visible.	Platform is central to the business model. Growth and monetization are predictable and sustainable.
Platform Strategy and Team Maturity	No unified vision. Decisions depend on individuals rather than principles.	Vision is defined. Dedicated teams start forming. Leadership sponsorship begins. Platform functions (capabilities) are clearly defined along with busienss model.	Vision, ownership, and collaboration are institutionalized. Platform governance and culture are strong.
Experience and Economization Maturity	User and developer experience is inconsistent. Costs are untracked.	Experience metrics and operational cost baselines appear. Efficiency efforts start.	Seamless experience is embedded in every layer. Continuous improvement and cost efficiency are cultural norms.
Technology Maturity	Fragmented tools. Manual operations dominate.	Automation, resilience, and observability are in progress.	Fully integrated, cloud-native, secure, and scalable technology foundation.
Architectural Maturity	Ad hoc design and undocumented decisions.	Modular patterns and integration guidelines introduced.	Adaptive, well-documented architecture supporting continuous evolution.
Developer and Engineering Maturity	High friction. Limited automation or documentation.	Improved tooling and developer experience. Feedback loops visible.	Self-service, automation, and inner-source practices enable rapid, reliable delivery.

Platform maturity is never uniform. In every organization I've worked with, one quadrant surges ahead while another quietly lags behind. Some teams have a sharp platform strategy and well-defined functions but weak technology maturity, creating a gap between intent and execution. Others excel at developer productivity yet lack architectural clarity, leading to friction no tooling can fix. And many build strong systems but struggle because business alignment, experience quality, or cost discipline remain immature. These imbalances are normal, and they are usually the source of the recurring issues you feel today.

The turning point comes when organizations stop treating maturity as a single score and start seeing it as a pattern. When leaders acknowledge uneven maturity openly, the real work can begin. The model helps you locate friction precisely and mature with intention rather than guesswork. Platforms don't fail because they are immature overall; they fail because one quadrant collapses under the weight of the others. The maturity matrix helps you see those fragile points early so your platform grows with adoption, alignment, and a foundation that stays.

A Moment of Reflection in Sam's Journey

To bring this to life and full circle, let's return to Sam, the curious platform manager we met earlier in our journey in the Introduction chapter.

Sam's company had been calling their internal developer platform "next-generation." But when he applied the maturity model, the reflection was sobering.

- **Business maturity:** The platform wasn't directly tied to measurable outcomes. Teams used it because they had to, not because it added business value.

- **Platform strategy and team maturity:** Ownership was split between two departments, creating confusion.

- **Experience and economization:** Developers often found onboarding slow, and support costs were spiraling.

- **Technology maturity:** Automation pipelines were half built, and observability gaps made troubleshooting painful.

- **Architecture:** There was no single reference model for design; everyone built their own patterns.

- **Developer and engineering:** Documentation was inconsistent, and most knowledge lived in private chats.

Sam realized that while the company had built something technically sound, it wasn't yet a mature platform. It was still functioning like a large, shared tool set – useful but unsustainable.

After mapping their current stage as "Scaling" in some areas and "Nascent" in others, the leadership team finally saw the truth: their maturity was uneven. That realization became the turning point.

They used the model not as a report card but as a mirror – a structured reflection that helped them focus their next twelve months on three priorities, even while teams and initiatives continued evolving in parallel: clarifying ownership, improving developer experience, and aligning business goals.

By the following year, their maturity radar looked different. It wasn't perfect, but it was balanced, and that made all the difference.

Using the Maturity Model in Your Context

1. **Start with honest reflection.**

   Gather a cross-functional group – architects, developers, product managers, and business leads – and discuss where you stand in each quadrant.

2. **Avoid aiming for maturity everywhere at once.**

   The goal is balance, not perfection. Overinvesting in technology while neglecting user experience or team maturity can destabilize progress.

3. **Repeat the assessment every 6–12 months.**

   Treat it as a living reflection of your platform journey. You'll notice that growth isn't always linear; some areas will advance faster than others, and that's normal.

4. **Connect results to your V-ARISE attributes.**

   For example, if your platform scores low on integration, that signals a weakness in the *integratable* aspect.

   If you lack cross-team adoption, it's a sign of low *Ecosystem-enabling* maturity.

5. **Translate findings into focused actions.**

   Each weak quadrant deserves one or two clear initiatives and no more.

   Maturity grows not through grand transformation programs but through deliberate, repeated improvements.

Reflecting on What Truly Matters

Many teams eventually discover that what they've been chasing isn't maturity; unfortunately, it's movement. However, someone needs to call once; let's assess our maturity.

They count the number of releases, measure velocity, and celebrate automation, yet the relevant indicators of health often go unnoticed: trust between teams, reuse across systems, satisfaction among users, and adaptability when priorities shift.

The Platform Maturity Model doesn't just evaluate your technology stack; it reveals coherence, whether your platform is growing faster than your organization's ability to sustain it. When that truth comes into focus, something changes. You stop asking "How much can we build?" and start asking "How much of what we build can sustain?"

That's when maturity becomes visible. It's that subtle shift from speed to stability, from doing more to doing better. That separates platforms that fade from those that last.

Key Takeaways

- Maturity is balance, not perfection. It's the harmony between innovation and governance, speed and steadiness, creativity and structure.

- The six quadrants of the Platform Maturity Model – Business, Strategy and Team, Experience and Economization, Technology, Architecture, and Developer and Engineering. It offers a mirror for honest reflection.

- Use this model regularly, not as a checklist but as a learning, evolving compass. Review your maturity every few months to track how your platform evolves.

- Focus on coherence across quadrants. If one area races ahead while another lags behind, your platform will eventually feel that strain.

- Let the **V-ARISE attributes** guide your progress – Adaptable, Repeatable, Integratable, Self-sufficient, and Ecosystem-enabling. They're the visible pillars that hold every strong platform together.

- Above all, maturity is not about arriving. Understanding your unique friction points. It's about evolving with awareness. The more consciously you assess and grow, the longer your platform will stay relevant, trusted, and alive.

SECTION VI

The Future of Platforms with AI (Transform)

Explores emerging AI-driven patterns, ethics, and the next wave of intelligent platforms.

CHAPTER 18

Future Architecture Patterns – From Cloud-Native to AI–Native

"The future of platforms will favour not those who move the fastest, but those who build trust, fairness, and deliver exceptional experiences."

The landscape of digital platforms is entering a profound new phase, shaped by rapid advancements in Artificial Intelligence (AI) and Machine Learning (ML). These technologies are redefining how organizations build, deploy, and evolve their ecosystems. This chapter explores emerging trends that will influence the future of platforms and highlights how to prepare for them by anchoring change in trust, fairness, and experience.

In this context, Generative AI refers to systems that create new text, images, code, or media. Machine Learning refers to predictive or optimization models that learn from data. Platform retains the meaning used throughout this book: a stable foundation with clear interfaces that enables others to build and scale value.

Late 2022 marked a turning point as we entered the era of Generative AI disruption, introducing advanced features and integrations at unprecedented speed. With these new capabilities, platforms can now summarize complex information, automate intricate workflows, and enhance user interactions with remarkable fluency. These shifts demand a re-evaluation of existing platform strategies to leverage applied AI and ML responsibly and effectively across industries.

The questions most organizations face today are familiar: How will AI and ML reshape existing platforms? Will traditional architectures transform completely or adapt gradually? What new forms of churn and opportunity will emerge? How can companies stay competitive and trusted in this changing world?

This chapter addresses these questions through the lens of the **Platform Success Blueprint**, showing how AI and ML can strengthen each side of the model while maintaining the principles that ensure platform longevity.

The Changing Shape of Platforms

We are already witnessing intelligent features quietly transforming everyday tools. Personalized recommendations on YouTube, Amazon, and Instagram, or auto-suggestion functions in writing tools, are now part of daily life. Platforms like Amazon and Netflix go further, generating personalized content, playlists, and descriptions in real time, adapting to each user's behavior. This shift has made digital interactions more fluid, contextual, and anticipatory.

The trend is clear: platforms are becoming more adaptive, learning from every user action to deliver deeper personalization. As this pattern spreads, it will change how we define user experience, productivity, and trust.

Over time, this shift will extend beyond digital environments. We are moving toward a world where we own fewer physical products and instead access them as services, managed through peer-to-peer transaction platforms and underpinned by secure, transparent technologies such as blockchain. This evolution reinforces the role of platforms as trusted mediators of value, not just distributors of functionality.

Despite all this change, the **core principles of the Platform Success Blueprint remain constant**. The pillars that define adaptability, fairness, and trust will continue to guide success. AI and ML may add new layers of complexity, but a foundation grounded in strategy, architecture, and experience ensures this complexity stays manageable.

V-ARISE in the Age of AI

The V-ARISE model continues to act as a guiding compass as platforms evolve into AI-powered ecosystems. While the technologies change, the principles remain timeless. What shifts is how they are expressed.

Adaptable

Platforms become truly adaptive when they support agentic behaviors, modular AI endpoints, and dynamic data flows. These allow systems to respond to new contexts, changing inputs, and evolving user needs without heavy rework.

Repeatable

Repeatability in the AI era means delivering consistent capability and context every time. Whether through vibe coding, agentic orchestration, creative templatization, or automated pipelines, repeatability reduces variance and enables dependable automation at scale.

Integratable

No AI platform can thrive in isolation. APIs, events, shared schemas, and model interfaces must interoperate cleanly. Integration is what allows AI components to work together and what enables a platform to scale in an economy where speed and composability are everything.

Self-sufficient

Self-sufficiency means that each platform function delivers complete value without depending unnecessarily on external systems. In the AI context, this could mean owning your fine-tuning pipeline, managing your own inference workflows, or ensuring that core capabilities do not collapse if a third party changes direction. A platform must stand on its own feet.

Ecosystem-enabling

AI platforms must create trusted environments where partners, developers, and creators can safely contribute. Ecosystem enablement means designing for collaboration, extensibility, shared governance, and responsible use. The goal is not just capability but productivity with trust.

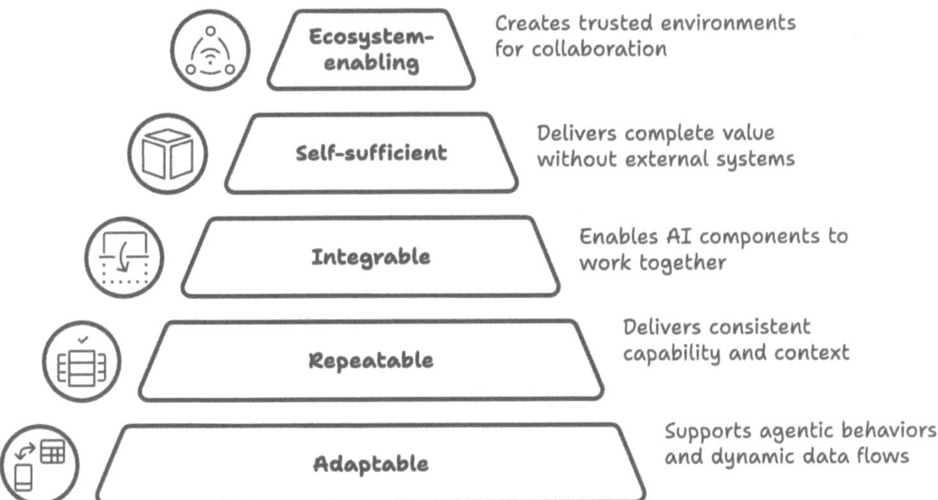

Figure 18-1. *V-ARISE Model for AI Platforms*

Anticipating the Next Wave

The coming decade will be defined by platforms that blend intelligence, automation, and trust. Many of these advancements may arrive sooner than expected, making this a decade of rapid experimentation and refinement.

Quantum technology, for example, is currently where conventional computing was in the 1960s – centralized and accessible mainly to research institutions and large technology companies such as IBM and Google. Though still experimental, quantum computing promises breakthroughs in simulation, optimization, cryptography, and secure communication[1]. It will eventually reshape aspects of platform design, especially where complex data models require high-speed computation. For now, it remains a technology to watch, not yet a core building block.

Challenges and Opportunities Ahead

Next-generation platforms will deliver increasingly immersive and personalized experiences powered by AI and ML. At the same time, they must address new challenges: ensuring fairness, complying with diverse regulations, protecting data privacy, and maintaining ethical transparency.

These changes create five key opportunity areas for platform leaders.

1. **The Role of Data Fabrics in AI Architectures**

    A data fabric is the shared layer that makes governed, real-time data available across systems with lineage and policy enforcement built in. It enables seamless data access and ensures consistency for AI workflows. A strong data fabric improves decision-making, accelerates insights, and enhances trust by showing how data is sourced and transformed.

2. **Ensuring Fairness and Transparency (Explainability and Auditability)**

    AI-driven platforms must adopt robust governance frameworks to detect and mitigate bias. Regular model audits, transparent reporting, and inclusive data practices are critical. Building an

---

[1] https://sloanreview.mit.edu/article/the-future-of-platforms/

internal AI Center of Excellence can centralize these efforts, ensuring consistency and continuous improvement across the organization.

3. **Scaling AI for Large Datasets**

   Handling massive, complex datasets requires adaptable, distributed architectures and cost-optimized storage. Platforms that succeed here will gain a significant advantage in agility and performance. The goal is not only speed but also efficiency, scalability, and sustainability.

4. **Compliance with Global Data Laws**

   As platforms expand across borders, they must adhere to local data protection laws while maintaining global performance. Achieving this requires data localization, encryption, and privacy-by-design principles integrated into every layer of the platform. Those who design compliance into their architecture from the start will move faster and expand with less friction.

5. **Balancing Automation with Human Oversight**

   As automation deepens, human oversight remains essential. Platforms that blend automation with meaningful human review will maintain accountability and trust. Embedding explainability, model auditability, and traceable decision flows ensures that automation enhances rather than replaces human judgment.

Responsible and Sustainable AI

AI introduces both opportunity and obligation. The environmental cost of training and operating large models is significant. To address this, platforms can prioritize energy-efficient algorithms, use smaller or distilled models where possible, and measure energy usage per request alongside financial cost. Running inference closer to users and scheduling noncritical workloads at off-peak times further reduces impact.

Responsible AI also requires transparency and governance. A minimal control set can help organizations stay compliant and credible:

- Document all data sources used for training and fine-tuning.

- Attach a model card version metadata to every release to describe purpose, data, and limitations.

- Keep humans in the loop for sensitive tasks.

- Log and review AI-generated outputs regularly.

- Conduct red-team testing before deployment.

- Establish incident response and rollback procedures for model errors.

These actions, simple yet vital, build trust with both regulators and users.

The Evolutionary Path: Three Stages of AI Platform Adoption

The future of platforms will evolve gradually rather than through abrupt revolutions. Organizations will typically move through three stages of AI and ML adoption, though mature companies may work on several in parallel.

Stage 1 – Integrating AI and ML Features

This initial phase focuses on adding AI-powered enhancements to existing platforms. Examples include predictive search, summarization, and customer support automation. These features deliver visible value quickly with minimal infrastructure change. Success at this stage depends on clear user experience boundaries, responsible output handling, and usage monitoring.

Stage 2 – Integrating Intelligent Platforms and Architectures

This phase involves embedding intelligent orchestration into both legacy and modern systems. Platforms at this stage use shared data fabrics, unified APIs, and event-driven architecture to enable consistent, hybrid experiences. Integration complexity increases, so maintaining stability, security, and governance becomes essential. When done well, this stage extends system lifespan and multiplies value.

Stage 3 – Running or Becoming AI and ML-Driven Platforms

In this advanced stage, organizations develop and operate their own AI-driven platforms. They manage the entire lifecycle – training, deployment, monitoring, and continuous improvement – aligned to domain-specific needs. For instance, an automotive company might build an AI platform to optimize supply chains or personalize vehicle features. While this demands advanced expertise, it creates strong differentiation and deeper ownership of innovation.

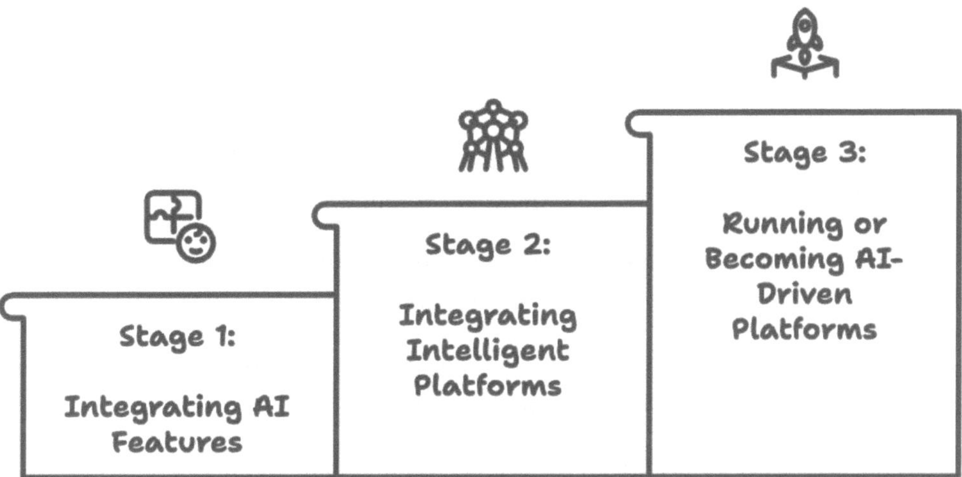

Figure 18-2. *AI Adoption Ladder*

These stages together create a ladder of capability. Each layer builds on the last, linking experimentation with maturity and translating innovation into measurable value.

Platform Users and Providers in the AI Era

For platform users, AI reduces friction and increases personalization, turning every interaction into a learning opportunity. The risk is opacity; users may not always understand how decisions are made. Building explainability into interfaces keeps trust intact.

For platform providers, AI adds an additional runtime to operate. Alongside managing software and infrastructure, providers must now manage models, prompts, evaluation systems, and ethical safeguards. The challenge is maintaining speed without losing governance. Providers that design governance as part of their architecture will lead this next wave.

Measuring Success in the AI Platform Era

To ensure meaningful and responsible progress, AI platforms should measure success across five dimensions:

> **Product value:** User satisfaction, feature adoption, and retention uplift that prove the AI is solving real problems

> **Model quality:** Accuracy, relevance, and drift detection, especially when models operate over long-lived data streams

> **Safety:** Rate of harmful outputs, incident resolution time, and human-review coverage for critical cases

> **Efficiency:** Cost per request, latency, and resource use, which directly determine scalability

> **Sustainability:** Estimated energy consumption and carbon footprint, both of which increasingly shape cost and architectural decisions

A concrete example of this in practice is **OpenAI's approach to reinforcement and live-drift monitoring**[2]. When a model's retrieval distribution shifts, it tracks relevance degradation, inference cost changes, and safety indicators in parallel. If relevance drops

---

[2] https://platform.openai.com/docs/guides/reinforcement-fine-tuning

but cost rises, the platform triggers an automatic retraining or re-ranking cycle rather than shipping degraded performance to users.

Reviewing such metrics routinely turns AI development from guesswork into an engineering discipline, grounded in feedback and not hype.

The Future: Evolutionary, Not Revolutionary

The future of platforms will unfold gradually, building on the foundations of trust, adaptability, and user focus. Quantum computing, advanced AI, and 6G technologies will expand what is possible, but progress will favor those who move with clarity, not haste.

Organizations that strengthen their current architecture and governance while experimenting with AI will gain the most. The goal is to evolve responsibly, transforming automation into augmentation and capability into coherence.

To begin this journey, start small but start now. Establish a strong data fabric, launch one responsible AI use case, and create one monthly review across value, safety, cost, and carbon. Let the **Platform Success Blueprint** and **V-ARISE** principles guide every next step.

Key Takeaways

- The future of platforms with AI and ML will be evolutionary, built on trust, fairness, and exceptional experience.

- Leverage your current data and information fabric to harness AI responsibly.

- Evolve progressively from AI feature integration to fully AI-driven platforms.

- Build governance, sustainability, and measurement into every decision.

- Use V-ARISE as your compass – the principles will remain timeless even as the technology changes.

The Future: Evolutionary, Not Revolutionary

CHAPTER 19

Intelligent Platform Design – The Next Wave

"When intelligence becomes native to systems, platforms stop being tools and start becoming co-creators of value."

We have now entered an age where artificial intelligence is not a layer added on top of platforms but a thread woven through every part of them. The way platforms are designed, operated, governed, and experienced is shifting. Intelligence changes not only what platforms can do but also how they behave, adapt, and create value. This chapter explores what happens when platforms meet AI, how new categories of intelligent platforms are emerging, and what this evolution means for builders, enterprises, and creative communities.

A New Design Discipline

As discussed in the previous chapter, the principles of trust, fairness, and measurable value remain constant even when technology transforms. What shifts now is the center of gravity. When intelligence becomes native across the stack, platform design evolves into its own discipline – **Intelligent Platform Design**.

This discipline unites architecture, data, and human-centered thinking. It demands a deeper level of consideration and asks questions we did not have to ask before:

How much autonomy should a system have?

How do we make trust visible and explainable?

How do we balance speed of decision with depth of judgment?

How should intelligent behaviors evolve over time without overwhelming users?

These questions will shape the platforms of the next decade more than any framework, tool, or architectural pattern. They define how platforms mature from being engines of capability to becoming intelligent collaborators.

© Shweta Vohra 2026
S. Vohra, *Decoding Platform Engineering Patterns*, https://doi.org/10.1007/979-8-8688-2555-2_19

Three Flavors of AI Platforms

To make sense of this changing landscape, we can broadly classify AI-era platforms into three categories, each with its own focus, dependency, and maturity curve. From these categories we can expect newer business models will emerge.

Platforms for Creative Consumption

These are the platforms most visible to individuals. They are designed for imagination, experimentation, and expressive output. Examples include conversational systems such as ChatGPT or Claude, creative tools like Canva and Runway, and the growing family of model-as-a-service offerings that allow anyone to generate content or assemble lightweight agents. New tools are emerging across every creative stream, but only a few will mature into true platforms. To stand out, creative platforms must embody the V-ARISE principles and consistently meet rising user expectations.

What makes this category remarkable is not just accessibility but the depth of personalization it offers. They power the freedom economy, where individual creators, educators, and small businesses can operate at near-industrial scale without industrial effort. Early observations across the industry show a clear trend: people are using these platforms to build new economies with very little friction – monetizing content, automating workflows, and reaching global audiences at a speed that was unimaginable a decade ago.

Their long-term success will depend on intuitive design, ethical data practices, and an emotional connection with users. Creative platforms thrive when they remove friction, amplify expression, and help people feel more capable than before.

At the same time, a new class of consumer platforms is emerging, where creativity blends with connected experiences. Think of travel platforms that unify discovery, booking, local experiences, and real-time assistance into a single journey. Consider interconnected wealth and banking ecosystems where investments, payments, advisory, and financial planning work together seamlessly. Mobile environments are evolving into "apps of apps," where users navigate fluidly across services without friction or context switching. We are also seeing early signals in areas such as connected health experiences that integrate diagnostics, care, and lifestyle, and intelligent home ecosystems that adapt continuously to user behaviour. These platforms extend creativity beyond content into life orchestration, where the experience is not just created, but continuously shaped around the user.

Platforms for Enterprise Enablement

Enterprises are adopting AI not just for productivity, but also for decision-making, operational intelligence, and workflow orchestration. This category of platforms sits at the heart of organizational work, where scale, security, and measurable outcomes matter the most. Unlike consumer AI tools that focus on individual creativity, enterprise enablement platforms operate inside controlled environments and are evaluated by their ability to improve accuracy, reduce effort, and support confident decision-making.

There are three broad flavors emerging in this space.

Productivity and Knowledge Platforms

These tools enhance writing, planning, analysis, coordination, and knowledge retrieval. Assistants like Microsoft Copilot, Google Gemini, and ChatGPT help teams manage context-heavy tasks, translate complexity into clarity, and reduce cognitive load. Workflow systems like Asana, Monday.com, and Notion weave AI into everyday processes, smoothing out inefficiencies that organizations previously accepted as the cost of doing business.

What makes them platforms is not the task itself but the ecosystem built around them – embeddings, plugins, enterprise connectors, knowledge graphs, and secure workspace integrations that allow other tools and teams to build on top of them.

Decision-Making and Intelligence Platforms

A more advanced class is emerging around data-driven decisions and organizational intelligence. Tools like Tellius, ThoughtSpot, and Qlik Sense are no longer just dashboards – they are bringing capabilities where AI participates in decision-making. They help identify patterns, predict outcomes, and surface insights that human teams would struggle to detect at scale.

These platforms behave like decision engines. They integrate data, apply models, and provide explainable insights, allowing leaders to trust recommendations without surrendering control. This is where the space is maturing quickly: enterprises want AI to think with them, not for them, and decision-intelligence platforms are evolving to meet that expectation.

Operational and Automation Platforms

The third flavor is operational platforms that power day-to-day execution. Tools like CoTester and AgentRx bring AI into software testing and auto-healing. Workflow engines and document processing platforms combine rules, machine learning, and agentic flows to automate complex, multi-step processes.

These platforms can and will qualify as platforms if they offer extensibility, APIs, and modular building blocks that teams can compose into their own operational systems. They don't automate one task; they automate a chain of tasks. They become part of the organization's operational backbone.

Why This Category Is Maturing Quickly

Enterprise AI enablement is evolving into a true platform space because organizations require

- Clarity of ownership

- Tight governance

- Security guarantees

- Data lineage and protection

- Integration into existing systems

- Auditability

- Measurable ROI

Enterprises will not adopt systems they cannot trust, explain, govern, or scale. As a result, vendors are increasingly building platform foundations – multi-tenant architectures, plugin frameworks, fine-grained permissions, and governance layers that make these tools enterprise-grade.

These platforms are no longer standalone applications. They are becoming ecosystems where teams can build, integrate, and extend based on their unique workflow demands.

The Purpose of Enterprise Enablement Platforms – their goal is not to replace human capability but to amplify it. They streamline work across engineering, operations, data, legal, finance, HR, and product teams – with safety and context awareness built in. The real power lies in how deeply they integrate with an organization's processes and how predictably they translate AI capabilities into business outcomes.

Enterprise enablement platforms are the pragmatic middle layer of the AI era, where creativity meets risk, and where innovation becomes measurable.

Platforms for Foundational Middleware and Infrastructure

At the foundation are platforms that build platforms – the invisible layer that everything else stands on. As discussed earlier in Chapter 5, these foundational systems include AI-enabled infrastructure, data orchestration platforms, and middleware that support model creation, deployment, automation, and scaling. Cloud offerings such as Amazon Bedrock, Azure OpenAI Service, and Google Vertex AI show how today's ecosystems are evolving from being simple service providers to becoming intelligent substrates for every other platform type above them.

But these cloud services, while powerful, are still only the **first generation** of intelligent infrastructure. They provide essential primitives, yet leave much of the real integration work to enterprises. The next wave is far more ambitious. It focuses on platform patterns that enable golden paths – predefined, opinionated workflows that give enterprises consistency, security, and scale without needing brittle integrations or custom glue code.

This is where intelligent platform design is heading.

We are moving toward middleware platforms that do not merely expose APIs but actively participate in the orchestration of the entire value chain. These platforms will understand context, enforce governance, optimize pipelines, and adapt automatically as business needs shift. They will manage data contracts, observe model behavior, trigger remediations, rebalance workloads, and maintain lineage – all without human intervention.

In this vision, platform providers will increasingly deliver **unified environments** where model training, evaluation, deployment, monitoring, and observability coexist as a single flowing system rather than scattered components stitched together manually. Imagine a future where

- Model versions auto-negotiate compatibility with downstream systems

- Policies enforce themselves in real time during model deployment

- Pipelines auto-heal based on drift or performance signals

- Logging, tracing, and governance become intrinsic behaviors, not add-ons

- Infrastructure adapts workloads based on patterns of usage and cost

This is the beginning of **intelligent middleware** – platforms that do not just run your models but understand them. They act as the connective tissue between business goals, engineering teams, and AI capabilities.

In other words, the future is not a collection of AI services. The future is AI-aware infrastructure.

Enterprises will rely on this layer to support the full lifecycle of AI systems, and this is where the most long-term innovation will concentrate. Once this foundation becomes stable, every layer above – enterprise enablement, creative platforms, and agentic systems – becomes easier to build, scale, and evolve.

This is the layer that will quietly power the next decade of platforms.

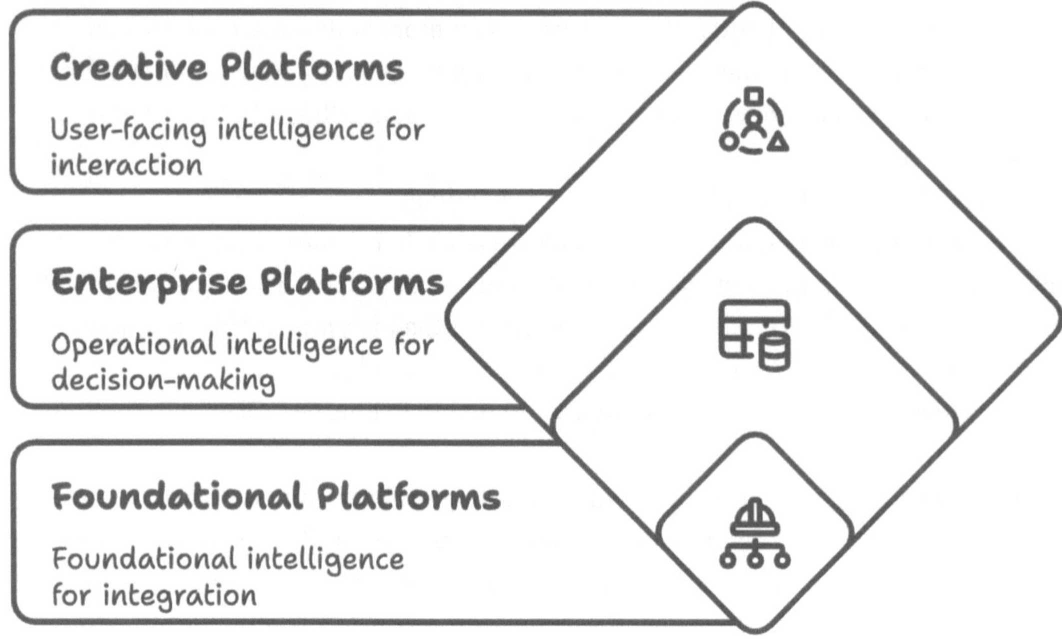

Figure 19-1. Intelligent Platform Pyramid - Next Wave

Each layer depends on the one beneath it, yet the flow of intelligence moves both ways. The creative layer shapes demand; the enterprise layer translates it into capability; the middleware layer provides the means to scale and govern it.

Agentic Convergence

If the first generation of AI platforms focused on specific tasks, the next generation will focus on orchestration. **Agentic platforms** act as conductors that coordinate multiple intelligent systems. A single request may invoke different agents for planning, data retrieval, evaluation, and presentation before returning an answer to the user.

This convergence will blur boundaries between the three platform types. A creative tool might call enterprise APIs for project management, while an enterprise assistant may rely on middleware agents for secure data access. The network of agents effectively becomes a meta-platform – a living ecosystem where intelligence flows dynamically between contexts.

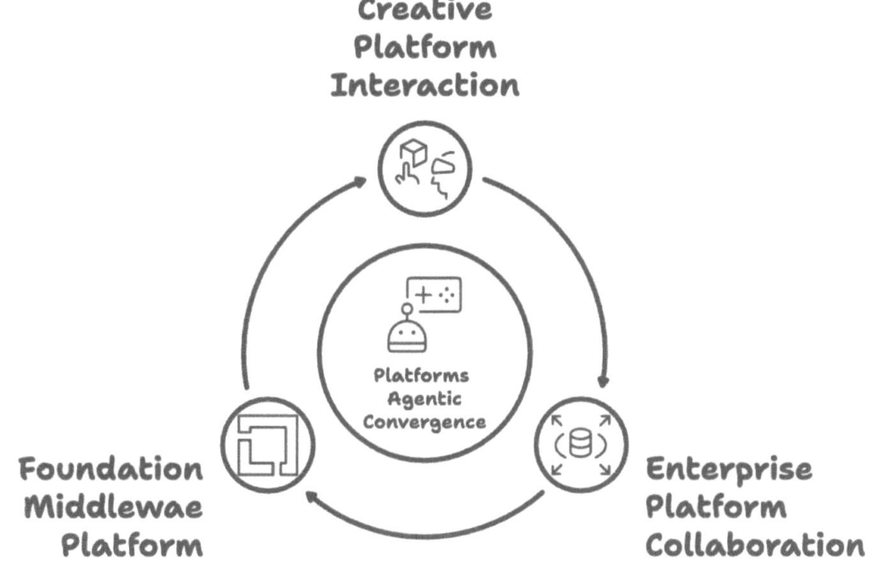

Figure 19-2. *Agentic Convergence Cycle*

While still at an early stage, this direction will redefine software ecosystems much like APIs did two decades ago. Agent-to-agent communication, model-to-model negotiation, and even AI-to-AI marketplaces will emerge. What remains uncertain is how governance will evolve to match this fluidity.

Trust Architecture for Intelligent Platforms

As autonomy increases, trust becomes even more important. When users can no longer see every decision a system makes, they must rely on the architecture of trust embedded within it. In the human world, trust is more of an emotion and belonging, whereas if you need to explain it to intelligent platforms, these need to be translated in the way machines understand and models contextualize.

A strong trust architecture rests on four core elements:

> **Responsibility:** Platforms are designed and operated with ethical, legal, and societal accountability at their core.

> **Explainability:** Users and stakeholders can understand *why* a system behaves the way it does or produces specific outcomes.

> **Observability:** Operators can trace, monitor, and audit system behavior across its lifecycle.

> **Recoverability:** Systems can safely correct themselves, roll back decisions, or recover from failures without causing harm.

Trust is not an add-on; it must be designed from the start, much like resilience or scalability. In this new context, explainability is the user interface of ethics.

Designing for Endurance

To thrive in the coming decade, platform builders need a new mindset – one that is evolving faster than anything we imagined even ten years ago. This mindset requires the ability to design systems that can explain their decisions, adapt to new contexts, and maintain trust even under pressure.

Three principles guide this shift:

1. **Convergence over collection:** Build for integration, not accumulation. Let agents and models collaborate through well-defined contracts rather than isolated endpoints.

2. **Transparency over opacity:** Make decision flows observable to humans and auditable by design. Trust cannot survive hidden reasoning; it needs explainability.

3. **Pace over race:** Adopt a rhythm of change that teams can sustain and users can absorb. Scale slowly enough to remain stable.

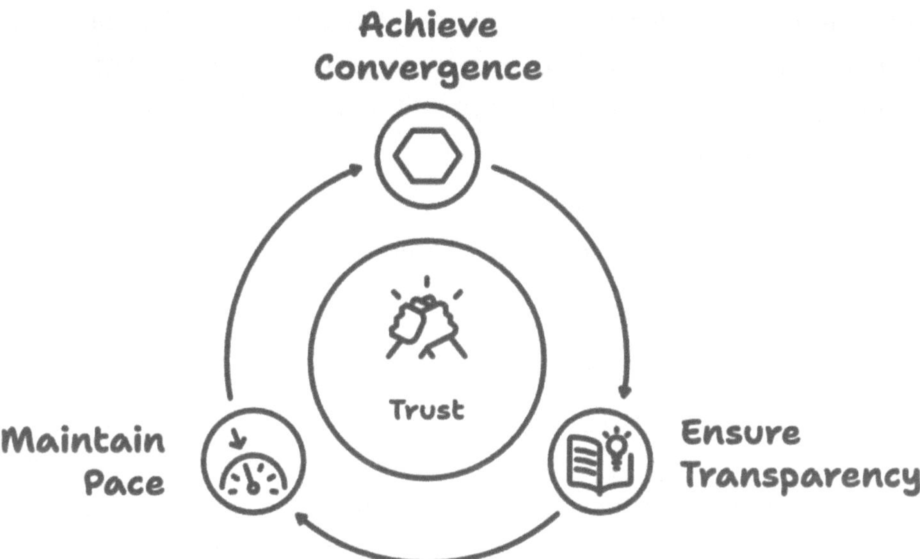

Figure 19-3. *Design Principles for Intelligent Platforms*

Evolving Business Models

AI is reshaping how platforms create and capture value. Traditional labels like B2B or B2C are becoming less helpful as value flows become more granular. We are beginning to see Developer-to-AI, AI-to-AI, and Agent-to-Model interactions that treat intelligence as both a participant and a contributor in the ecosystem.

In these emerging models, value is not measured only in transactions but in feedback loops. The more a system is used, the better it becomes. Learning itself becomes an economic asset.

Future marketplaces will not trade purely in services but in intelligence assets: prompts, embeddings, fine-tuned models, evaluation pipelines, and reusable workflows. Governance, attribution, and revenue sharing for these assets will become the defining differentiators for platform ecosystems.

The Unfinished Work of Every Era

Every technological wave leaves questions unanswered, and Chapter 2 explored this in detail. Cloud left sustainability and cost optimization as unfinished business. Platforms left interoperability and standardization unresolved. AI will leave its own marks: coherence, explainability, bias, and the ongoing tension between autonomy and accountability.

Recognizing these unfinished threads allows builders to design at a maintainable pace. It reminds us that progress without pause creates fragility. As intelligence spreads across systems, the temptation to rush will grow. The wiser path is deliberate integration and responsible evolution.

Enduring Intelligent Platforms for Humans

As platforms meet AI, a new chapter begins. It is not defined by speed or novelty, but by how well we make sense of what we build. Creative platforms will make expression effortless. Enterprise platforms will deepen decision intelligence. Middleware and infrastructure platforms will quietly power the intelligence underneath. Agents will weave these layers together into fluid, adaptive ecosystems.

But the most important design choice remains human. We must decide whether we are building systems that merely act or systems that meaningfully serve. Technology has always been a human endeavor. We do not build platforms so machines can entertain other machines. We build them so people can create, learn, collaborate, and grow.

A world where chess is played only by models, where art is admired only by algorithms, or where travel is designed for robots is not advancement. It is misdirection. Platforms matter because they extend human capability, not because they replace it.

As we move forward, let us design with clarity, integrate with even more care, and evolve at a pace that sustains trust and explainability. This era offers immense promise, but it will reward those who build with intention rather than haste.

As we started in previous chapter - "The future of platforms will favour not those who move the fastest, but those who build trust, fairness, and deliver exceptional experiences."

Key Takeaways

- Intelligent platform design now brings together architecture, data, and human judgment into one discipline.

- AI platforms fall broadly into three categories – creative, enterprise, and middleware – each adding a different layer of value.

- Agents and more autonomous systems will gradually weave these layers together, enabling more adaptive and interconnected ecosystems.

- Trust, explainability, and responsible pace are becoming as important as capability or scale.

- The future of platforms will be defined not by how fast they move, but by how well they endure and uplift the humans they serve.

Index

© Shweta Vohra 2026
S. Vohra, *Decoding Platform Engineering Patterns*, https://doi.org/10.1007/979-8-8688-2555-2

Q

R

User interface (UI), 44, 125
UX/UI design, 126

V

V-ARISE model, 139
V-ARISE platform, 50
Vendor ecosystem, 141
Version Control, 166
Vertical integration, 216
Virtualization, 24

W, X

WordPress, 127

Y

YouTube, 94

Z

Zendesk, 127
Zoom, 123